HISTORY AND MEMORY
AFTER AUSCHWITZ

∾

OTHER WORKS BY DOMINICK LACAPRA

Emile Durkheim:
Sociologist and Philosopher

History and Criticism

History, Politics, and the Novel

Madame Bovary on Trial

A Preface to Sartre

Representing the Holocaust: History, Theory, Trauma

Rethinking Intellectual History: Texts, Contexts, Language

Soundings in Critical Theory

The Bounds of Race:
Perspectives on Hegemony and Resistance
edited

Modern European Intellectual History:
Reappraisals and New Perspectives
edited with Steven L. Kaplan

HISTORY AND MEMORY
AFTER AUSCHWITZ

Dominick LaCapra

CORNELL UNIVERSITY PRESS

ITHACA AND LONDON

First published 1998 by Cornell University Press.
First printing, Cornell Paperbacks, 1998.

Printed in the United States of America.

Cornell University Press strives to utilize environmentally responsible suppliers and materials to the fullest extent possible in the publishing of its books. Such materials include vegetable-based, low-VOC inks and acid-free papers that are also either recycled, totally chlorine-free, or partly composed of nonwood fibers.

Library of Congress Cataloging-in-Publication Data

LaCapra, Dominick, 1939–
History and memory after Auschwitz / Dominick LaCapra.
p.   cm.
Includes bibliographical references and index.
ISBN 0-8014-3496-3 (cloth:alk. paper).
ISBN 0-8014-8496-0 (pbk:alk. paper).
1. Holocaust, Jewish (1939–1945)—Historiography.
2. Holocaust, Jewish (1939–1945)—Psychological aspects.
3. Holocaust, Jewish (1939–1945)—Influence.   I. Title.
D804.348.L33   1998
940.53'18—dc21   97-41845

Cloth printing   10 9 8 7 6 5 4 3 2 1
Paperback printing   10 9 8 7 6 5 4 3 2 1

For Jane

For me, ethics and aesthetics are associated with the word *essay*.

It is said to come from "weighing," and is mostly used by scholars only to characterize the smaller excrescences, those not written with full commitment, of their life's work; it is also called "attempt." I can also make use of it in this latter sense, to which, however, I would like to give a different content.

Is the essay something left over in an area where one can work precisely [in the sense of the natural sciences]. . . . Or: the strictest form attainable in an area where one can*not* work precisely.

I will seek to demonstrate the second sense.

Now, a rational course of thought can be true or false, as can an affective one, but aside from that it "speaks to us" or doesn't speak to us. And there are trains of thought that really work only through the mode of feelings. For a person who has no ear for them they are completely confusing and incomprehensible. But here it is nevertheless visibly a matter of an entirely legitimate means of understanding, even if it is not of binding general validity. The number of such ways of reaching understanding among people is, moreover, greater than assumed (chimpanzee couples, effect of a leader through charisma, etc.). Even the individual person has the experience that the same thought can be dead for him at one time, a mere series of words, alive at another.

Robert Musil, fragment ["On the Essay" 1914?]

CONTENTS

ACKNOWLEDGMENTS

A version of chapter 2 appeared in *History & Memory,* and a version of chapter 4 in *Critical Inquiry.* The other chapters are published here for the first time.

For their reading and response to Chapter 4, I would like to thank members of a workshop on psychoanalysis at Cornell (especially David Bathrick, Brett de Bary, Nelly Furman, Mary Jacobus, Biddy Martin, Tim Murray, David Rodowick, Suzanne Stewart, and Nancy Wood) as well as the participants at the 1996 session of the School of Criticism and Theory. I thank Michael Roth for his reading of the entire manuscript and for his insightful comments. I would particularly like to thank Geoffrey Hartman both for his reading of the manuscript and for his carefully reasoned and eloquent response to Chapter 4 when it was presented at a typically engaging and argumentative colloquium of the School of Criticism and Theory.

For their reactions to a number of the essays in this book, I thank Ben Brower, Leigh Ann Eubanks, Adam Hoffman, Tracie Matysik, Kathleen Merrow, Richard Schaefer, Judith Surkis, and Jeremy Varon. I also thank Kathleen Merrow for her assistance in gathering materials for Chapter 5, and Tracie Matysik for her assistance in preparing the index. For her reading of the manuscript and her many helpful comments, I am (as always) grateful to Jane Pedersen. Finally, I thank Grey Osterud for carefully reading and copyediting the manuscript.

D. LaC.

HISTORY AND MEMORY
AFTER AUSCHWITZ

Introduction

The problem of memory has recently become a preoccupation of historians and critical theorists. A journal, *History & Memory*, is even devoted to the topic, and Pierre Nora has edited a multivolume study of memory sites.[1] But the relations between memory and history have still to be sorted out, and exceptionally vexed is their import for aesthetic, ethical, and political issues. What aspects of the past should be remembered and how should they be remembered? Are there phenomena whose traumatic nature blocks understanding and disrupts memory while producing belated effects that have an impact on attempts to represent or otherwise address the past? What, in general, is the significance of trauma in history? Do some events present moral and representational issues even for groups not directly involved in them? Do those more directly involved have special responsibilities to the past and the way it is remembered in the present? Can—or should—historiography define itself in a purely scholarly and professional way that distances it from public memory and its ethical implications? Should it, on the contrary, ground itself in memory as its matrix and muse? Or is there a more complex and nuanced interaction between history and memory? Does art itself have a special responsibility with respect to traumatic events that remain invested with value and emotion? I hope to shed some light on these questions, for my fo-

---

[1] *Les lieux de mémoire* (Paris: Gallimard, 1984). Translated as *Realms of Memory*, ed. Lawrence Kritzman, trans. Arthur Goldhammer (New York: Columbia University Press, 1996).

cus in this book is on the interactions among history, memory, and ethicopolitical concerns as they emerge in the aftermath of the Shoah.

Each chapter approaches these questions from a distinctive perspective that is meant to interact in a thought-provoking but nontotalizing manner with the angle of vision in other chapters. Yet to some extent the first chapter frames the others. It examines the relations between history and memory as they have been construed by various historians and theorists, and it offers a specific critical and analytic approach to the problem. It focuses especially on the Holocaust or Shoah as a complex phenomenon at the intersection of history and memory with which we are still trying to grapple. In this respect, it examines certain arguments in Saul Friedlander's *Memory, History, and the Extermination of the Jews of Europe* in the attempt to formulate better the question of how to understand and remember the Nazi genocide and its attendant traumas.[2] Especially important here is the attempt to elucidate the notion of a negative sublime as it applies to the acts of at least certain perpetrators.[3]

In the first chapter and throughout this book, I resist a rash generalization that would indiscriminately apply such a concept as the "negative sublime" and associated behavior to the overwhelming majority of Germans. But it is nonetheless noteworthy that there were significant numbers of cases of perpetrator behavior toward Jews, in such sites as work and death camps, forced marches, and police battalions, that involved extreme cruelty, gratuitous abuse, practices of degradation, perverse carnivalesque glee, and even "sublime" elation.[4] In Chapter 1,

---

[2] Bloomington: Indiana University Press, 1993.

[3] The role of a negative sublime in the ideology, experience, and actions of Nazi perpetrators raises obvious problems for analysts, notably in one's own appeal to the sublime (which always harbors a negative dimension) in the treatment of the Shoah. The appeal to the sublime in the critique of representation and the insistence on the way trauma exceeds cognition have become prevalent motifs in recent thought, especially in the aftermath of Jean-François Lyotard's analyses (notably in *The Differend: Phrases in Dispute*, trans. George Van Den Abbeele [1983; Minneapolis: University of Minnesota Press, 1988]) and Shoshana Felman's contributions (especially in Shoshana Felman and Dori Laub, M.D., *Testimony: Crises of Witnessing in Literature, Psychoanalysis, and History* [New York: Routledge, 1992]). The possible role of the sublime with reference to Nazi perpetrators does not disallow or "contaminate" all appeals to the sublime, including its use in the analysis of the Holocaust. But it does raise the question of whether one is, however unintentionally, repeating the views of perpetrators without sufficient critical framing of those views to distinguish them from one's own voice and one's carefully delimited use of certain concepts.

[4] Such cases of perpetrator behavior are extensively chronicled yet become the basis for a rash generalization concerning Germans in Daniel Jonah Goldhagen's controversial, best-selling book, *Hitler's Willing Executioners: Ordinary Germans and the*

I discuss Heinrich Himmler's famous Posen speech of October 1943, addressed to upper-level SS officers, for it may be taken as the paradigmatic assertion of the sublimity and "glory" of extreme transgression and unheard-of excess in the Nazi treatment of Jews. Often such features are marginalized or downplayed in the emphasis on factors such as the banality of evil, the well-nigh inevitable consequences of totalization (or totalitarianism), the role of bureaucratic routine and cold duty, the inertial force of social pressure, the effects of depersonalizing and fragmented relations to the other, and the significance of a massive technological framework, instrumental rationality, and industrialized mass murder. The point is not to dismiss these factors, which are important and have been objects of extensive research. Indeed none of the features or factors I have mentioned is insignificant, and it is misguided to downplay some of them in order to assert the dominant if not exclusive role of others. Yet unusually baffling, hence demanding as much elucidation as possible, is the conjunction of extremes involving the insertion, in the presumably uncongenial context of advanced "modernity," of that which seems utterly out of place and appears, deceptively, as a regression to barbarism. Such "barbarism" may perhaps be better apprehended as an uncanny return of the repressed in the form of phobic ritualism and paradoxical sacrificialism bound up with a desire for purification and regenerative, even redemptive, violence toward victims.[5] Indeed the sublime itself may be

---

Final Solution (New York: Alfred A. Knopf, 1996). For a nuanced analysis that contests Goldhagen's representation of the near ubiquity of "eliminationist" anti-Semitism in Germany, see Saul Friedländer, *Nazi Germany and the Jews* (New York: Harper Collins, 1997). In this book, Friedländer complements his earlier analysis in *Memory, History, and the Extermination of the Jews of Europe* by elaborating and applying a concept of redemptive anti-Semitism to characterize the Nazi treatment of Jews. For Friedländer, redemptive anti-Semitism "was born from the fear of racial degeneration and the religious belief in redemption" (p. 87). Moreover, "Nazism was no mere ideological discourse; it was a political religion commanding the total commitment owed to a religious faith" (p. 72). (The reader should note that the author's name appears without an umlaut in *Memory, History, and the Extermination of the Jews of Europe* but with an umlaut in *Nazi Germany and the Jews.*)

[5] The concept of a regression to barbarism rests on an indiscriminate and self-serving view of other societies to which modern, presumably advanced societies are compared. It also frequently assumes an idea of progress leading from "them" to "us." Neither of these assumptions is required by a notion of the return of the repressed. Indeed the latter is related to a very different understanding of temporality in which any features of society deemed desirable must be recurrently rewon, and less desirable ones pose a continual threat that reappears in different guises over time. Moreover, it is conceivable that other societies have negotiated certain temptations and threats, such as excess or extreme transgression, better than have so-called modern societies.

seen as a secular sacred and involve the attempt to transvalue trauma into a disconcerting source of elation and transcendence.

In Chapter 2 I return to the so-called Historians' Debate of 1986—a debate that raised some fundamental issues, especially concerning the functions of historical memory with respect to the issue of national identity. The position-setting views of Jürgen Habermas and Ernst Nolte help to frame these issues while intimating the continuing significance of the controversy. Particularly important, from the perspective I take, are the implications of the debate for historical self-understanding and for the public role of memory as it bears on the possibility of mourning in a national context. Although the Historians' Debate threatened to be eclipsed by the reunification of Germany in 1989, one may argue that its pertinence was underscored by reunification. In different but related ways, the Historians' Debate and German reunification presented the spectacle of a resurgent yet embattled nationalism conjoined with the problem of collective identity, and in certain respects the earlier phenomenon may be read as a problematic dress rehearsal for the later, more "world-historical" one.

In Chapter 3 I move from Germany to France and from the general to the particular, and explore the problem of relating historical understanding to the analysis of literature. Albert Camus's 1956 novel *The Fall* (*La chute*) seems especially remarkable as a case in which a major postwar intellectual and writer attempted to address the Holocaust. Even Sartre, Camus's principal contender for the role of intellectual guide in France and elsewhere in the West, said virtually nothing about the specific nature of the Holocaust and its bearing on the Jews. In his well-known postwar study, *Antisemite and Jew,* Sartre did not even mention the Holocaust.[6] Camus, on the other hand, did make some effort to come to terms with the Shoah. The question, however, is the extent to which this trauma came belatedly to function as a screen to diminish the impact of a subsequent traumatic series of events: the French-Algerian war and its relation to French colonialism and postwar problems, notably with respect to French Algerians.

Chapter 3 takes Shoshana Felman's analysis of Camus as a challenging counterpoint to the view I elaborate. The important and influential book she co-authored with Dori Laub, *Testimony: Crises of*

[6] Trans. George J. Becker (New York: Schocken, 1948). The French title of Sartre's work is *Réflexions sur la question juive* (Paris: Gallimard, 1946).

Witnessing in Literature, Psychoanalysis, and History, contains many suggestive insights. But in my judgment it also harbors some of the more dubious possibilities of a particular combination of poststructuralism and psychoanalysis in the seeming attempt to address historical issues that have a continued importance for the present and future. For this broader reason, Felman's arguments merit careful attention, and the critical engagement with her approach extends into the next chapter as well.

In Chapter 4, I discuss Claude Lanzmann's film *Shoah* (1985), which has been widely praised as the greatest film on the Holocaust and even as the greatest documentary ever made. Lanzmann himself, however, has argued that his film is not a documentary but should be seen primarily as a work of art. He has made many other arresting comments that have tended to become the primary framework in terms of which critics (such as Felman and Gertrud Koch) have interpreted the film. This chapter closely examines Lanzmann's views, especially his attribution of primacy to art, his absolute refusal of attempts to understand the Holocaust (particularly the motivation and nature of perpetrators), and his pronounced interest in survivors who relive or act out their past suffering, thereby providing him as filmmaker with objects of identification. The chapter tries to raise certain critical questions about Lanzmann's views and to offer different avenues for approaching his film and its historical dimensions.

Camus's *The Fall* would generally be classified as a work of high or elite culture. Lanzmann's *Shoah* would also probably be seen as "high-cultural" or even as an "art film," although that label seems curiously inappropriate. But both are demanding works that cross the line between elite and mass or popular culture, and both have received the sustained attention of "elite" critics and had many readers or viewers in the general public. Art Spiegelman's *Maus,* the subject of Chapter 5, audaciously tries to address the Holocaust in a comic-book format. It thus inserts what is for many the unspeakable or the *tremendum* into the context of possibly one of the most vulgar and commodified vehicles of popular culture. For some, this is enough to raise crushing doubts about the venture. Yet the comic book has at times been an experimental form exploring contested areas of modern culture, and Spiegelman's effort is serious and deserving of careful scrutiny. In fact, an implicit comparison with Lanzmann's accomplishment in *Shoah* underlies my discussion. One contestable aspect of this implicit comparison is my feeling that, although *Shoah* might appear to be a work of a different order of magnitude from *Maus*, Spiegelman is a less dubious presence in, and more convincing commentator on, his achievement than is Lanzmann with respect to his.

In Chapter 6, I try to draw out some general implications of the earlier chapters and reflect more extensively on their problematic aspects. I especially attempt to bring out my conception of the relations among history, memory, ethics, and politics. What helps to articulate these relations is, I think, a potential to be informed by a rethinking of psychoanalysis that addresses such problems as transference, acting-out, and working-through, which are intimately connected with both mourning and other forms of social action requiring the ability to remember in a desirable way. This view of psychoanalysis is relatively nontechnical and does not strictly conform to the principles of any given school. Rather it selectively appropriates aspects of the work of Freud and of those responding to him in ways I judge to be fruitful for reconfiguring historical understanding as a process that requires a critical exchange with the past bearing on the present and future.[7]

I would conclude by pointing out that the word "after" in the title to this book does not have a merely chronological meaning. Things changed because of the Shoah, and even events that occurred before it (including, say, texts of Heidegger or Nietzsche) could not be understood or "read" in the same way. Without becoming a *telos* of prior history, the Holocaust had retrospective effects and prompted belated recognitions that posed new questions to aspects of history that earlier had a different face. Were Auschwitz and everything for which it stood therefore unique? One might argue that the Shoah was both unique (this kind of genocide had not happened before) and comparable (how did Hitler's camps compare with Stalin's gulags?). At the same time, it was neither unique nor comparable, for there is a sense in which comparatives (especially in terms of magnitude) are irrelevant, and even superlatives (in Spiegelman's phrase, "the central trauma of the Twentieth Century") are questionable except perhaps as hyperbolic expressions of one's own inadequacy in trying to come to terms with problems. At best, assertions of uniqueness or of compara-

---

[7] For an elaboration of this approach to historical understanding, see Dominick La-Capra, *Representing the Holocaust: History, Theory, Trauma* (Ithaca: Cornell University Press, 1994) and "History, Language, and Reading: Waiting for Crillon," *American Historical Review* 100 (1995), 799–828.

bility have to be justified in problematic ways that vary with one's sub-ject-positions and judgments concerning the needs of a situation or context. During the Historians' Debate, when tendencies toward nor-malization were prevalent, assertions of the uniqueness of the Holo-caust might have been defensible, especially when made by Germans. To justify Israeli policies or to establish one's own special status, such assertions are suspect. But the more general point, as I intimate in the first chapter, is that the Holocaust was "unique" in a specific, nonnu-merical, and noninvidous sense. In it an extreme threshold or outer limit of transgression was crossed, and whenever that threshold or limit is crossed, something "unique" happens *and* the standard oppo-sition between uniqueness and comparability is unsettled, thereby de-priving comparatives (especially in terms of magnitude) of a common measure or foundation.

CHAPTER ONE

History and Memory:
In the Shadow of the Holocaust

Recently the concern with the problem of memory has become so wide-spread and intense that one is tempted to take a suspicious view and re-fer to fixation. In certain of its forms, the preoccupation with memory may indicate a failure of constructive will and divert attention from the needs of the present and the necessity of attempting to shape the future. One particularly dubious phenomenon is the nostalgic, sentimental turn to a partly fictionalized past that is conveyed in congenially ingra-tiating, safely conventionalized narrative form. Indeed the immersion in memory and its sites may at times have the quality of junk-Proustian *Schwärmerei*. But the recent turn to memory may have more than a symptomatic value, at least when a concern with memory includes a de-sire to be attentive to the problem of history insofar as it bears on the present and future, involving the need for a self-critical examination of one's own implication in the problems one treats. Memory—along with its lapses and tricks—poses questions to history in that it points to prob-lems that are still alive or invested with emotion and value. Ideally, his-tory critically tests memory and prepares for a more extensive attempt to work through a past that has not passed away.

I would initially mention two pressing sets of reasons for the turn to memory and its relation to history. First, there is the importance of trauma, notably including the deferred recognition of the significance of traumatic series of events in recent history, events one might well prefer to forget. The traumatic event has its greatest and most clearly unjustifiable effect on the victim, but in different ways it also affects everyone who comes in contact with it: perpetrator, collaborator, bystander, resister, those born later. Especially for victims, trauma brings about a lapse or rupture in memory that breaks continuity with the past, thereby placing identity in question to the point of shattering it. But it may raise problems of identity for others insofar as it unsettles narcissistic investments and desired self-images, including—especially with respect to the Shoah—the image of Western civilization itself as the bastion of elevated values if not the high point in the evolution of humanity.

The traumatic event is repressed or denied and registers only belatedly (*nachträglich*) after the passage of a period of latency. This effect of belatedness has of course been a manifest aspect of the Holocaust as it impinged not only on Germany and Germans but also on other nations and groups. Even in Israel, the immediate aftermath of the Shoah was typified by denial and resistance as Israelis forged a concept of the redemptive nation and its heroic inhabitants that presented the Diaspora as a time of erring that culminated in catastrophe for nationless, hence powerless, Jews. Survivors were often constrained to adopt a new identity and be silent not only about the old one but about the way it was destroyed or devastated. The role of the Holocaust in Israel has changed over time, and it has been a cause of contention among various groups.[1] In other countries as well, the aftereffects and aftershocks of the Holocaust have not dissipated, and the events marking it have still to be worked through. It is also unclear how its status will be affected by major developments such as the breakup of the former USSR and Yugoslavia or the reunification of Germany, developments that have favored the return of suppressed or repressed anti-Semitism and ethnic rivalry as well as the desire to normalize history by having the Holocaust fade into the misty vistas of *la longue durée*.

On a more microsocial and interpersonal level, the increased awareness of the prevalence of child abuse has given new prominence to the issue of the relation between actual event and fantasy in the genesis of trauma. As child abuse and childhood trauma have become common concerns, so has the preoccupation with "false memory syndrome" as one of the more socially consequential forms that the tricks of memory may take.

---

[1] On this issue see Tom Segev, *The Seventh Million: The Israelis and the Holocaust* (1991; New York: Hill and Wang, 1993).

A second, broadly cultural reason for the recent turn to memory has been the interest in *lieux de mémoire* (memory sites), in the phrase of Pierre Nora, as well as in what Claude Lanzmann calls *non-lieux de mémoire* (what I would term trauma sites). The point here is that a memory site is generally also a site of trauma, and the extent to which it remains invested with trauma marks the extent to which memory has not been effective in coming to terms with it, notably through modes of mourning. In certain cases it is unclear whether one should refer to arrested or aborted mourning, because an attempt at mourning may not even be made and the need for it may be rationalized away. This was in good measure the case in postwar Germany, and the tendentious role of rationalization that obviates the need for mourning has appeared again in the views of certain participants in the *Historikerstreit* (Historians' Debate), notably Ernst Nolte and his defenders. Indeed in postwar Germany, the economic miracle served as a pretext for evasion or facile transcendence of the past, and it was at times unclear whether the object of even unsuccessful mourning and of the melancholy accompanying manic economic activity was the victims of the Holocaust or the lost glories of the *Hitlerzeit*. These glories reappear in bitter-sweet, more or less addled form in such later media events as Joachim Fest's biographical film on Hitler (as well as his 1973 book, *Hitler: Eine Biographie*, with its excessive focus on Hitler's preHolocaust early years and its obsession with the question of whether Hitler achieved at least "negative greatness") or Hans-Jürgen Syberberg's imposing but deeply equivocal *Hitler—Ein Film aus Deutschland* of 1977 (distributed in the United States as "Our Hitler"). Yet the memory lapses of trauma are conjoined with the tendency compulsively to repeat, relive, be possessed by, or act out traumatic scenes of the past, whether in more or less controlled artistic procedures or in uncontrolled existential experiences of hallucination, flashback, dream, and retraumatizing breakdown triggered by incidents that more or less obliquely recall the past. In this sense, what is denied or repressed in a lapse of memory does not disappear; it returns in a transformed, at times disfigured and disguised manner.

The recent past has been marked by the proliferation of museums, monuments, and memorials dedicated to the Holocaust. But of special significance among sites for memory and trauma are survivor testimonies, which find an important place in museums and exhibits themselves. Along with physical sites, the testimonies of survivors, perpetrators, and more or less complicitous bystanders form the core of Claude Lanzmann's important film *Shoah* (1985). For the serious student, the most significant repository of survivor testimonies is the Yale Fortunoff collection, which by the end of 1996 included approximately 3,700 witness accounts. The testimonies that are to be gathered under the auspices of Steven Spielberg will dwarf the Yale collection, for his Survivors of the Shoah Foundation plans to record the testimony of 50,000 survivors. "With offices in Los Angeles, New York and Toronto, and soon in Washington, D.C.; Jerusalem; Paris; and Sydney, Australia, the non-profit project scans the globe for survivors."[2] Whatever else one may think of it, Spielberg's initiative is an indication that the testimony has recently become a prevalent and important genre of nonfiction that raises the problem of the interplay between fact and fantasy. And witnessing—typically, witnessing based on memory—has emerged as a privileged mode of access to the past and its traumatic occurrences.

Testimonial witnessing typically takes place in a belated manner, often after the passage of many years, and it provides insight into lived experience and its transmission in language and gesture. So great has been the preoccupation with testimony and witnessing that they have in some quarters almost displaced or been equated with history itself.[3] Yet this equation is deceptive. Testimony is a crucial source for history. And it is more than a source. It poses special challenges to history. For it raises the issue of the way in which the historian or other analyst becomes a secondary witness, undergoes a transferential relation, and must work out an acceptable subject-position with respect to the witness and his or her testimony. Transference here implies the

---

[2] Sherry Amatenstein, "A Rescue Mission with a Time Clock," *USA Weekend* (5–7 May 1995), p. 4. The Max Charitable Foundation, which Spielberg also created, provided funding for the establishment of the Steven Spielberg Film and Video Library at the United States Holocaust Memorial Museum in Washington. Its goal is "to acqure and organize all significant film and video images of the Holocaust and related aspects of World War II not yet in the Museum's collection." *The Year in Review*, 1994–1995, publication of the United States Holocaust Memorial Museum, p. 7. Of course the recent interest in memory is an overdetermined phenomenon. Among the many reasons for it, one may also mention the rise in self-consciousness, the concern with the past, and the need to rewrite history from different perspectives manifested by various groups, including African Americans, Native Americans, and Hispanic Americans.

[3] See especially Lawrence Langer, *Holocaust Testimonies: The Ruins of Memory* (New Haven: Yale University Press, 1991), and Shoshana Felman and Dori Laub, M.D., *Testimony: Crises of Witnessing in Literature, Psychoanalysis and History* (New York: Routledge, 1992).

tendency to become emotionally implicated in the witness and his or her testimony with the inclination to act out an affective response to them. These implications and responses vary with the subject-positions of the witness and the interviewer, historian, or analyst as well as with the work done on those subject-positions to reenact or transform them.

One basis for the intensity of the recent interest in testimonies is the advanced age of survivors and the feeling that time is short before living memory of the Holocaust by its victims will itself be a thing of the past. An equally pressing concern is created by negationists and "revisionists" who attack the validity of that memory and deny or normalize the abominations of the *Hitlerzeit*, foremost among which is of course the Shoah. Figures such as Robert Faurisson are able to appeal to extremes in denying the excesses of the past, for they may turn either to hyperbolic neopositivism that demands absolute verification to establish the mere existence of gas chambers or to equally exaggerated relativism and constructivism that affirm the ultimately fictive, subjective nature of all narrative and interpretive schemas. One of the forces behind the turn to memory is the threat posed by negationists and the wish-fulfilling desires or demands they satisfy, a threat that looms ever larger to the extent that survivors with primary memory of events pass from the historical scene.

Witnessing is a necessary condition of agency, and in certain cases it is as much as one can expect of someone who has been through a limit-experience. It is altogether crucial as a way in which an intimidated or otherwise withdrawn victim of trauma may overcome being overwhelmed by numbness and passivity, reengage in social practice, and acquire a voice that may in certain conditions have practical effects (for example, in a court of law). But just as history should not be conflated with testimony, so agency should not simply be conflated with, or limited to, witnessing. In order to change a state of affairs in a desirable manner, effective agency may have to go beyond witnessing to take up more comprehensive modes of political and social practice.

Before proceeding further, I would like to indicate briefly the way certain historians have addressed the problem of memory and its relation to history. One important tendency is to dwell, at times obsessively, on the danger I evoked in opening this discussion—the danger of an obsession with, or fixation on, memory. This tendency is epitomized in the recent book by Eric Conan and Henry Rousso, *Vichy, un passé qui ne passe pas.*[4] In Rousso's earlier book, *The Vichy Syndrome: History and Memory in France since* 1944,[5] he made explicit use of a psychoanalytic framework and concluded with a discussion of a collective French obsession with Vichy since the mid-70s. In the more recent book, he and Conan dispense with the explicit psychoanalytic framework, including its more critical dimensions, yet retain one of its more problematic features: the pathologization of historical processes. Moreover, the mere mention, without sufficient elaboration, of the earlier book's treatment of incomplete mourning, repression, and return of the repressed in post-Vichy France gives a somewhat unsituated and excessive prominence to the putative role of obsession in the more recent past and seems simply to oppose it to—rather than present it as intimately linked with—repression, denial, and "taboo." Conan and Rousso's argument is also rendered rather questionable by a somewhat unguarded invocation in the title of the book of the phrase made famous, if not infamous, by Ernst Nolte in the German historians' debate of 1986.[6] Since a detailed discussion of Conan and Rousso's book would, in the present context, take me too far afield, I shall turn to an article that encapsulates some of its crucial dimensions, especially the more thought-provoking ones: Charles Maier's "A Surfeit of Memory? Reflections on History, Melancholy and Denial."[7]

Maier quickly removes the question mark from his title by arguing emphatically that there has been a surfeit or excess of memory in the recent past, specifically among intellectuals. "It is apparent that in the past few years the intellectuals' fascination with memory continues unabated; not just with the times past that we seek to remember—although historical retrieval has also become a culture industry—but with the act of remembering itself, with its psychic phenomenology" (p. 137). Maier tends to pathologize the turn to memory: "I . . . believe we have in a sense become addicted to memory. . . . I think it is time to ask whether an addiction to memory can become neurasthenic and

---

[4] Paris: Fayard, 1994. Another way to formulate this tendency is in terms of a meta-obsession, or obsession with the problem of obsession.

[5] Trans. Arthur Goldhammer (Cambridge: Harvard University Press, 1991).

[6] "Vergangenheit, die nicht vergehen will," *Frankfurter Allgemeine Zeitung*, 6 June 1986. Translated with other documents related to the historians' debate in James Knowlton and Truett Cates, *Forever in the Shadow of Hitler? Original Documents of the Historikerstreit, the Controversy concerning the Singularity of the Holocaust* (Atlantic Highlands, N.J.: Humanities Press, 1993), pp. 18–23.

[7] *History & Memory* 5 (1993), 136–51.

disabling. At the least we should ask what characteristics of our time may have helped to bring about this indulgence" (pp. 140–41). Here one might pause over the attempt to follow an admittedly impressionistic judgment about a surfeit of memory with a pathologizing gesture that leads to an attempt at causal explanation. I would, however, prefer to focus on the more genuinely challenging sides of Maier's argument. For it readily becomes apparent that he is preoccupied not simply with a quantitative excess that signals a morbid preoccupation but with a specific quality or kind of memory to which he objects.

Indeed the memory that upsets him is itself something one indulges in with bitter-sweet melancholy (pp. 138–39). It is the chocolate-covered madeleine of the psyche on which one overdoses. Memory in this phenomenological sense presumably gives direct access to experience, often vicarious experience, that may be sacralized or seen as auratic—notably the traumatic experience of victimization (p. 144). Thus construed, memory involves fixation on the past that inhibits action in the present oriented to a more desirable future. Moreover, Maier is particularly concerned with the questionable functions of Holocaust commemoration for American Jews. As he puts the point:

> There has been from time to time another function or subtext of Holocaust commemoration. It has served to impose a certain unity on the Jewish community in the United States. Like the loyalty oaths that professors had to sign in the 1950s, the Holocaust museum implies a bland statement that establishes group cohesion not by imposing stringent codes, but precisely by calling for a pledge of allegiance that seems so undemanding that only the really disloyal could object.
>
> To pose an alternative heuristic question: why not a museum of American slavery? Would it not be a more appropriate expenditure of national land and funds to remember and make vivid crimes for which our own country must take responsibility rather than those perpetrated by a regime which, in fact, Americans gave their lives to help destroy? Or why not a museum of American Indian suffering from smallpox to Wounded Knee and the alcoholism of the reservations? Of course, the affected groups might not want this sort of museum. If we polled spokespersons for African Americans and American Indians, they might prefer a museum which integrated the proud moments of their history and culture with its moments of victimization in some linear or historical order. Why does the new Jewish museum center on

the catastrophe? And why is it this catastrophe and not the slave auction block or Andrew Jackson's ethnic cleansing of the Cherokee that is remembered on the Mall? (p. 146)

The force of Maier's questions is not eliminated by the fact that the Holocaust museum in Washington does include other victims of Nazi oppression, such as homosexuals and "Gypsies," and it also exhibits the unwillingness of the United States to change immigration laws or take other steps to assist victims of the Nazis during the Second World War. Nor should one be diverted from the questions Maier poses by the hyperbolic aspects of his account. (For example: "In fact, modern American politics, it might be argued, has become a competition for enshrining grievances. Every group claims its share of public honor and public funds by pressing disabilities and injustices. National public life becomes the settlement of a collective malpractice suit in which all citizens are patients and physicians simultaneously" [p. 147].) Instead I shall conclude with Maier's thought-provoking political argument:

The surfeit of memory is a sign not of historical confidence but of a retreat from transformative politics. It testifies to the loss of a future orientation, of progress toward civic enfranchisement and growing equality. It reflects a new focus on narrow ethnicity as a replacement for encompassing communities based on constitutions, legislation and widening attributes of citizenship. The program for this new ethnicity is as symbolic as it is substantive. It aspires preeminently to the recognition by other groups of its own suffering and victimhood. Finally, it cathects to landscape and territory because territoriality has been abandoned as a physical arena for civic action and is nurtured instead as an enclave of historicism. (p. 150)

This quasi-Habermasian critique of memory may be fruitfully related to other critiques of narrow identity politics, such as those found in Judith Butler or Paul Gilroy.[8] In my judgment, it incriminates not all

---

[8] See especially, Judith Butler, *Bodies That Matter: On the Discursive Limits of "Sex"* (New York: Routledge, 1993), and Paul Gilroy, *The Black Atlantic: Modernity and Double Consciousness* (Cambridge: Harvard University Press, 1993). One may note that, in the liturgical or iconic reception of the Holocaust and its traces or representations, one has a paradoxical use of it as a founding trauma that may attempt to establish identity rather than to pose the question of identity problematically. The complex issue of the founding trauma extends beyond the Holocaust and deserves further investigation.

concern for memory—or even some fantastic quantitative surplus of memory—but a certain kind of memory that may indeed be politically diversionary and self-indulgent. Maier's critique serves as a reminder that another kind of memory is more desirable, memory requiring the kind of memory-work Freud related to working through the past. Memory in this sense exists not only in the past but in the present and future tenses. It relates acknowledgment and immanent critique to situational transcendence of the past that is not total but is nonetheless essential for opening up more desirable possibilities in the future.

The kind of memory I would see Maier as cogently criticizing is itself locked in a binary opposition with history or simply conflated with it rather than implicated in a more problematic, mutually questioning relation to it. Other historians in the recent past have indeed anxiously opposed history to memory or, on the contrary, avidly approximated it to, if not confounded it with, memory. In the first instance, memory is crucial because it is what history must define itself against, whether happily or sadly. Memory in brief becomes the antithesis or "other" of history. In the second instance, memory's importance stems from its putative position as the ground or essence of history. Memory is then understood as basically the same as history or at least as history's matrix and muse.

The first tendency often leads to a neopositivistic understanding of history as a dry and sober matter of fact and analysis and to a suspicion of memory as inherently uncritical and close to myth. Memory not only plays tricks; it is purportedly constituted by its tricks, which make it intrinsically unreliable as a historical source. The second tendency induces a fictionalizing if not mythologizing idea of history that is insensitive to the tricks memory plays and to the reasons for those tricks. Instead there is a tendency to go with memory's flow, mingle fact and fancy, provide ingratiating personal anecdotes or autobiographical sketches, and moot the question of the relation between history and fiction. This second tendency is evident not only in certain approaches to history but in such genres as the television docudrama.[9] Need-

---

[9] For a controversial historical work making use of fiction, see especially Simon Schama, *Dead Certainties* (New York: Knopf, 1992). I shall later discuss a book that might be taken as the theoretical complement of the tendency to ground history in memory merged with the imaginary: Patrick H. Hutton's *History as an Art of Memory* (Hanover, N.H.: University Press of New England, 1993).

less to say, these two tendencies are not genuine alternatives but enemy brothers that feed symptomatically off each other.

The binary opposition between memory and history is very prevalent in recent thought. I shall simply provide two examples, one of which seems to valorize history over memory and the other, memory over history.[10] In the first, history is a demythologizing form of secular enlightenment; in the second, it is the destroyer of a more authentic, existentially rich, living memory.

Arno Mayer writes:

Compared to the Muse of memory, the Muse of history is sworn to certain ideas and rules for recording and interpreting the past. Since the Enlightenment, historians have shared certain commonsense notions of causality and accuracy. They have also presumed the past to be accessible by virtue of being profane, not providential. In addition, rather than give free rein to their subjectivity, they are supposed to master it. At a minimum, historians are expected to avow their own prejudices and to probe those of their sources. No less important, they invite critics, both friendly and hostile, to verify the authenticity and reliability of their evidence as well as to debate the logic of their constructions and the coherence of their explanations. Historians must also develop a lateral and wide-angled vision, for they are enjoined to probe for linkages between events that were unclear or unknown to contemporaries.[11]

This seemingly unexceptionable statement not only tends to conflate memory with myth or ideology. It also positions history in a purely enlightened realm that may divert attention from the continual need to engage in a critique of ideology and to examine one's implication in the problems one studies—issues that are pronounced with respect to extremely traumatic phenomena in which one's investment is great and the problem of subject-position and voice is particularly acute. I have elsewhere devoted an extensive analysis to Mayer's book and problems related to it.[12] Here I shall simply observe that the result of Mayer's procedure is to reproduce a rather "mythical" or "ideologi-

[10] See also the opposition between history and memory in Yosef Hayim Yerushalmi, *Zakhor: Jewish History and Jewish Memory* (New York: Schocken, 1987).

[11] *Why Did the Heavens Not Darken? The "Final Solution" in History* (New York: Pantheon, 1988), p. 17.

[12] *Representing the Holocaust: History, Theory, Trauma* (Ithaca: Cornell University Press, 1994), chap. 3.

cal" opposition in the very attempt to master the problem of myth and its secular displacements. Despite its symptomatic interest, this procedure provides an insufficient basis for an attempt to work critically through one's implication in the problems one treats. In Mayer's account it is related to a one-sided, reductive effort to construe Nazi anti-Semitism as a "parasite" (Mayer's term) on anti-Bolshevism and to explain the Holocaust as the consequence of failed instrumental rationality or, more precisely, as the unintended consequence of the Nazis' eastern campaign against the Soviet Union. In the process there is an evacuation of the displaced and deranged sacrificial, scapegoating dimensions of Nazi practice as well as a pacification of the very trauma of the Holocaust. The more traumatic and disturbing dimensions of the Nazi period are the incentive for the turn to the problem of memory, yet they become normalized or domesticated in the placid opposition between memory and history.

The specific nature of Pierre Nora's opposition between memory and history differs from Mayer's. But I would contend that there is a similar neutralization of trauma and an insufficient basis for a critical attempt to work through one's transferential implication in the processes one studies. Nora's opposition comes in his important introductory essay to the three-volume study he edited, *Les lieux de mémoire*.[13] For Nora, memory and history, "far from being synonyms," are "opposed" (p. xix). Indeed "it is the very mode of historical perception that, with the assistance of the media, has prodigiously expanded and substituted the ephemeral film of topicality for a memory that folds back on the legacy of its own intimacy [c'est la mode même de la perception historique qui, media aidant, s'est prodigieusement dilaté, substituant à une mémoire repliée sur l'héritage de sa propre intimité la pellicule éphémère de l'actualité]" (p. xviii). Nora goes on to elucidate this rather enigmatic and lyrical assertion:

> Acceleration: what the phenomenon finally reveals to us in brutal
> fashion is all the distance between true, social, and untouchable mem-
> ory, for which so-called primitive or archaic societies have represented
> the model and carried off the secret—and history, which is what our
> societies, condemned to forgetfulness, make of the past because they
> are carried away by change. Between an integrated memory, dictatori-

[13] Paris: Gallimard, 1984. All translations are my own.

al and unconscious of itself, a memory with a past that eternally brings back a legacy, referring the ancestral past to the undifferentiated time of heroes, origins, and myths—and ours, which is only history, trace, and sifting. A distance that has only deepened as men have accorded themselves, more and more in modern times, a right, a power, and even a duty to change. Distance that today finds its convulsive culminating point.

It is as if this tearing away of memory under the conquering and crushing pressure of history has an effect of revelation: the rupture of a very ancient bond of identity, the end of what we live as self-evident: the equivalence [adéquation] of history and memory. (p. xviii)

It is difficult not to read this pathos-charged, exaggerated, if at times equivocal evocation of memory (the past-we-have-lost) as a distant echo of Lévi-Strauss's opposition between "hot" and "cold" societies, an echo whose own mythologizing resonance is only accentuated by the fact that it was put forth in almost willful oblivion of Derrida's painstaking deconstruction of the opposition on which it is based. But what is also symptomatically evoked in this passage is a sense of trauma that is both veiled and displaced by the romantically folkloric form it takes. Nora feels that something essential has been lost, and—whether or not the loss is itself imaginary—the very opposition between history and memory serves to commemorate and assuage it.

One is tempted to interject here what should be obvious. Of course memory is not identical with history. But neither is it the opposite of history. Their relation over time may vary, but not as a function of a categorical opposition between "us" and "them." And the problem of their actual and desirable interaction is oversimplified by a stark opposition between the two. Memory is a crucial source for history and has complicated relations to documentary sources. Even in its falsifications, repressions, displacements, and denials, memory may nonetheless be informative—not in terms of an accurate empirical representation of its object but in terms of that object's often anxiety-ridden reception and assimilation by both participants in events and those born later. For example, the prevalent idea among victims and others that Nazis made soap of Jews is empirically false, but it has a figurative value both in terms of the very real Nazi tendency to reduce Jews to objects and in terms of its inversion of Nazi ritual and hygienic anxiety over contamination by Jews. (Here the homeopathic remedy—the "poison" that in an appropriate dosage becomes the cure or the putative contaminant that is turned into a cleansing force—is distorted into a bitter irony.) Moreover, a critically informed memory is crucial in the attempt to determine what in history deserves preservation in living traditions, either as something to be criticized and avoided or as something to be respected and emulated. Conversely, history serves to question and test memory in critical fashion and to specify what in it is empirically accurate or has a different, but still possibly significant, status. Indeed once history loses contact with memory, it tends to address dead issues that no longer elicit evaluative and emotional interest or investment. Here one might argue that history has at least two functions: the adjudication of truth-claims and the transmission of critically tested memory. One may even contend that history may legitimately have a ritual component insofar as it is not confined to neopositivistic protocols but rather engages, at least discursively, in its own variant of the form of memory-work and working-through that is embodied in mourning, a process that may be called for with respect to victims of traumatic events. In any case, one's judgment concerning the appropriateness of a historical account—one's very sense of whether or not the language used is "fitting"—may require, at least with respect to limit-cases, an appeal to ritual as well as to scientific and aesthetic criteria.

In the foregoing respects one might contend that history and memory have a supplementary relation that is a basis for a mutually questioning interaction or open dialectical exchange that never attains totalization or full closure. Memory is both more and less than history, and vice-versa. History may never capture certain elements of memory: the feel of an experience, the intensity of joy or suffering, the quality of an occurrence. Yet history also includes elements that are not exhausted by memory, such as demographic, ecological, and economic factors. More important, perhaps, it tests memory and ideally leads to the emergence of both a more accurate memory and a clearer appraisal of what is or is not factual in remembrance.

I would here distinguish between primary and secondary memory. Primary memory is that of a person who has lived through events and remembers them in a certain manner. This memory almost invariably involves lapses relating to forms of denial, repression, suppression, and evasion, but it also has an immediacy and power that may be compelling. Secondary memory is the result of critical work on primary memory, whether by the person who initially had the relevant experiences or, more typically, by an analyst, observer, or secondary witness such as the historian. The participant and the observer-participant meet on the ground of secondary memory, where they may conceivably agree on certain things that constitute accurate memory. They may even debate the relevance of that memory for social and political life in the present and future. In any case, the elaboration of an accurate, critically tested secondary memory on the basis of primary memory and other evidence is the specific task of the historian, which goes beyond but certainly includes being an attentive listener or secondary witness with respect to the testimony of witnesses. This secondary memory may come to take the place of, or at least supplement, primary memory and be internalized as what one indeed remembers. Secondary memory is also what the historian attempts to impart to others who have not themselves lived through the experience or events in question. This procedure may require a muted or diminished transmission of the traumatic nature of the event but not a full reliving or acting out of it. It also requires an interpretation and estimation of what in memory is other than factual.

In addition, it is obvious but important to note that no memory is purely primary. It has always already been affected by elements not deriving from the experience itself. To the extent an event is traumatic, it creates a gap or hole in experience. Otherwise it is processed—and affected by processing—as it is experienced through the mediation of forms, types, archetypes, and stereotypes that have been assimilated or elaborated in the course of life. With respect to trauma, memory is always secondary since what occurs is not integrated into experience or directly remembered, and the event must be reconstructed from its effects and traces. In this sense there is no fully immediate access to the experience itself even for the original witness, much less for the secondary witness and historian. Conversely, to the extent there is immediate access through the reliving or acting-out of the event, memory is inhibited, and working-through requires that acting-out be supplemented by secondary memory and related processes (for example, narration, analysis, bodily gesture, or song).

Just as history goes beyond or falls short of memory, so memory has a comparable relation to history. There may be aspects of memory that have no place in history, for example, aspects of my personal life that do not bear on—and may even be diversionary, tendentious, or irrelevant with respect to—certain issues. For this reason, the turn to anecdote and autobiography must be carefully motivated if it is not to be dubious. For example, if I were able to elaborate them in a certain way or at least provide enough material to enable others to do so, it might be relevant in understanding my interest in the Holocaust, at least on the level of motivation (not justification), to know that although I was raised as a Catholic, I grew up in a Jewish neighborhood, had many close Jewish friends, and was a Sabbath goy. It might also be relevant to know that I left this neighborhood at about the time of puberty while simultaneously losing the Catholic faith—losses I experienced as difficult if not traumatic. For a few years following the move, I even returned regularly to my old neighborhood to refind my friends who still lived there. I now realize that some of the people I knew there were undoubtedly Jewish emigrés from Nazi-controlled areas of Europe. Indeed these aspects of my life might be especially significant in that they involved disruptions and belated recognitions that might be a precondition for becoming sensitive to larger and more catastrophic disruptions in history. Other aspects of my life might be less relevant and of little more than narcissistic interest in a discussion of the Shoah.[14]

These formulations barely begin to scratch the surface of a complex set of problems. But they may be enough to cast doubt on the opposition between memory and history and to suggest that the problem is instead their actual and desirable interaction. The opposition does nonetheless have symptomatic value: it attests to the pressure exerted by certain concerns that induces even astute and insightful historians to resort to questionable modes of conceptualization, especially in the case of traumatic events that still carry an intense affective and ideological charge and bear upon contemporary issues and social problems. The French Revolution has been, and in limited ways continues to be, this kind of event, although at present one might suspect that the tendency among *Annales* historians to devote disproportionate attention to it and to facets of the old regime has functioned in the past (and may still function) as a palliative screen that obscures more recent traumas, especially that of France under Vichy. The Shoah and attendant phenomena constitute a traumatic series of events with which we are still attempting to come to terms, and it is psychoanalytically significant

---

[14] It is, however, also important to note that the study of the Holocaust has now passed beyond the confines of Jewish studies or a sector of German studies and has become a problem of general concern. One need provide no autobiographical or other particular motivation to account for one's interest in it, and the important consideration is what results from that interest.

that often the transition from restricted, indirect allusions to extended and more or less specific discussions of it among important French thinkers such as Derrida, as well as those in this country who take them as reference points (including myself), was at least in part motivated by displacement in the technical sense, that is, by way of the discovery of Paul de Man's early journalism and the resurgence of the controversy over Heidegger's Nazi turn. In and of themselves these two phenomena are of relatively minor significance with respect to the Holocaust and might at most warrant a footnote in a general history of it.

In any event, the more general problem of trauma has been prominent in recent thought. In the (curiously named) field of "trauma theory," there is a great temptation to trope away from specificity and to generalize hyperbolically, for example, through an extremely abstract mode of discourse that may at times serve as a surrogate for a certain form of deconstruction, elaborate an undifferentiated notion of all history (or at least all modernity) as trauma, and overextend the concept of victim or survivor. But the turn to trauma is important, and it poses the dual challenge of not avoiding the disconcerting dimensions of the past and of consistently relating theory to specific problems in historical, social, and political analysis.

Splitting off history from memory may mitigate trauma. But mitigation or even avoidance may also result from the counterpart to splitting or dissociation: the conflation of history and memory. In this respect Patrick H. Hutton's *History as an Art of Memory* is especially interesting, for it by and large omits the problem of trauma in its attempt to ground history in memory. Although there is much useful information and discussion in the book, its general approach makes it subject to Eric Santner's analysis of narrative fetishism:

> By narrative fetishism I mean the construction and deployment of a narrative consciously or unconsciously designed to expunge the traces of the trauma or loss that called that narrative into being in the first place. . . . [It] is the way an inability or refusal to mourn employs traumatic events; it is a strategy of undoing, in fantasy, the need for mourning by simulating a condition of intactness, typically by situating the site and origin of loss elsewhere.[15]

[15] "History beyond the Pleasure Principle," in Saul Friedlander, ed., *Probing the Limits of Representation: Nazism and the "Final Solution"* (Cambridge: Harvard University Press, 1992), p. 144. On Hutton, see note 9.

Hutton objects to what he sees as the postmodern emphasis on representation and wants, phenomenologically and hermeneutically, to go back to the thing itself: lived experience, its perpetuation in traditions of living memory, and its imaginative reliving in historicism. One need not be an unqualified advocate of postmodernism to note that some figures whom Hutton discusses (such as Foucault) or mentions disparagingly in passing (such as Derrida) have been preoccupied with the problems of trauma, disruption, and disorientation, albeit at times in too general or allusive a fashion. Hutton simply overlooks these postmodern concerns and does not indicate how they might be related to his attempt to determine the relation of memory to history. He insistently asserts:

> It is not enough to describe the past through its representations, for
> that presupposes a detachment that is alien to the lived experiences
> that memory bears into the present. Living memory is ultimately the
> ground of the historians' interest in the past, just as it was once the
> foundation of the identity of the historical actors that they now seek to
> understand. It inspires the historians' inquiry, just as the search for
> that which has been forgotten serves as their goal. (p. 72)

One may agree that history is not limited to describing the representations and uses of the past, however important these tasks may be. But one may ask how precisely memory carries lived experiences into the present and question Hutton's seeming belief in unmediated access to the past through imaginatively reliving its experiences as they are handed down in living traditions. The past itself for him is construed as a pure, positive presence that is not beset with its own disruptions, lacunae, conflicts, irreparable losses, belated recognitions, and challenges to identity. It is thus utterly idealized and mythologized. Indeed Hutton's procedure might lead one to suggest that it is not so much memory per se as certain modern constructions of it that lend themselves to misleading mythologization. In fact his conception of reimagining and reliving the past threatens to confuse acting-out (that is, compulsively reliving past experience) with reenacting selective aspects of it found to be desirable on the basis of critical judgment and memory as the achievement of working through problems.

With respect to historiography, Hutton ignores the intricate relation between any form of empathy or identification and critical distance, a relation that is necessary not only for understanding but also for any attempt to form cogent judgments about what is desirable in the past and deserves to be reworked or flexibly reenacted (in contrast to compulsively acted out) in the present. His conception of experience, tradition, and memory remains abstractly positive, even nostalgically mystified, and this conception is furthered by the fact that he provides no historical examples of the kinds of experience and living memory he wants to affirm. In addition, he understands Freud as unproblematically within historicist and hermeneutic traditions. One gets little if any idea of the way Freud addressed the dislocation of experience and memory in trauma or of the difficulties that, for him, beset the process of working through problems toward memory and renewed agency in the face of the uncanny, the repetition compulsion, and acting-out.

Hutton's hero is Philippe Ariès, who he thinks shares his approach to history and draws from family values and localism as personal bases for the understanding of memory as the ground of history. Indeed, family and locality as viewed through the idealizing prism of personal memory remain the only examples of the kinds of experience and tradition that Hutton offers the reader. Moreover, he devotes a long chapter to the French Revolution while confining his references to the Nazi period and Vichy to rare allusions that do not confront the dilemmas these historical phenomena pose for his advocacy of tradition and living memory. The result is a variant of neoconservative historiography that is not defended argumentatively. Instead it is ideologically encrypted in an overly general plea for memory and tradition. I shall conclude my discussion of Hutton by quoting his opening lines, which set the tone for the discussion that follows them:

> I have always cherished local memories for the way they lead into a
> larger past. I grew up in what remains for me an enchanted landscape.
> Princeton, New Jersey, where I was raised, was saturated with com-
> memorative places, to which a wonderful, old teacher . . . led me and
> my third-grade classmates on her last walking tour of the historic
> houses of Princeton. Then there is my Irish heritage, with its senti-
> mental lore, though this past is more obscure. On my mother's side,
> we had a famous ancestor. (p. xi)

The world seems to change as we turn to Saul Friedlander, who had a different past and whose struggles with history and memory are also quite different from Hutton's. Friedlander's *Memory, History, and the*

Extermination of the Jews of Europe is centrally concerned with all the problems that Hutton ignores or marginalizes.[16] The Nazi period reminds us, if such reminding is necessary, that there are deadly "living traditions" such as racism and anti-Semitism and that even values such as genuine love of the locality, or *Heimat,* can be perverted. Unfortunately, their perversion may be precisely the place from which one has to start in any contemporary attempt to rehabilitate them. Edgar Reitz's monumentally uncritical film *Heimat* (1984), in which the film-maker seems to share the limited memory and lapses of his characters, at least serves to show that a homey sense of locality may well be preserved by preventing disturbing forces from impinging too directly on one's consciousness. Friedlander has coined the term *Heimatsgeschichte* to designate the type of history that mitigates or evades threats to identity and a desired self-image: these threats are blurred or confined to the periphery of awareness, while the central focus remains fixated on the more normal sides of everyday life that lend themselves to endearing nostalgia.

Friedlander's idea of the way in which the Holocaust is distinctive or even unique is thought-provoking yet combines two contentions. "The Nazi regime attained what is, in my view, some sort of theoretical outer limit: one may envision an even larger number of victims and a technologically more efficient way of killing, but once a regime decides that groups, whatever the criteria may be, should be annihilated there and then and never be allowed to live on Earth, the ultimate has been achieved. This limit, from my perspective, was reached only once in modern history: by the Nazis" (pp. 82–83). I would propose that Friedlander's first contention frames his second and even that it makes the more important point. The essential consideration is that an outer limit was reached and that, once this limit is reached, something radically transgressive or incommensurable has occurred. The limit may be reached more than once in history and still remain distinctive or even unique in a specific, very important sense. To say that in fact the limit was reached only once changes the sense of uniqueness and may even banalize it, notably by prompting a dogmatic assertion of absolutes, a grim competition for first place in victimhood, or the type of research into similarities and differences that easily becomes diversionary and pointless.

Friedlander also notes certain limited ways in which his approach

[16] Bloomington: Indiana University Press, 1993.

to the Shoah may approximate deconstruction, notably in "the avoi ance of closure, the ever-questioning commentary, and the 'excess carried by the Shoah" (p. 131). Without repudiating these family resemblances to deconstruction, he nonetheless insists on the "simultaneous acceptance of two contradictory moves: the search for ever-closer historical linkages and the avoidance of a naive historical positivism leading to simplistic and self-assured historical narrations and closures" (p. 131). Thus the critique of closure, totalization, and simplistic, self-assured narration is not accompanied by what is often rashly imputed to deconstruction: an unqualified affirmation of free play or uncontrolled dissemination. It is rather combined with a search for more comprehensive articulations and forms of understanding that nonetheless remain self-critical and open to contestatory voices, in particular the disturbing voices of victims themselves. In this effort, Friedlander finds especially useful such key psychoanalytic concepts as transference, acting-out, and working-through.

Before turning to these concepts, I would note that in attempting to elucidate "the unease in historical interpretation," the excess and the blockage to understanding embodied in the Shoah, Friedlander quotes and comments on a section of what has perhaps become a proof-text of Nazi ideology and, in certain ways, of important currents in modern thought more generally: Heinrich Himmler's 1943 Posen speech to upper-level SS officers. Friedlander looks to this speech as a way of elucidating the *Unheimlichkeit* ("strangeness" or "uncanniness") of the Shoah and the manner in which it presents the historian with "some imponderables which indeed seem to escape us, included in the overall notion of 'Rausch'" (p. 109). (Friedlander translates *Rausch* as elation, but it can also mean intoxication, delirium, or ecstasy.) Moreover, he notes that "for further analysis, we would need a new category equivalent to Kant's category of the sublime, but specifically meant to capture inexpressible horror" (p. 115).[17]

I shall quote a longer portion of Himmler's speech than that found in *Memory, History, and the Extermination of the Jews of Europe:*

> I also want to make reference before you here, in complete frankness, to
> a really grave matter. Among ourselves, this once, it shall be uttered
> quite frankly; but in public we will never speak of it. Just as we did not

[17] In *Representing the Holocaust,* esp. pp. 105–10, I have tried, perhaps too simply, to approach this category in terms of a negative sublime, an issue to which I shall return.

June 30, 1934, to do our duty as ordered, to stand up against
nrades who had transgressed, and shoot them, also we have
about this and never will. It was the tact which I am glad to
r of course to us that made us never discuss it among our-
talk about it. Each of us shuddered, and yet each one knew
do it again if it were ordered and if it were necessary.
ı am referring to the evacuation of the Jews, the annihilation of the
Jewish people. This is one of those things that are easily said. "The
Jewish people is going to be annihilated" says every party member.
"Sure, it's in our program, elimination of the Jews, annihilation—we'll
take care of it." And then they all come trudging, 80 million worthy
Germans, and each of them has his one decent Jew [*seinen anständigen
Juden*]. Sure, the others are swine, but this one is an A-1 Jew [*ein prima
Jude*]. Of all those who talk this way, not one has seen it happen, not
one has been through it [*keiner hat es durchgestanden*]. Most of you
know what it means to see a hundred corpses lie side by side, or five
hundred, or a thousand. To have stuck this out, and—excepting
cases of human weakness [*abgesehen von Ausnahmen menschlicher
Schwächen*]—to have kept our integrity [*anständig geblieben zu sein*],
that is what has made us hard. In our history this is an unwritten,
never-to-be-written page of glory, for we know how difficult we
would have made it for ourselves if today—amid the bombing raids,
the hardships and the deprivations of war—we still had the Jews in
every city as secret saboteurs, agitators, and demagogues. If the Jews
were still ensconced in the body of the German nation, we probably
would have reached the 1916–17 stage by now.[18]

I have commented on these passages elsewhere and will not repeat
what I have already written.[19] The portion of the speech Friedlander
quotes is as follows:

Most of you know what it means when 100 corpses are lying side by
side, when 500 lie there or 1,000. Having borne that and neverthe-

[18] Lucy Dawidowicz, ed., *A Holocaust Reader* (West Orange, N.J.: Behrman House,
1976), pp. 132–33.
[19] See *Representing the Holocaust*, pp. 105–10. I would, however, repeat the basic
point that silence itself is typically seen as an "appropriate" response in the face of the
sublime—a response that suggests the relation of the sublime to a secular sacred. Moreover, one may argue that, in referring to the "spectacle" of an increasing number of
corpses, Himmler alludes to a kind of initiatory, radically transgressive limit-experi-

less—some exceptional human weaknesses aside—having remained decent [*anständig geblieben zu sein*] has hardened us. . . . All in all, we may say that we have accomplished the most difficult task out of love for our people. And we have not sustained any damage to our inner self, our soul and our character [*und wir haben keinen Schaden in unserem Inneren, in unserer Seele, in unserem Charakter daran genommen*]. (Quoted, p. 105)

Friedlander traces the horror and uncanniness of these lines to two sources: an inversion of values related to the dissonance between breaking the most fundamental of human taboos ("wiping from the face of the earth each and every member of a specific human group") and the "declaration that this difficult task was being accomplished satisfactorily, without any moral damage"; and the awareness that what is for Himmler and elite SS the most glorious page in their history must remain secret and unwritten because it will not be understood by future generations. Friedlander further notes that Hitler's unquestioned obsession with anti-Semitism is not apparent in the case of Himmler and his Posen audience. More important for Himmler

---

ence for Nazi perpetrators—an unspeakable rite of passage involving quasi-sacrifice, victimization, and regeneration through violence. One may also underscore the problem of relating the discourses and practices of pest control and deranged sacrificialism. In his important book, *The Architect of Genocide: Himmler and the Final Solution* (Hanover, N.H.: University Press of New England, 1991), Richard Breitman concludes that Himmler "became a strong racial anti-Semite well before he met Hitler; afterward he became a complete fanatic" (p. 245). When he attempts to offer at least a minimal interpretation of Himmler's actions and motivations in the Holocaust, Breitman uses the language of both sacrifice and pest control without trying to relate them: "Himmler was a human being—above average intellectually, below average physically and emotionally—who became willing to sacrifice tens of millions of people for what he regarded as the future of the German people. He did not really consider his victims human, so was not at all concerned about their suffering or their fate. They were like pests and vermin that any farmer had to dispose of if he was going to sustain himself and his family" (pp. 249–50). One may agree that Jews, for Nazis like Himmler, were never on the same level of humanity as themselves, but Jews' radical otherness might situate them both below that level (with pests or vermin) and somehow above it as phantasmic, powerful, polluting, anxiety-producing, and at times eroticized creatures engaged in harmful conspiracies. Moreover, Himmler's notorious chronic stomach cramps might indicate that problems were not as easy for him to resolve as Breitman seems to believe and that some ideological mechanism, however absurd or cynical, was necessary for Himmler to live with what he was doing. In addition, one has to inquire further into the nature of "sacrifice" in the displaced and deranged form it took in the Nazi genocide as well as into its relation to a seemingly contradictory or antinomical phenomenon such as pest control. One may also note that Kafka's *Metamorphosis* (1915) offers in some small way an uncanny prefiguration of these problems.

were the bond with the Führer ("Führer-Bindung") and the *Rausch* (p. 107).

One may supplement Friedlander's account of the *Rausch* by reference to a 1988 collection of documents entitled *"The Good Old Days": The Holocaust as Seen by Its Perpetrators and Bystanders*, edited by Ernst Klee, Willi Dressen, and Volker Riess.[20] The phrase "The Good Old

[20] 1988; New York: The Free Press, 1991; trans. Deborah Burnstone. It is illuminating to read this book along with a viewing of Leni Riefenstahl's *Triumph of the Will* (1934), a film that was made before the activities of the *Einsatzgruppen* and that touches primarily on the less obviously compromised aspects of Nazi spectacle and *Rausch*. Also worth seeing is the recent film *Profession Neo-Nazi*, which documents the activities of a young neo-Nazi leader, Ewald Althans, who takes Himmler and Heydrich as role models and Ernst Zundel as a new Führer. I would further note that certain implications of *"The Good Old Days"* for understanding perpetrators are both further substantiated through extensive archival research and carried to an interpretive extreme in Daniel Jonah Goldhagen's *Hitler's Willing Executioners: Ordinary Germans and the Holocaust* (New York: Alfred A. Knopf, 1996). Goldhagen tends to reverse Hannah Arendt's notion of the banality of evil and to propose a new rendition of the *Sonderweg* ("special path") view of German history by presenting the Germans as steeped in a national tradition of anti-Semitism that prepared them to participate voluntarily, even whole-heartedly and almost mystically, in the state-sponsored, malicious, cruel torture and killing of the Jews. "The Holocaust was a *sui generis* event" that was enabled by "the long-incubating, pervasive, virulent, racist, eliminationist antisemitism of German culture," and "it was only in Germany that an openly and rabidly antisemitic movement came to power—indeed was elected to power—that was bent upon turning antisemitic fantasy into state-organized genocidal slaughter" (p. 419). I agree with Goldhagen's view of the legitimating role of culture and ideology, although his understanding of them is narrowly, even jargonistically "social-scientific." I also agree with his critique of the reduction of anti-Semitism to a dependent variable, the attribution of primary or even exclusive explanatory force to bureaucratization or the industrialization of mass murder, and the restriction of deep-seated anti-Semitism to a small elite of fanatical Nazis. Indeed Goldhagen adduces extensive evidence to show the prevalence of anti-Semitism in Germany, and he assembles crucial information on perpetrators in "work" camps, death marches, and police battalions. But he is tendentiously fuzzy on the importance of the comparative point that anti-Semitism was virulent in other nations or areas and on the specific relation of anti-Semitism to other factors in explaining the Nazi rise to power and the Holocaust. Moreover, he goes beyond even his extensive evidence both by failing to analyze countertendencies to anti-Semitism in Germany and by generalizing about German society as a whole in a manner that allows for only rare exceptions to "the ubiquity of eliminationist antisemitism" (p. 435). And, despite his criticism of Christopher Browning's normalizing or essentializing tendencies in believing that everyone must have—and thus overcome— inhibitions or moral scruples in order to make genocide possible (see *Ordinary Men: Reserve Police Battalion 101 and the Final Solution in Poland* [New York: Harper Collins, 1992]), Goldhagen relies on his own "normal" reactions as a standard of comparison for those imputed to "ordinary" Germans. He also repeatedly invokes "eliminationist antisemitism" as an ultimate explanatory category and often dichotomizes between voluntarism and the explicit threat or actuality of external coercion (which typically did not exist in the case of police battalions). He thus cannot account for the disturbingly ambiguous status of certain extreme phenomena, the more complex

Days" [*Die Schöne Zeiten*] comes from a caption in a private photo album kept by concentration camp commandant Kurt Franz of Treblinka. Among the photos is one of Franz's dog Barry, which he used to set on prisoners with a command that inverts the status between canine and Jew: "Man, grab the dog!" The legend to the photo tells us that "'Barry' tore many Jews to pieces, on numerous occasions biting off their genitals" (p. 248).

We have perhaps become overly accustomed to accounts of Nazi horrors. But *"The Good Old Days"* is especially disturbing for the way its documents mingle extreme cruelty with kitsch sentiment, notably in the letters of German SS and army personnel to beloved wives and girlfriends, and for the elated, carnivalesque atmosphere that often surrounds the killing of Jews, for both perpetrators and bystanders. The scenes of laughter and cheering are particularly chilling. The quotation that serves as legend to the photo of the so-called Death-dealer of Kaunas (Lithuania), a handsome young, blond man leaning on a club that is almost as tall as he, reads: "Each time a victim was beaten to death they started to clap" (p. 23). The report of a German *Oberst* (army colonel) notes: "At first I thought this must be a victory celebration or some type of sporting event because of the cheering, clapping and laughter that kept breaking out. . . . When I stepped closer, however, I became witness to probably the most frightful event that I had seen during the course of two world wars" (p. 28). As Hugh Trevor-Roper (Lord Dacre) observes in his foreword: "In Kaunas, Lithuania, where Einsatzkommando 3 operated, the Jews were clubbed to death with crowbars, before cheering crowds, mothers holding up their children to see the fun, and German soldiers clustered round like spectators at a football match. At the end, while the streets ran with blood, the chief murderer stood on the pile of corpses as a triumphant hero and played the Lithuanian national anthem on an accordion" (p. xii). This scene is extreme, but not atypical of other incidents documented in the book. Such scenes might lead one to conclude that Himmler underestimated the capacity of those outside the upper ranks of the SS to appreciate, indeed to share, his sentiments.

---

workings of ideology, or his own emotional response to problems. Indeed his inability to elucidate further the nature of "eliminationist antisemitism" and the brutally victimizing, cruel, elated, and often mockingly carnivalesque behavior attending it leads him to translate into the concept of "political culture" what seems close to a stereotype of Germans as anti-Semitic.

It is worth observing that *"The Good Old Days"* is important in its own context as a politically and ethically significant act of memory. The dust-jacket of the book informs the reader that Ernst Klee is a teacher, film-maker, and writer; Willi Dressen, deputy director of the Central Bureau for the Judicial Authorities of the German Länder; and Volker Riess, a historian. The collaboration of three Germans from different professions is indicative of the cross-disciplinary resonance and the entry into public consciousness of the memory of the Holocaust as a political and cultural problem in Germany. Indeed the book marks a high point in a process, which took the often covert or repressed private sentiments concerning the Shoah and the official public representations or avoidances of it that typified the immediate postwar generation and brought them more or less dramatically and disturbingly together, typically through the literal mediation of the media, spectacle, and consumer culture. *"The Good Old Days"* is one of the most thought-provoking and genuinely searching instances of this uneven and at times contentious process, which included such phenomena as Joachim Fest's film *Hitler—A Career* (1977), the broadcast of the American television series *Holocaust* (1979), Edgar Reitz's sixteen-hour television epic and film *Heimat* (1984), and the Historians' Debate (1986).[21]

---

[21] For an informative and stimulating discussion of the broader developments in postwar Germany, see Michael Geyer and Miriam Hansen, "German-Jewish Memory and National Consciousness," in Geoffrey H. Hartman, ed., *Holocaust Remembrance: The Shapes of Memory* (Oxford: Blackwell, 1994), pp. 175–90. Geyer and Hansen's essay is itself self-consciously part of the history it traces. One should not give way to pointless casuistry in certain matters, but it may be worth noting the problem in understanding the relation between the carnivalesque elation in scenes described in *"The Good Old Days"* and the sublime horror and elation alluded to by Friedlander. One may argue that the sublime has modalities varying from the immanent to the transcendent. In this respect, it parallels the sacred of which it may be the secular displacement, and the prototypical sublime-sacred spectacle may be (as René Girard intimates) the traumatic, violent killing of the sacrificial victim. From the perspective of a radically transcendent conception of the sublime, such as that of Jean-François Lyotard, the immanent sublime (notably including sacrifice) would be a degradation of an unrepresentable, radical alterity that is misappropriated when it is rendered immanent or "spectacularized." But other approaches, such as those of Edmund Burke or Ernst Jünger, situate the sublime in more immanent fashion. Even in Kant, from whom Lyotard draws, the sublime, while stemming from a mental projection and in some sense transcendent with respect to worldly objects or phenomena, may be triggered or excited by immanent scenes or spectacles. The carnivalesque (which, contrary to Bakhtin's utopian and idealized populism, may at times involve scapegoating and sacrificial elements) is related to an immanent, possibly spectacularized or secularized sacred. Moreover, in becoming desublimated or immanent the sublime may turn into the grotesque, and the carnivalesque is bound up with an aesthetic of the grotesque rather

Of *Rausch* Friedlander writes:

> Could one of the components of "Rausch" be the effect of a growing
> elation stemming from repetition, from the ever-larger numbers of the
> killed others: "Most of you know what it means when 100 corpses are
> lying side by side, when 500 lie there or 1000." This repetition (and
> here indeed we are back, in part, at Freud's interpretation) adds to the
> sense of *Unheimlichkeit*, at least for the outside observer; there, the per-
> petrators do not appear anymore as bureaucratic automata, but rather
> as beings seized by a compelling lust for killing on an immense scale,
> driven by some kind of extraordinary elation in repeating the killing
> of ever-huger masses of people (notwithstanding Himmler's words
> about the difficulty of this duty). Suffice it to remember the pride of
> numbers sensed in the Einsatzgruppen reports, the pride of numbers
> in Rudolf Höss's autobiography; suffice it to remember Eichmann's
> interview with Sassen: he would jump with glee into his grave know-
> ing that over five million Jews had been exterminated; elation created
> by the staggering dimension of the killing, by the endless rows of vic-
> tims. The elation created by the staggering number of victims ties in
> with the mystical Führer-Bond: the greater the number of the Jews ex-
> terminated, the better the Führer's will has been fulfilled. (pp. 110–11)

The Eichmann evoked in this statement is not Hannah Arendt's, nor
does he resemble the Nazi officials in Claude Lanzmann's *Shoah*. Perhaps the point is that the "banality of evil" may apply to the personalities of individual perpetrators but not to the unimaginable deeds
these mediocrities performed. One may recall as well Freud's notion
of the repetition-compulsion, which he related to the death-drive and
to endless acting-out of traumatic scenes. With reference to Friedlander's mention of the sublime, one might suggest that the sublime
itself seems to involve at least three components: a rupture or block-

---

than the sublime. The more extreme, immanent, and confused forms of a negative sublime may, however, be difficult to distinguish from comparable forms of the grotesque
and carnivalesque. In addition, complex, overdetermined events may mean different
things to different people or even to the same person both over time and at any given
time. What would seem most prominent in the Nazi phenomenon is the role of an immanent or desublimated sublime related to a certain kind of carnivalization as well as
to sacrificialism, regenerative violence, and victimization or scapegoating. One may
also argue that the prohibition of representation is a safeguard against—or foreclosure
of—the immanent sacred, notably including the role of sacrifice.

age of some sort (for example, of understanding); a flooding of the system or potentially traumatizing excess (for example, of anxiety, terror, or at least something beyond understanding—in Kant, the unsettling apprehension of that which cannot be comprehended); and elation (for example, at surviving the risk of rupture and excess, or perhaps for some more unfathomable reason). If this analysis is accurate, it would seem that, for Friedlander, the historian's account somehow repeats (with a difference?) the anxiety-producing rupture and excess active in the object of study but resists or recoils at elation or *Rausch*.

> However, precisely at this point—the elation created by the dimensions of the killing—our understanding remains blocked at the level of self-awareness, and this after the events and because of these events. As the British philosopher Alan Montefiore put it very aptly: "The unimaginable belongs to that part of my darkest imagination— or, at least, that imagination which, whether it be mine or not, I may have to recognize within me—to which my whole conscious, 'normally' sensitive being refuses the very right of existence." Thus, the greater the moral sensitivity, the stricter the repression will be of a subject deemed too threatening to both the individual and society. The historian can analyze the phenomenon from the "outside," but, *in this case, his unease cannot but stem from the noncongruence between intellectual probing and the blocking of intuitive comprehension.* (p. 111)

Here one may supplement Friedlander's account with the argument that the unease provoked by noncongruence should be conjoined with an explicit act of critical distancing and an attempt to check acting-out and the repetition compulsion as well as to counteract the fascination of certain extreme phenomena. This checking depends on critically framing and working through problems by appealing to informed (secondary) memory, judgment, and responsible agency. The inability to recognize oneself, at least potentially, in Himmler may derive from insufficient insight into the self—from what may be radically disorienting or even blinding if it is seen. In other words, it may, as Friedlander intimates, be due to repression or even to the denial of the other within oneself. But an awareness or recognition of the other, to the extent it is desirable, in no sense entails affirmation or acceptance. On the contrary, it requires vigilance and the mounting of conscious resistance to deadly tendencies that are fostered but never simply determined by certain historical conditions whose genesis should be controverted in every legitimate manner.

My comments imply that one way to see the sublime is as involving a transvaluation of trauma that brings to the subject an experience of elation or *Rausch*. They also indicate the need for discriminating among modalities of the sublime and recognizing the temptation and threat of possibilities that should meet with active resistance.

As Friedlander intimates, Kant sets many of the parameters for subsequent discussions of the sublime. Without attempting to go into all the complexities of Kant's account, one may note that for him the sublime is incomparably or absolutely great; surpasses every standard of the senses; stems from the mind and is projected onto nature yet is excited by scenes of wild disorder and desolation; is produced by a momentary checking of vital powers and a consequent stronger outflow of them; and is marked by attraction-repulsion and pleasure in pain. Moreover, the epitome of the sublime is in one's strangely disconcerting, deeply ambivalent relation to a hidden, radically transcendent divinity. And the sublime is evoked by the near-death experience, by coming to the brink of the abyss or of annihilation while escaping death and destruction oneself. Kant even finds the sublime in an aesthetic response to the soldier and war:

> For what is that which is, even to the savage, an object of the greatest admiration? It is a man who shrinks from nothing, who fears nothing, and therefore does not yield to danger, but rather goes to face it vigorously with the most complete deliberation. Even in the most highly civilized state this peculiar veneration for the soldier remains, though only under the condition that he exhibit all the virtues of peace, gentleness, compassion, and even a becoming care for his own person; because even by these it is recognized that his mind is unsubdued by danger. Hence whatever disputes there may be about the superiority of the respect which is to be accorded them, in the comparison of a statesman and a general, the aesthetical judgment decides for the latter. War itself, if it is carried on with order and with a sacred respect for the rights of citizens, has something sublime in it, and makes the disposition of the people who carry it on thus only the more sublime, the more numerous the dangers to which they are exposed and in respect of which they behave with courage. On the other hand, a long peace generally brings about a predominant commercial spirit and,

along with it, low selfishness, cowardice, and effeminacy, and debases the disposition of the people.[22]

There is already a good measure of "inexpressible horror" in Kant's view of the sublime. And, while Kant's evocation of soldiering and war relies on an idealized version of premodern warfare, it is nonetheless noteworthy that Himmler makes some effort to render the sublime horror he evokes compatible with integrity and the avoidance of moral damage to the self.

Given his recognition of the role of repulsion as well as attraction in the sublime, Kant noted that the "satisfaction" brought by it "deserves to be called negative pleasure" (p. 83). Yet Kant was not entirely captivated by the boundlessness of the sublime, and insisted that "the concept of the sublime is not nearly so important or rich in consequence as the concept of the beautiful" (p. 84). With respect to the purposiveness of nature, the theory of the sublime, for Kant, was a "mere appendix" to aesthetic judgment (p. 85). One may wonder whether Kant's analytic of the sublime goes well beyond the bounds of these restrictive comments and whether his principal argument is displaced by its appendix or dangerous supplement. In any case, the sublime after Kant does tend to become prominent if not prepossessing in Romanticism, post-Romanticism, and important sectors of poststructural and postmodern thought.

[22] *The Critique of Judgement*, trans. J. H. Bernard (New York: Collier Macmillan, 1951), p. 102. It is out of the question to try to provide even a sketch of the history of views of the sublime, and my comments are intended as little more than suggestive. One may nonetheless note that Nietzsche was appropriated by Nazis, and certain dimensions of his thought—reinforced by a hyperbolic, elated, at times oracular style—are open to interpretation in terms of Dionysian ecstasy or intoxication, radically transgressive and cruelly festive experimentalism, tradition-shattering transvaluation, and this-worldly regeneration. Yet there are also countercurrents in Nietzsche, including often self-directed irony and parody, in addition to important tendencies critical of scapegoating and victimization. For an attempt to trace the uses and abuses of Nietzsche by Nazis, see Steven E. Aschheim, *The Nietzsche Legacy in Germany 1890–1990* (Berkeley: University of California Press, 1992), chap. 8, and Aschheim, *Culture and Catastrophe: German and Jewish Confrontations with National Socialism and Other Crises* (New York: New York University Press, 1996), chap. 4. In the latter book Aschheim also observes that, during the Weimar Republic, "the perception of decline and impending European catastrophe and the concomitant radical 'will to rupture, revolution, and awakening' was . . . by no means limited to the right. Many of the same strains animated much of what was new on the intellectual left and, often in interdependent ways, the Jewish radical revival" (p. 35). Among those within the Jewish revival, Aschheim focuses on Ernst Bloch, Gershom Scholem, Franz Rosenzweig, and Walter Benjamin. For radically critical and revolutionary strains in Heidegger related to a thematic of the uncanny and the sublime, see my *Representing the Holocaust: History, Theory, Trauma*, chap. 5.

Walter Benjamin of course saw fascism in terms of an aestheticiza-tion of politics. This observation, which has attained the status of a commonplace in contemporary criticism, should not obscure either other dimensions of fascism (including both displaced religiosity and bureaucratic rationality) or the way other ideological tendencies may also aestheticize politics or be in quest of a political sublime, often pos-tulated as having redemptive value. The early Benjamin of the *Critique of Violence* (1921) might himself be seen as involved in that quest, no-tably in his view of the proletarian general strike and his invocation of "divine" violence, and such involvement is one reason for his far from totally negative interest at that time in the work of Georges Sorel and Carl Schmitt. Thus Benjamin's later comment on the aestheticization of politics could be read as in part a self-critique, although it was not made to apply to the redemptive, politically sublime side of one vari-ant of Marxism. Still, a general problem in modern thought is the man-ner in which the sublime is believed to appear or is sought not only in the relatively safe haven of art but in other areas, notably politics and social action, involving displaced religious quests for redemption or salvation. Indeed, open to question is the extent to which the sublime itself may be interpreted as a displaced secular sacred that is uncom-fortably housed in art and that tends to migrate or be actively moved into other areas, with reactions to this tropism ranging from resistance to encouragement and celebration.

Edmund Burke is another touchstone for treatments of the sublime. And while anxiety, terror, and pleasure-in-pain may be found in Kant, they are even more pronounced in Burke's notion of the sublime. Yet the later Burke recoiled at the aestheticizing "sublimation" of politics, and his *Reflections on the Revolution in France* can be read as an argu-ment against a quest for the political sublime that of course also con-veys an ambivalent fascination with it. In the writings of Ernst Jünger, ambivalence tends to be resolved in distinctly dubious ideological di-rections, and sociopolitical action is an avenue to sublimity. Sublime elation is generated by the experience of battle, and the heroic male un-dergoes a secularized sacrificial process of regeneration through vio-lence. Moreover, the high point of heroism for the sensitive soul is to remain hard in the heat of battle and to transvalue trauma into proof of one's superiority, virility, and election. Jünger took his distance from the Nazis, whom he saw as too vulgar for his tastes, but in obvious ways his writings are symptomatic of tendencies that took a more in-sistently destructive and negative cast in Nazi ideology and played a part in fascist thought more generally (for example, in Drieu la Rochelle or Marinetti).

Friedlander at least implicitly links the sublime and the *unheimlich* (uncanny). Yet he does not discuss their relation to the return of the repressed. One may argue that sublimation in Freud involves a movement beyond the senses into "higher" spheres in which otherwise repressed erotic or destructive energy is converted into works of civilization. In this sense sublimation counteracts the return of the repressed and is a domestication or territorialization of the sublime, an attempt to render it less uncanny through either a dialectical elevation (*Aufhebung*) or a more problematic movement of displacement. More disconcertingly, Freud saw the uncanny as the once familiar that was defamiliarized through repression and that induced a compulsive return to the same place. The instance Freud emphasized was the uncanny nature of the female genitals associated with the mother's womb as the once familiar but repressed *Heimat* that becomes *unheimlich*. One might suggest that the sacred and religion in general often tend to have a denied or repressed (rather than an explicitly displaced, sublimated, and partly controlled) position in secular life that may induce an often destructive and violent return of the repressed in disguised, distorted, and extreme forms. Indeed the figuration of the sacred in many modern thinkers has been in terms of sublime scenes of violence, scapegoating, and victimization, scenes often involving misogynistic male fantasies or the acting-out of intergroup (as well as interspecies) prejudice. This is of course a restricted view that may say more about modern orientations toward religion than about the nature of religion in general. (Here the work of Georges Bataille is emblematic, both symptomatic and at times analytically critical of these tendencies.) As I have noted, one may ask whether the sublime itself may be seen as a secular sacred that may even be associated with a strained attempt to transvalue violence and trauma.

In *Representing the Holocaust,* I not only suggested the role of a negative sublime in at least certain Nazis but also cautiously speculated that the victimizing excesses of the Nazi genocide were related to a deranged sacrificialism in the attempt to get rid of Jews as dangerous, at times fascinating, phobic or ritually impure objects that polluted the *Volksgemeinschaft* (community of the people). This self-purifying sacrificialism had a complex relation to racialized biology, eugenics, an "aesthetic ideology" of totalization or beautiful wholeness, and modes of bureaucratization and medicalization, all of which were also manifest in the Nazi genocide. Moreover, this sacrificialism might be interpreted as a return of the repressed, but such an interpretation would not imply a simple regression to some primitive, pre-civilized, or barbarous state. Indeed the problem for understanding would be the disorienting linkage of such sacrificialism to specifically modern conditions, such as bureacratization, formal rationality, and industrialized murder, in which the repressed would return precisely as the repressed or as what *seemed* totally out of place and *unheimlich*. Here I would note that Nazis, or at least some Nazis, may also have resorted to what has been analyzed as "cynical reason." Slavoj Žižek has written of this phenomenon:

> In the *Critique of Cynical Reason* [1983], a great bestseller in Germany, Peter Sloterdijk puts forward the thesis that ideology's dominant mode of functioning is cynical, which renders impossible—or, more precisely, vain—the classic critical-ideological procedure. The cynical subject is quite aware of the distance between the ideological mask and the social reality, but he none the less insists upon the mask. The formula, as proposed by Sloterdijk, would then be: 'they know very well what they are doing, but still, they are doing it.' Cynical reason is no longer naïve, but is a paradox of enlightened false consciousness: one knows the falsehood very well, one is well aware of a particular interest hidden behind an ideological universality, but still one does not renounce it.[23]

I would resist going to the extreme of postulating the irrelevance of ideology in older forms involving belief and false consciousness that require critique. But the possible role of cynical reason is an important consideration that may shed light on aspects of the Nazi genocide. One often asks how Nazis could have taken seriously the more idiotic aspects of their ideology, especially the image of the Jew. Moreover, one may well ask how a sacrificialism, however deranged or disguised, could possibly apply to victims who were ideologically presented as

---

[23] *The Sublime Object of Ideology* (London: Verso, 1989), p. 29. Here one may also suggest a formula for the open secret which the Holocaust at a certain point became in Germany: they know enough to realize that they do not want to know more. On this issue, see especially David Bankier, *The Germans and the Final Solution: Public Opinion under Nazism* (Oxford: Blackwell, 1992).

vermin or filth that was utterly devoid of value. Here the notion of cynical reason may be combined with bureaucratic rationality in helping to account both for the way an ideology may be affirmed in spite of an awareness of its idiocy and for the possible operation of a certain kind of sacrificial mechanism. Here the formula would be: "I know Jews are, according to our ideology, unworthy sacrificial victims (pests, vermin), but I shall sacrifice them anyway." Moreover, cynical reason may well interact with more traditional ideology in a larger constellation. Thus the Nazi genocide could also be sustained by *Rausch* and ecstatic elation in the *Führerbindung* with the belief that, in eliminating Jews, one was doing the will (or obeying the sacred orders) of the supreme leader.

These comments imply that the historian begins with a positive, negative, or ambivalent transferential relation to the object of study as well as to other inquirers into that object. Transference is inevitable to the extent that an issue is not dead, provokes an emotional and evaluative response, and entails the meeting of history with memory. When confronting live issues, one becomes affectively implicated and tends to repeat in oneself at some level the processes active in what one tries to understand. With respect to traumatic events, and certainly with respect to the extremely traumatic limit-event, one must, I think, undergo at least muted trauma and allow that trauma (or unsettlement) to affect one's approach to problems. In treating these events, a kitsch, harmonizing, or fetishistic narrative that denies trauma is particularly objectionable. But one should not remain at the level of acting-out or absolutize the latter in the form of an attempt actually to relive or appropriate others' traumas, even in the case of victims whose traumas cannot be identified with Himmler's reactions. Even if trauma cannot be fully overcome, as it may not be for victims of limit-cases or even for attentive secondary witnesses, it may be counteracted by the attempt to work through problems, mourn the victims of the past, and reengage life in the interest of bringing about a qualitatively better state of affairs. Working through problems would also involve an attempt to acquire greater insight into the tangled web I have evoked, the web linking trauma, the uncanny, the sublime, the secularized sacred, and sacrificialism.

In conclusion, I would change metaphors and note the role of a tragic grid that achieved a paramount place in the Holocaust but in other ways is also evident elsewhere in history. It is the grid that locks together perpetrator, collaborator, victim, bystander, and resister, and that also threatens to encompass the secondary witness and historian. A goal of working-through should be the better understanding of this grid and the attempt to overcome it toward a more desirable network of relations.

In limit-cases the perpetrator may be traumatized. And the perpetrator may suffer from hallucinations, nightmares, and other symptoms of trauma. Himmler, as is well known, suffered from chronic stomach cramps that his masseur, Felix Kersten, saw as psychosomatic in origin. And Himmler's aggressive associate, Erich von dem Bach-Zelewski, was prey to hallucinations and nocturnal fits of screaming connected with the killing of Jews and related activities in the East. But perpetrator trauma, while attended by symptoms that may be comparable to those of victims, is ethically and politically different in decisive ways. The denial or repression of that crucial difference is one basis of the projective attempt either to blame the victim or apologetically to conflate the perpetrator or collaborator with the victim. The traumas of victims are often a reason for the initial lack of resistance when a mode of aggression departs so far from expectations that it is unbelievable and met with incredulity and a total lack of preparedness. As Freud noted, trauma is attended by an absence of *Angstbereitschaft*, the readiness to feel anxiety. One of the purposes of studying history, notably the history of the limit-case, is to generate that anxiety in tolerable, nonparanoid doses so that one is in a better position to avoid or counteract deadly repetitions.

The historian must work out a subject-position in negotiating transference and coming to terms with his or her implication in the tragic grid of participant-positions. The conventional stance for the historian is often closest to that of the innocent bystander or onlooker.[24] But this safe position is particularly questionable in the case of the Holocaust and other extreme or limit-events. The most tempting position is probably that of the resister with marked sympathy for the victim and antipathy for the perpetrator or collaborator. This stance is, however, too easily taken up, especially by someone who has not earned it or been tested by limit-events. I think the historian should attempt to work out a complex position that does not simply identify with one or another participant-position. While acknowledging in particular the need to

---

[24] Even Michael Marrus tends to gravitate toward this blandly conventional position in his very important, extremely informative book, *The Holocaust in History* (New York: Meridian, 1987).

honor the resister and to listen attentively to and respect the position of the victim (or the multiple and variable positions of victims), as well as to appreciate the complexities introduced by what Primo Levi called the gray zone of relations induced by the Nazi policy of trying to make accomplices of victims, the historian should attempt to prepare the way for overcoming the entire complex of relations defined by the grid: perpetrator–collaborator–victim–bystander–resister. These are distinctions whose historical importance one recognizes but that one does not unproblematically valorize or deconstruct. There is an important sense in which one deconstructs only what one valorizes, however ambivalently.[25] These distinctions articulate a network of interrelated subject-positions that one investigates empirically, analyzes carefully and critically, in certain ways attempts to avoid replicating in one's own voice, and tries to overcome in practice. To the extent that it is at all feasible, the purpose of this overcoming would be the generation of a transformed network of relations that counteract victimization and allow for different subject-positions and modes of agency. Working through the past in any desirable fashion would thus be a process (not an accomplished state) and involve not definitive closure or full self-possession but a recurrent yet variable attempt to relate accurate, critical memory-work to the requirements of desirable action in the present.

[25] Here a further distinction is important, that between deconstruction and critique. One deconstructs texts, corpuses, or phenomena (for example, a philosophical tradition, social movement, or institution) that provide the wherewithal for self-criticism in that their more dubious tendencies (such as misogyny or stereotyping) may be countered or contested by other significant dimensions of the text, corpus, or phenomenon. One criticizes texts, corpuses, or phenomena that do not provide sufficient material to contest their own prominent or even dominant tendencies. Thus one may deconstruct Freud and Nietzsche on the basis of the way in which their misogynistic tendencies may be placed in question through other significant dimensions of their writing. By contrast, one criticizes the early journalistic writings (particularly a couple of anti-Semitic texts) of Paul de Man, and even more so Hitler's *Mein Kampf* or Himmler's 1943 Posen speech, in that the ways in which they place themselves in question are relatively weak or largely contained, if not overwhelmed, by their more dominant and very dubious forces. Of course there are problematic cases calling for both deconstruction and critique. But to treat the early journalism of de Man as one would treat his later texts or those of figures such as Nietzsche or Freud indicates a collapse of judgment and a tendency to reprocess projectively (with apologetic implications) rather than to read critically. The goal of deconstruction may well be a situation wherein the more decisive sides of critique are suspended or unnecessary, but, even if one admits the value of this goal, one may doubt whether, on the way to it, one is able to dispense with critique. One may, however, note that forms of immanent critique are close to deconstruction in their assumptions and applicability.

CHAPTER TWO

Revisiting the Historians' Debate:
Mourning and Genocide

My basic premise in this chapter is that the fundamental concepts of psychoanalysis (such as transference, resistance, denial, repression, acting-out, and working-through) undercut the binary opposition between the individual and society, and their application to individual or collective phenomena is a matter of informed argument and research. Freud developed these concepts in a clinical context and thought they applied to collective processes only through analogy; a recurrent concern is how it is possible to extend them to collectivities. I believe that this concern, both in Freud and in others, is based on mistaken individualistic ideological assumptions and gives rise to misguided questions. One should rather call into question the very idea that one is working with a more or less flimsy analogy between the individual and society and argue instead that there is nothing intrinsically "individual" about such concepts as repression and working-through. These concepts refer to processes that always involve modes of interaction, mutual reinforcement, conflict, censorship, orientation toward others, and so forth, and their relative individual or collective status should not be prejudged.[1]

[1] On these issues as well as other questions raised in this chapter, see my *Representing the Holocaust: History, Theory, Trauma* (Ithaca: Cornell University Press, 1994). The present essay takes up, develops further, and supplements lines of analysis and argument in Chapter 2 of *Representing the Holocaust*, occasionally repeating formulations of the earlier essay. In general, it has a dialogical relation to that essay, briefly recalling the position-setting views of Jürgen Habermas and Ernst Nolte and elaborating several points that were only adumbrated in the earlier essay (for example, in the analy-

Mourning may obviously take collective forms, for example, in rituals. *Lieux de mémoire* (in Pierre Nora's phrase) may be *lieux de trauma* as well as commemorative sites, and the question is whether and how they may become *lieux de deuil* (mourning sites) for working through traumatic events. But to what extent are such modern sites as memorials and museums viable in making mourning possible? Can mourning be effective on the level of massive, "imagined" communities such as nation-states? What is the role of smaller, "face-to-face" groups, for example, support groups for victims of trauma? Are they possible bases or at least suggestive paradigms for more durable institutional forms of activity? Can they function as sites for mourning and, more generally, for working through problems? Indeed, can even interviews and testimonies as well as other modes of discourse, dialogue, and debate—including historiography itself—to some extent function as such sites? If so, under what conditions? I shall try to lay the basis for addressing these questions, which should be taken as the horizon of my discussion.

Mourning should be seen in the larger context of Freud's concept of working-through, which has received relatively little elaboration in important forms of post-Freudian psychoanalysis, for example, that influenced by Jacques Lacan. Freud compared and contrasted melancholia with mourning. He saw melancholia as characteristic of an arrested process in which the depressed and traumatized self, locked in compulsive repetition, remains narcissistically identified with the lost

---

ses of transference and cultural representation). Moreover, the present chapter examines the Historians' Debate retrospectively, placing it in relation to later developments in Germany and taking for granted certain analyses in *Representing the Holocaust* (for example, with reference to the problem of "normalizing" the past). On the problem of violence, see my "Violence, Justice, and the Force of Law," *Cardozo Law Review* 11 (1990), 1065–78. The issue of the *Cardozo Law Review* in which this essay appears, entitled *Deconstruction and the Possibility of Justice*, also contains Jacques Derrida's essay, "The Force of Law: The 'Mystical' Foundation of Authority," to which my essay was a response at a conference. The follow-up book of the same title (ed. Drucilla Cornell et al. [New York: Routledge, 1992]) omitted my essay. The earlier version of Derrida's essay to which I responded did not contain two interesting and crucial addenda concerning the problem of Nazism and the Holocaust that do appear in the *Cardozo Law Review* (a footnote after Part I, pp. 977–78 and a "Post-scriptum" after Part II, pp. 1040–45). The first time I saw these addenda was in the published version of Derrida's essay in the *Cardozo Law Review*, where they appear as somewhat unmotivated supplements to Derrida's principal text. They were apparently prompted at least in part by comments in my essay that raised questions about Derrida's reading of Walter Benjamin's "Critique of Violence."

object. Mourning brought the possibility of engaging trauma and achieving a reinvestment in, or "recathexis" of, life that allowed one to begin again. In line with Freud's concepts, one might suggest that mourning be seen as a homeopathic socialization or ritualization of the repetition-compulsion that attempts to turn it against the "death drive" and counteract compulsiveness by re-petitioning in ways that allow for critical distance, change, resumption of social life, and renewal. In any case, the broader concepts that include, without being restricted to, melancholia and mourning are acting-out and working-through: melancholia as a mode of acting-out and mourning as a crucial mode of working-through.[2]

In acting-out one has a mimetic relation to the past which is re-generated or relived as if it were fully present rather than represented in memory and inscription. In psychoanalytic terms, the acted-out past is incorporated rather than introjected, and it returns as the repressed. Mourning involves introjection through a relation to the past that recognizes its difference from the present and enacts a specific performative relation to it that simultaneously remembers and takes at least partial leave of it, thereby allowing for critical judgment and a reinvestment in life, notably social life with its demands, responsibilities, and norms requiring respectful recognition and consideration for others. But with reference to trauma, acting-out may be a necessary condition of working-through, at least for victims and in certain ways, for all those directly involved in events.Even the secondary witness or empathetic observer who resists full identification with, and the dubious appropriation of the status of, victim may nonetheless undergo muted trauma. Indeed the muting or mitigation of trauma that is nonetheless recognized and, to some extent, acted out may be a requirement of working through problems. Acting-out and working-through are in general intimately linked but distinguishable processes, and it may be argued that creating conditions in which working-through could counteract (while never fully transcending) the force of acting-out and the repetition-compulsion would generate different possibilities in thought and life.

The danger in much contemporary theory is a restriction of possi-

---

[2] See "Remembering, Repeating and Working Through" (1914), *The Standard Edition of the Complete Psychological Works of Sigmund Freud*, trans. James Strachey, vol. 12 (London: Hogarth Press, 1958), pp. 145–56, and "Mourning and Melancholia" (1917), *Standard Edition*, vol. 14 (1957), pp. 237–60.

bilities to the phantasm of total mastery, full ego-identity, "totalitarian" social integration, and radically positive transcendence (whether poetic or political), on the one hand, and acting out repetition compulsions with endless fragmentation, aporias, and double-binds, on the other.[3] Sometimes evident as well is a perspective fixated on failed transcendence or irremediable loss in which any mode of reconstruction or renewal is seen as objectionably recuperative or naive.[4] What is not theorized in this frame of reference is the possibility of working-through in which totalization (as well as radical transcendence, whether putatively successful or failed) is actively resisted and the repetition-compulsion counteracted, especially through social practices and rituals generating normative limits that are affirmed as legitimate yet subject to disruption, challenge, change, and even radical disorientation. This possibility may seem foreclosed in modern societies precisely because of the relative dearth of effective rites of passage, including rituals of mourning. But this historical deficit should not be absolutized into a universalistic notion of a necessary constitutive lack or an indiscriminate conflation of all history with trauma.

Indeed, the dual temptations to be countered are the conversion of ontological absence into historical lack or loss and the complementary

---

[3] For a fuller discussion of this problem, see my *Representing the Holocaust: History, Theory, Trauma,* especially pp. 190–94. I find this danger in the works of Paul de Man, Jacques Lacan, and Slavoj Žižek among others. Even Judith Butler, in her important book *Bodies That Matter: On the Discursive Limits of "Sex"* (New York: Routledge, 1993), at one point restricts theoretical possibilities to phantasmic total mastery and the disruptive repetition-compulsion when she stresses the "difference between a repetition in the service of the fantasy of mastery (i.e., a repetition of acts which build the subject, and which are said to be the constructive or constituting acts of a subject) and a notion of repetition-compulsion, taken from Freud, which breaks apart that fantasy of mastery and sets its limits" (p. 244n). The implication here seems to be that only the repetition-compusion sets limits to the phantasy of total mastery, thereby foreclosing the possibility of a form of working-through that checks compulsive repetition but is not tantamount to total mastery. In Butler's formulation, one remains fixated at two extremes—total mastery and the endless repetition-compulsion—that attest to the unquestioned predominance of an all-or-nothing logic. This logic also threatens to confine critical theory to various modalities of acting out posttraumatic conditions. Butler makes the important move of redefining "construction" as displacement, that is, as repetition with alteration, notably in normative institutional practices. But her conception of theoretical possibilities at times remains too confined, and her very notion of normativity is primarily negative and delegitimating. The problem she adumbrates without sufficient elaboration is that of a different form of normativity, subjectivity, agency, and institutional life that would not situate homosexuality in an abject, excluded position—indeed, a form of normativity that might overcome the need to scapegoat, abject-ify, and exclude or eliminate certain "others."

[4] On this problem, see my "Temporality of Rhetoric" in *Soundings in Critical Theory* (Ithaca: Cornell University Press, 1989), pp. 90–124.

ontologization of historical lack or loss that absolutizes or universalizes it. In the former instance, one has the notion of a punctual "death of God" or the phantasm of a lost golden age of total community, purity, and integrity, which may give rise to a redemptive quest to reinstate the lost origin in a revolutionary future. In the latter case, which is perhaps more tempting for those who accept the deconstruction or demystification of lost origins, one moves too quickly and without sufficient mediation from a historical loss or lack to a traumatizing hole in being or a constitutive absence construed as a necessary lack that stimulates endless desire, absolutely resists symbolization, and may obliterate all distinctions. The attendant difficulty is either the avoidance of trying to come to terms with specific historical traumas, such as the Shoah, or the tendency to address them only in excessively allusive, underspecified, indiscriminate, and at times obfuscating ways. Both the historicization of absence and the transhistorical absolutization of lack or loss tend to eliminate alternative possibilities: modalities of working-through that address the role of institutions or practices that both mitigate trauma without denying its force and allow for more desirable sociocultural and political configurations. Indeed the fascination with excess and the fixation on an all-or-nothing frame of reference may blind one to the significance of everything between the excremental and the sublime.

Another way to formulate this point is to argue for a problematic distinction between structural or existential trauma and historical trauma that enables one to pose the problem of relations between the two. One may argue that structural or existential trauma appears in different ways in all societies. It may be evoked or addressed in various fashions: in terms of the passage from nature to culture, the eruption of the pre-Oedipal or pre-symbolic in the symbolic, the entry into language, the encounter with the Real, the inevitable generation of the aporia, and so forth. Structural trauma is often figured as deeply ambivalent, as both painfully shattering and the occasion for *jouissance*, ecstatic elation, or the sublime. Although one may contend that structural trauma is in some problematic sense its precondition, historical trauma is related to specific events, such as the Shoah or the dropping of the atom bomb on Japanese cities. It is deceptive to reduce, or transfer the qualities of, one dimension of trauma to the other, to generalize structural trauma so that it absorbs historical trauma, thereby rendering all references to the latter merely illustrative, homogeneous, allusive, and perhaps equivocal, or, on the contrary, to "explain" all posttraumatic, extreme, uncanny phenomena and responses as exclusively caused by particular events or contexts.[5] Indeed the problem of specificity in analysis and criticism may be formulated in terms of the need to explore the problematic relations between structural and historical trauma without reducing one to the other.

The important Historians' Debate (*Historikerstreit*) in Germany provides a test case of the role of psychoanalytic concepts in illuminating both historiographical issues and social problems, especially problems in the formation of national identity. It also helps to disclose how mourning and working-through are relevant to collective traumas and how such processes may be arrested by forms of acting-out in which the past is compulsively relived rather than remembered and critically confronted. At times it indicates the problematic nature of the generalization of trauma and victimage to cover perpetrators in a manner that occludes the specificity of perpetrator trauma and even obfuscates the very existence or differential role of perpetrators who are transformed into victims.

Extreme or limit-events involving trauma pose especially severe problems for processes of coming to terms with the past.[6] In Germany the question of how to respond to the Shoah has of course been a major problem since the end of the Second World War, and it has gone through a number of important permutations. The reunification of Germany in 1989 created new difficulties and possibilities in the process of what Germans term *Vergangenheitsbewältigung* (mastering the past). It also poses problems for the understanding of issues raised

[5] Confusion results when Slavoj Žižek counters reductive contextualization with equally reductive generalization and leveling of problems: "All the different attempts to attach this phenomenon [concentration camps] to a concete image ('Holocaust', 'Gulag' . . .), to reduce it to a product of a concrete social order (Fascism, Stalinism . . .)— what are they if not so many attempts to elude the fact that we are dealing here with the 'real' of our civilization which returns as the same traumatic kernel in all social systems?" *The Sublime Object of Ideology* (London: Verso, 1989), p. 50.

[6] I am using "limit-event" here in the sense of the radically transgressive event in social life, for example, the "crime against humanity." This use should not be conflated with the limit-event or experience that goes to the verge of transgression without going over the edge. The latter is explored in particularly challenging forms of art and writing that may be understood as relatively safe havens for acting out problems and at times intimate modes of working through them, modes that may involve deep play or what Thomas Mann (borrowing from Goethe) termed a jesting in earnest. The exploration of the limit-experience was the ambition of Maurice Blanchot, and his *Death Sentence* (*L'Arrêt de mort*, 1948) is a telling instance of the complex relation between this fascinating exploration and the role of more ordinary evasiveness with respect to dubious elements in one's past.

in the Historians' Debate that must resurface in the newer context created by reunification and initiatives towards European integration.

It is significant that participants in the Historians' Debate made spontaneous, often self-serving use of psychoanalytic concepts in their exchanges. This use signals the need for a more critical, vigilant, and reflective elaboration of these concepts, and it may even indicate how a debate among professional historians may itself function as an attempt to come to terms with the past in a manner that involves such processes as acting-out and working-through. Indeed, the debate reveals many aspects of arrested or averted mourning through denial and repression as well as certain attempts to delineate the requirements of effective mourning in working through the past toward a more desirable future (notably in Jürgen Habermas's interventions).

The Historians' Debate took place in the course of 1986. Conducted not in professional journals but in the popular press and large-circulation periodicals, it raised the question of the relation between the public sphere and the work of specialized professionals. Appropriately enough, it was catapulted to the status of a heated public controversy if not a *cause célèbre* by two articles in *Die Zeit* by the philosopher Jürgen Habermas, written in response to a June 6 article in the *Frankfurter Allgemeine Zeitung* by the historian Ernst Nolte.

By the end of 1986 contributions had been made by a long list of scholars, especially historians whose names read like an honor roll of the profession in Germany: Karl Dietrich Bracher, Joachim Fest, Imanuel Geiss, Klaus Hildebrand, Andreas Hillgruber, Eberhard Jäckel, Jürgen Kocka, Christian Meier, Horst Möller, Hans Mommsen, Wolfgang J. Mommsen, Thomas Nipperdey, Hagan Schulze, Michael Stürmer, and Heinrich August Winkler. A close reading of their contributions reveals often subtle differences in position as well as lines of argument that are not subject to easy summary.[7] But the crux of the debate on a popular level was the extent to which certain interpretive

[7] These contributions have been translated by James Knowlton and Truett Cates, *Forever in the Shadow of Hitler? Original Documents of the Historikerstreit, the Controversy Concerning the Singularity of the Holocaust* (Atlantic Highlands, N.J.: Humanities Press, 1993). See also Peter Baldwin, ed., *Reworking the Past: Hitler, the Holocaust, and the Historians' Debate* (Boston: Beacon Press, 1990); Richard J. Evans, *In Hitler's Shadow: West German Historians and the Attempt to Escape from the Nazi Past* (New York: Pantheon, 1989); Ian Kershaw, *The Nazi Dictatorship: Problems and Perspectives of Interpretation* (second ed.; London: Edward Arnold, 1989); and Charles Maier, *The Unmasterable Past* (Cambridge: Harvard University Press, 1988). See also *New German Critique* 44: *Special Issue on the Historikerstreit* (Spring/Summer 1988).

procedures, notably the comparison of Nazi crimes with other modern genocidal phenomena (particularly Stalin's Gulags), tended to relativize, normalize, or even "air-brush" Auschwitz in order to make it fade into larger historical contexts and out of conscious focus. To the extent this normalizing fade-out effect was successful, it would mitigate or obliterate the trauma caused by the Shoah and obviate the need to come to terms with it and to mourn the principal victims of the Holocaust; indeed, it would deny that need and foreclose the possibility for mourning. And it would focus if not fixate attention on the way Germans too were victims. Thus a positive identity could be sought without working through the differential implication of members of one's nation in the events and aftermath of the Shoah.[8]

The process of shifting or blurring the focus on the past served to foreground acceptable continuities in German history as a basis for an idealized self-image and an affirmative, pro-Western identity. Here one has a very dubious but important use of contextualization as well as of an uncritical appeal to "experience."In and through such uses, past traumas are not allowed to register as traumatic in significantly different ways for different groups but are preemptively filled in through harmonizing modes of narration. Such narration tends to repeat the processes of avoidance, denial, and willed ignorance through which bystanders could remain indifferent to—or somehow be able to live with—persecution and genocide. Harmonizing narration could take the form of a specific kind of *Alltagsgeschichte* or history of everyday life which Saul Friedlander, alluding to Edgar Reitz's TV-film series, called *Heimatsgeschichte*. *Heimatsgeschichte* (literally, history of the homeland) focuses on the more normal or normalized aspects of life on which the Shoah impinged in marginalized, contained ways as a phenomenon at best on the periphery of consciousness.Experience, including the role of memory in recalling events that are presumed to be experientially integrated, contains the past through a self-legitimating, even sentimentalizing process that may well involve the repression of its more

---

[8] The opposite but complementary danger would of course be fixation on the Holocaust. I do not think such a fixation was active in major participants in the Historians' Debate, although any focus (which is not to be conflated with a fixation) has possible ideological uses in contemporary debates and politics. Still, there was to my knowledge no analogue of Menachim Begin in the Historians' Debate, and the danger of fixation in the German context was a red herring invoked by those with normalizing tendencies. For a controversial, well argued history of the uses of the Holocaust in the very different Israeli context, see Tom Segev, *The Seventh Million: The Israelis and the Holocaust* (New York: Hill & Wang, 1993).

unsettling aspects. "Experience" in this specific sense counters mourning and any desirable process of critically working through problems. In *Stranded Objects: Mourning, Memory and Film in Postwar Germany*,[9] Eric Santner provides an acute analysis of the technique of containment in Reitz, which is also operative in certain (not all) social histories:

> The scene that is most emblematic of the activity of repression—the labor of absorbing textual irritants into the voice of experience—comes in the first episode. It is 1923; Eduard and Pauline make an afternoon excursion to Simmern, the largest town near Schabbach. Pauline wanders off alone and finds herself looking at the window display of the town watchmaker and jeweler. Suddenly a group of young men run up behind her—including Eduard, armed as usual with camera and tripod—and begin throwing rocks at the window of the apartment above the watchmaker's shop where, as the film later discloses, a Jew—in this case also branded as a separatist—resides. They are chased off by police but the shards of fallen glass have cut Pauline's hand. Robert Kröber, the watchmaker, signals her to come into the shop where he cleans her wound, thereby initiating the love story of Pauline and Robert. Later on in the film—it is 1933—the audience hears that the now-married Pauline and Robert are buying the Jew's apartment. As Robert remarks, "The house belongs to him and now he wants to sell it . . . .The Jews don't have it so easy anymore."
>   This small *Kristallnacht* shows how the shards of the Jew's shattered existence—he is never seen in the flesh—are immediately absorbed into a sentimental story of courtship and matrimony, that is, into experience. (p. 92)

In reading Santner's analysis, one is reminded of Theodor Adorno's statement that "for countless people it wasn't all that bad under fascism. Terror's sharp edge was directed only against a few relatively well-defined groups." Adorno made this point to caution against the role of a "diminished faculty of memory" that abets repression and denial, thereby inhibiting the ability to work through problems posed by the Nazi regime.[10] A diminished faculty of memory corresponds to the role of more or less open secrets in a nation's practice and its history,

[9] Ithaca: Cornell University Press, 1990.
[10] See "What Does Coming to Terms with the Past Mean?" in Geoffrey Hartman, ed., *Bitburg in Moral and Political Perspective* (Bloomington: Indiana University Press, 1986), pp. 120–21.

for the Shoah was a relatively open secret at the time of its occurrence and has often maintained that status in the postwar period. A diminished faculty of memory would also increase chances that the secreted or "encrypted" aspects of the Nazi past would be passed on to those born later as a disorienting and destabilizing "phantom" or unworked-through heritage that would, at times mysteriously, haunt descendants and possibly create the basis for a renewed fascination with fascism.[11] (Such an encrypted and phantomlike past could easily be misinterpreted as a secular analogue of "original sin.")

One irony of the Historians' Debate itself, which this commentary will perforce compound, is that major participants were for the most part non-Jews writing about the problem of the elimination of Jews and other oppressed groups. The fact that, forty years after the fall of the Nazis, Jews had to be represented by others attested to the effectiveness of the Nazi genocide in Germany and central Europe, and it forced even those who insisted on the duty to remember and mourn the victims of a "past that will not pass away" to become involved, however unintentionally, in a scenario that on some level repeated the suppression or repression of Jewish voices. One may also recall parenthetically that at present in areas of central Europe there is what might be called imaginary or fetishized anti-Semitism, that is, anti-Semitism in the absence or minimal presence of Jews, which can also have crucial implications for remaining Jews. This phenomenon helps bring out the staying power of unburied and unmourned phantoms from the past as well as the more general role of the imaginary and its relation to paranoid discourse in anti-Semitism, which can make use of any facts, however contradictory, to reinforce its scapegoating procedures. An anti-Semitic animus is primarily projective and performative even though it has effects on real "referents," and it cannot be disconfirmed or confirmed by facts about its objects although such facts may be used to regenerate or stoke it. In this sense accurate information and cogent counterarguments are necessary but not sufficient to combat it.

Manifest in the Historians' Debate was the intense involvement of all participants in the attempt to come to terms with a traumatic, highly "cathected" past, an undertaking that, as I suggested earlier, may be

[11] For the important notions of the crypt and the phantom, see Nicholas Abraham and Maria Torok, *The Shell and the Kernel*, vol. 1, ed. and trans. Nicholas T. Rand (Chicago: University of Chicago Press, 1994).

approached at least in part through the medium of psychoanalytic concepts such as transference, repression, denial, acting-out, and working-through. The pertinence of these categories becomes particularly pronounced with respect to limit-events whose traumatizing nature and potential are extreme yet of course vary with the different subject-positions of participants, witnesses, and commentators. Moreover, their pertinence does not rule out, but rather should enhance, the crucial role of related activities, including political analysis and struggle, in engaging both anti-Semitism and the effects of an unworked-through past.

Transference of course involves personal relations among people in social contexts, such as the family, the school, and the nation. A close investigation of these relations would be crucial for any more complete analysis of the problems I discuss. What I shall focus on, however, is the dimension of transference in which there is the tendency to repeat, in one's own analysis (or other behavior), forces that are active in one's object of investigation. With reference to the Holocaust or Shoah, this tendency arises even on the basic level of terminology, for no terms are innocent and there is the danger of using dubious terms in one's own voice. Thus there is an ineluctable difficulty in naming the events in question. Indeed each name creates a somewhat different site for memory and mourning. "Holocaust" connotes a burnt sacrificial offering and threatens to sacralize events, although this possibility is counteracted at present by the prevalent use of the term in ordinary contexts. "Shoah" seemingly places events in one religious and ethnic tradition and has, at least for those not within that tradition, an exoticizing potential. (It also brings out the cultural and even linguistic power of film in the recent past. In France and even more generally, the term "Shoah" became prevalent after the appearance of Claude Lanzmann's film in 1985.) Other terms such as "final solution" or "annihilation" repeat Nazi terminology, often of course with the use of scare quotes as a distancing frame or alienation effect. Neologisms such as "Judeocide" (Arno Mayer's term without quotation marks) recall neutralizing bureaucratic jargon favored by the Nazis.[12] "Genocide" may have a

---

[12] Mayer's *Why Did the Heavens Not Darken? The "Final Solution" in History* (New York: Pantheon, 1988) is mistakenly seen as "conclusive" by Fredric Jameson in his essay on Paul de Man in *Postmodernism, or the Cultural Logic of Late Capitalism* (Durham: Duke University Press, 1991) , p. 258. On Mayer's book, see my *Representing the Holocaust: History, Theory, Trauma,* chap. 3; on Jameson's interpretation of it, see pp. 133–35.

leveling effect, but "Nazi genocide" may be one of the better terminological compromises. Still, the best option may be to use various terms with an awareness of their problematic nature and not to become riveted on one or another of them. In any case it is significant that, particularly with respect to extremely traumatic events, the transferential problem arises on the elementary discursive level of naming.

To act out a transferential relation is to repeat the past compulsively as if it were fully present, to relive it typically in a manic or melancholic manner. I noted that acting-out may be necessary with respect to trauma, especially in the case of victims, and in cases of extreme trauma there may never be a full transcendence of acting-out. But fixation on acting-out blocks mourning and working-through in general. One cannot give a full, adequate definition of working-through. Indeed, any inclusive and exhaustive definition would distort the concept. But it is nonetheless important to make theoretical space for the concept, to attempt however tentatively to elicit its components, and to reflect critically on it and its institutional and practical implications.

To work through problems requires acknowledging them. It also involves an attempt to counteract the tendency to deny, repress, or blindly repeat them, and it enables one to acquire critical perspective allowing for a measure of control and responsible action, notably including a mode of repetition related to the renewal of life in the present. It also requires an interactive context that mitigates isolation, depression, and melancholy and may have to extend beyond both self-reflection and a one-on-one relationship such as that between analyst and analysand or writer and reader. Since working-through may never fully transcend acting-out, undo denial, or totally heal the wounds of a traumatic past, it should be distinguished from the phantasm of total mastery (evoked in the unfortunate term *Vergangenheitsbewältigung*). Yet, as I have intimated, a prevalent tendency in recent thought is to restrict even theoretical

---

Mayer argues that Nazi anti-Semitism was subordinate to anticommunism and anti-Bolshevism and that the "Final Solution" arose because of contingencies stemming from difficulties encountered during Hitler's invasion of Russia: "In fact, the war against the Jews was a graft or parasite upon the eastern campaign, which always remained its host, even or especially once it became mired in Russia" (*Why Did the Heavens Not Darken?*, p. 270). Mayer's argument not only is close to certain revisionist positions in the Historians' Debate; it also echoes one important line of interpretation in East German historiography before the unsettlement leading to the fall of the regime in 1989. See, for example, Heinz Kühnrich, *Der KZ-Staat. Rolle und Entwicklung des faschistischen Konzentrationslager* (Berlin: Dietz, 1961).

options to phantasmic total mastery and the endless disruption or re-traumatizing role of the repetition-compulsion—a tendency that may conflate melancholy and mourning (more generally, acting-out and working-through) or at the very least devote insufficient attention to working-through.[13] (In accordance with this tendency, one may also restrict performativity to acting-out.) The problem, as Freud intimates, is not to conflate but rather to elaborate a tense mutual articulation of acting-out and working-through in coming to terms with trauma.

The two principal protagonists in the *Historikerstreit*, with reference to whose writings other participants framed issues, were Ernst Nolte and Jürgen Habermas. Although certain nuances are lost in the procedure, it is worthwhile to summarize their position-setting views. Acting out the past in a rather uncontrolled manner, normalizing traumatic events, and obscuring the specific role of perpetrators—indeed, blaming the actual victim—marked important aspects of Ernst Nolte's "Vergangenheit die nicht vergehen will" ("The Past that will not Pass") and related interventions, while Habermas (although in limited and at times insufficiently qualified ways) broached problems of working through a traumatic past and warned of the dangers of denying, repressing, or acting it out.

One issue often stressed by participants in the debate was that of the comparability or singularity of Nazi crimes. This issue could easily become diversionary in that all events are both comparable and singular or unique, and the historical question concerns the nature and function—including the function in the historian's own context of enunciation—of comparisons that delineate a specific configuration of similarities and differences. Nolte at times stressed similarities to the virtual exclusion of differences and, through a sophistic use of rhetorical questions, took comparison in the dubiously metaphysical (perhaps magical) direction of making Nazi crimes derivative or mimetic of a more basic original: Stalinist crimes. The Gulag was presumably the *fons et origo* of Auschwitz. Moreover, in a move that made the Shoah seem old hat and assimilated it to other genocidal phenomena with only a seemingly negligible qualification, Nolte asserted that "a no-

---

[13] This tendency may even at times be at play in Benjamin's *Origin of German Tragic Drama* (1963; London: Verso, 1985), which would seem to address primarily the issue of melancholy and arrested or aborted mourning. In any case the question of the relation of acting-out to working-through provides a basis for rereading various theorists, including such important figures as Paul de Man, Jacques Lacan, and Slavoj Žižek.

table shortcoming of the literature about National Socialism" was the failure to admit that all Nazi deeds "had already been described in the voluminous literature of the 1920s . . . with the sole exception of the technical process of gassing" (*Forever in the Shadow of Hitler?*, pp. 21–22). He even suggested that Hitler's policies should be seen as pre-emptive with respect to an archetypal Bolshevik menace. He thereby brought to life the hackneyed apologetic claim that at least the Nazis opposed the Bolsheviks and defended the interests of the West:

> The following question must seem permissible, even unavoidable: Did the National Socialists or Hitler perhaps commit an "Asiatic" deed merely because they considered themselves and their kind to be potential victims of an "Asiatic" deed? Was not the Gulag Archipelago primary to [or more original (*ursprünglicher*) than] Auschwitz? Was the Bolshevik murder of an entire class not the logical and factual pre-condition of the "racial murder" of National Socialism? Cannot Hitler's most secret deeds be explained by the fact that he had *not* for-gotten the rat cage? Did Auschwitz in its root causes not orginate in a past that will not pass? (*Forever in the Shadow of Hitler?*, p. 22; transla-tion modified)

"Ursprung," as Heidegger etymologically reworks the concept in *The Origin of the Work of Art*, means origin as initiatory, primal leap, and for Nolte Stalinist crimes were the origin of Nazi crimes in this strong and easily mystified sense.[14] Nolte also uses the ploy of posing pre-sumably daring, experimental questions that the norms of liberalism and pluralism would require one to entertain in open-minded schol-arship. But the ploy is deceptive because the apparent questions are rhetorically converted into pseudo-interrogatives whose dogmatic, in-cantatory effect is to suggest the actuality of an implausible if not his-torically absurd postulation.

For Nolte the Gulag may have "caused" Auschwitz, although pre-cisely how is unclear. Somehow the Nazis were "copy-cats" who did it because the Russians did it first, and the Nazis were afraid that the

[14] Nolte studied with Heidegger and considered himself a disciple. A more exten-sive investigation of Nolte's thought would require a careful analysis of his relation to Heidegger, including its transferential dimensions. Nolte's intervention in the Histo-rians' Debate could be read as an apology for Heidegger's prevarications concerning his past and his silence or occasional equivocations concerning the Holocaust. On the latter issues, see my *Representing the Holocaust: History, Theory, Trauma*, chap. 5.

Russians might do it to them. Given his discursive style, it is also unclear whether Nolte takes up the racial slur concerning an "Asiatic deed" in his own voice. As Eberhard Jäckel observed in a September 12 article in *Die Zeit*, Nolte's arguments "are not only unconvincing— they can be disproven with some certainty". For Jäckel:

> Hitler often said why he wished to remove and to kill the Jews. His explanation is a complicated and structurally logical construction that can be reproduced in some detail. A rat cage, the murders committed by the Bolsheviks, or a special fear of these are not mentioned. On the contrary, Hitler was always convinced that Soviet Russia, precisely because it was ruled by Jews, was a defenseless colossus standing on clay feet. Aryans had no fear of Slavic or Jewish subhumans. The Jew, Hitler wrote in 1926 in *Mein Kampf*, "is not an element of an organization but a ferment of decomposition. The gigantic empire in the East is ripe for collapse." Hitler still believed this in 1941 when he had his soldiers invade Russia without winter equipment. (*Forever in the Shadow of Hitler?*, p. 78)

In part to offset Nolte's exaggerated emphasis on similarities between Nazi and Bolshevik policies, Jäckel offered an oft-quoted delineation of the singularity of Nazi crimes: "I, however, claim (and not for the first time) that the National-Socialist murder of the Jews was unique because never before had a nation with the authority of its leader decided and announced that it would kill off as completely as possible a particular group of humans, including old people, women, children, and infants, and actually put this decision into practice, using all the means of governmental power at its disposal" (*Forever in the Shadow of Hitler?*, p. 76). (It might be preferable here to speak of the distinctiveness of the Shoah. As I noted earlier, if it is not redefined to refer to the transgression of an outer limit, the concept of uniqueness easily becomes an emblem in a grim competition for first place in victimhood.) Jäckel noted that the rat cage was interpreted by Hitler himself as referring to Lubjanka prison, and Orwell's *1984*, to which Nolte alluded as describing the technique of torture, did not appear until 1949 (p. 77). In a more sober follow-up article in *Die Zeit* on October 31, Nolte asserted that he believed Hitler was referring not to the prison *per se* but to a process in Lubjanka that had become known worldwide through Orwell's novel and had been reported in the press during the early post–World War I years as a reality in the prisons of the Cheka (p. 150). Whether or not these reports were true, Hitler, for Nolte, "was apparently convinced of their validity," although once again Nolte provided no proof for this assertion about Hitler's beliefs. Nolte also specified that "the Gulag Archipelago is primary to [or more original than] Auschwitz precisely because the Gulag was in the mind of the originator of Auschwitz; Auschwitz was not in the minds of the originators of the Gulag" (p. 151). He did not tell the reader what evidence enabled him either to read Hitler's mind or to assume that Hitler shared his own obsessions.

The rat cage is a little detail that reveals much about the nature and effects of Nolte's discursive and argumentative procedures. It indicates the role of displacement in Nolte's account: displacement in the technical sense of a movement upwards as well as a movement to a small and seemingly insignificant object (the rat cage) that is affectively invested or cathected as a substitute for a larger, truly significant problem (the origins of the Shoah). The rat cage in certain accounts (for example, in Poe and Freud) refers to the placement of a cage of ravenous rats over the bare buttocks of a victim, but Nolte refers to the scene in Orwell's 1984 where the cage is placed next to the protagonist-prisoner's face.

Although his postulation of some sort of causal priority for Bolshevism is gratuitous, it is conceivable that there is an element of validity in Nolte's speculations about Hitler's own confused stereotypes and anxieties concerning rats and Jews. The rat has long been a marker of subterranean filthiness and at times of homophobic anxiety, and Hitler (as well as Nazi propagandists in general) did see Jews as vermin. Moreover, one may qualify Jäckel's argument by pointing out that Hitler may have had a paranoid fear of Jews and Jewish "contamination," including the possibility that he himself had some Jewish "blood." But the basic point is that Nolte did not carefully frame his views as speculations but presented them as seeming facts or at least as solidly based conclusions, and he inserted them into dubious associative trains of thought rhetorically constructed as pseudo-interrogatives or as tendentious arguments that could easily serve apologetic purposes. He thus did more to reinforce paranoid anxieties and questionable inferences than to provide a basis for their critical analysis. In an earlier essay, he even went to the extreme of suggesting that Hitler might have been justified in interning Jews as prisoners of war because of Chaim Weizmann's "official declaration in the first days of September 1939, according to which Jews in the whole world would fight on the side of England."[15] Here Nolte's rhetorical strategy is based on a blatantly projective inclination to blame the victim.

Certainly, one would not want to deny the prevalence of atrocity in the twentieth century. But Nolte seemed to insist on this prevalence not so much to emphasize its importance as to mitigate if not evade specifically Nazi atrocities. Moreover, in light of his insistence on the role of Communism as a root cause of modern evil, Nolte's argument itself takes on a circular, paranoid structure which makes it impermeable to counter-evidence. His argument also has the earmark of uncontrolled transference in its uncritical repetition of features of his object of study. An approach such as Nolte's forecloses the possibility of mourning precisely because it denies the need for it. It instead opens the way for endless acting-out of unresolved aspects of the past in the attempt to create a positive national identity in the present—an attempt that must fail insofar as what has not been worked through returns to create new sources of disorientation and misguided action in the present and future.

Nolte's views are often opposed to those which Jürgen Habermas has championed. In his initial response to Nolte, "A Kind of Settlement of Damages" published on July 11, Habermas saw revisionist tendencies not only in professional historiography but in plans for the German Historical Museum in Berlin and the House of History of the Federal Republic in Bonn. He may have associated Nolte with other historians such as Hillgruber and Stürmer to give an insufficiently qualified and overly unified view of a movement in the profession toward apologetic revisionism. Moreover, Habermas's own self-image and his understanding of the tradition of critical rationality he wishes to defend have led him to make allowance in his own approach only for rather reduced variants of notions that disorient rationality without simply denying it (such as Freud's notion of the unconscious). And his understanding of those whom he sees as his "postmodern" adversaries, such as Foucault and especially Derrida, is often truncated and misleading. But Habermas's intervention in the *Historikerstreit* enabled him to bring important problems to public attention and to elaborate in more telling fashion certain of his basic arguments. (For example, he

[15] "Between Myth and Revisionism? The Third Reich in the Perspective of the 1980s" in H. W. Koch, ed., *Aspects of the Third Reich* (London: Macmillan, 1985), p. 27.

even returned to psychoanalysis and attempted to link it to social theory—a Frankfurt School project he had tended to leave behind after *Knowledge and Human Interests.*[16]) I think that attempts to insert Habermas's arguments into an overall, synchronic idea of his philosophy, to oppose them on a general level to views of postmodernists or post-structuralists, and to dismiss them as apologies for liberalism, humanism, or enlightenment tend to be overly abstract and insensitive to problems of context.[17] They may also obscure how Habermas was trying to delineate ways of engaging the past to enable mourning and working-through in the interest of creating the basis of a desirable democratic identity in the present.

The Bitburg incident forms part of the larger context in which the *Historikerstreit* must be seen. In 1985 Ronald Reagan tried to justify a decision not to visit a concentration camp during his trip to Germany commemorating the fortieth anniversary of the end of the war—a decision he changed only because of public pressure. And he persisted in his determination to visit Bitburg cemetery despite the revelation that it contained SS graves. He regressed to immediate post–World War II tendencies by demonizing events and attributing "the awful evil . . . an evil that victimized the whole world" primarily to one man, Hitler. He also asserted: "I think that there is nothing wrong with visiting that cemetery where those young men are victims of Nazism also, even though they were fighting in German uniform, drafted into service to carry out the hateful wishes of the Nazis. They were victims, just as surely as the victims in the concentration camps."[18] Apparently for Reagan everyone was equally a victim of the war and thus deserved to be mourned, if only by the gesture of visiting a cemetery. The indiscriminate generalization of victimhood, homogenization of mourning,

[16] Trans. Jeremy J. Shapiro; Boston: Beacon Press, 1971.

[17] For such attempts, which include arguments that are worth taking seriously, see Vincent P. Pecora, "Habermas, Enlightenment, and Antisemitism" and Sande Cohen, "Between Image and Phrase: Progressive History and the 'Final Solution' as Dispossession," both in Saul Friedlander, ed., *Probing the Limits of Representation: Nazism and the "Final Solution"* (Cambridge: Harvard University Press, 1992). See also Friedlander's insightful Introduction to this volume, as well as his *Memory, History, and the Extermination of the Jews of Europe* (Bloomington: Indiana University Press, 1993), where he explores the use of psychoanalytic concepts such as transference and working-through. Friedlander is a notable exception to my earlier generalization concerning the predominant role of non-Jews in the Historians' Debate. See especially his exchange of letters with Martin Broszat, "A Controversy about the Historicization of National Socialism," *New German Critique* 44 (1988), 85–126.

[18] *New York Times*, 19 April 1985.

and convenient dissociation of the Army and even the SS from Nazism were among the more egregious initiatives in the attempt to provide Germany with a positive identity as an ally of the United States.

Reagan's gesture went beyond the more general and rather prevalent attempt to dissociate Germans from Hitler and the Nazis. This tendency was active in American propaganda during the war, in contrast to the racially marked depiction of the Japanese enemy as homogenized, invariably yellow-skinned "Japs." It even plays a role in Claude Lanzmann's very important film *Shoah* which, despite its many qualities, provides insufficient insight into the problem of the involvement of the German population—not simply a few Nazi officials—in the events it evokes.[19] It is more objectionably at work (insofar as it is not countered by other forces) in Steven Spielberg's 1993 film *Schindler's List*, which presents stereotypical Nazis.[20] Spielberg's film has a strong element of harmonizing *Heimatsgeschichte* American-style, and its ending involves the transcendence of the equivocations earlier portrayed in Schindler's personality (including his patronizing, nonreciprocal relation to his Jewish associate-accountant played by Ben Kingsley) as the Schindler-figure is converted into saint and martyr. (At the end of the film Kingsley is himself converted into a Gandhi-Moses figure who leads the Jewish survivors into some unspecified promised land over the horizon.) Whatever acceptable working-through of the past may be, this film is not it, athough its mere existence and the fact that it has reached many people may make it the occasion for the type of reflection its own workings do relatively little to promote. The abiding presence of Reaganism in contemporary culture may, moreover, be indicated by the way in which both *Schindler's List* and Agniezska Holland's 1991 film *Europa Europa* have

[19] It is also unclear to what extent Lanzmann's approach to interviewing, especially in the case of victims, gets beyond the unintentional reliving or acting-out of the past to become a site for mourning and working-through. Needless to say, Lanzmann's film remains of fundamental importance despite these difficulties. (For an elaboration of these points, see Chapter 4.)

[20] The rest of the German population is represented by a little girl shouting the comparatively bland "Goodbye Jews," and the Polish population, by another little girl making the throat-cutting gesture. A third little girl, made unique by the representation of her red dress in living color, has a bizarrely Antonioni-type function as she evanescently appears at different intervals and alludes sentimentally to the killing of Jewish children. Color appears again only at the end of the film when an upbeat Hollywood ending has surviving "Schindler-Jews" participate in an elevating, somewhat utopian ritual of mourning as they deposit stones on a grave at which they arrive after travelling down what looks like a yellow-brick road.

as their central figure a confidence man who tends to be an object of positive identification on the part of the audience and whose questionable equivocations tend to be obscured or even transcended by the end of the film. Indeed the fact that Schindler is a Nazi is easily forgotten, as are the ways in which the protaganist in *Europa Europa* is a wannabe-Nazi.[21]

I shall not go into the manner in which the article Habermas wrote on Bitburg prefigured some of the points he would make in the salvo that opened the *Historikerstreit*.[22] I shall simply note that, in the second of his interventions in the Historians' Debate, Habermas put forth a striking formulation of the relationship between collective responsibility and the public role of memory:

> There is first of all the obligation that we in Germany have—even if no one else any longer assumes it—to keep alive the memory of the suffering of those murdered by German hands, and to keep it alive quite openly and not just in our own minds. These dead justifiably have a claim on a weak anamnestic power of solidarity, which those born later can only practice in the medium of memory which is constantly renewed, often desperate, but at any rate alive and circulating. If we brush aside this Benjaminian legacy, our Jewish fellow citizens, the sons, the daughters, the grandchildren of the murdered victims, would no longer be able to breathe in our country. That also has political implications. ("On the Public Use of History" in *Forever in the Shadow of Hitler?*, p. 165; translation modified)

The kind of public memory Habermas invokes, which is not purely individual or contained within a "private sphere," is, one may suggest,

---

[21] It should of course be noted that *Europa Europa* is a more complicated film than *Schindler's List* and open to more diverse and divergent interpretations. For example, the German title of *Europa Europa* is *Hitlerjunge Salomon*, which gives the film a parodic relation to the 1933 Nazi propaganda film *Hitlerjunge Quex*. Still, there is something questionable in representing the plight of a Jew under the Nazis in terms of what is, in one important sense, a remake of *The Adventures of Felix Krull*. Daniel Jonah Goldhagen's desire to counteract the tendency to dissociate the Germans from Hitler leads him to the opposite extreme of seeing virtually all Germans under Hitler and for generations before him as "eliminationist" anti-Semites; see his *Hitler's Willing Executioners: Ordinary Germans and the Holocaust* (New York: Alfred A. Knopf, 1996).

[22] See "Die Entsorgung der Vergangenheit: Ein kulturpolitisches Pamphlet," *Die Zeit*, 24 May 1985; translated by Thomas Levin as "Defusing the Past: A Politico-Cultural Tract" in Hartman, ed., *Bitburg in Moral and Political Perspective*, pp. 43–51.

a prerequisite for any process of mourning and working through collective traumas. Habermas also argued for a critical rather than a blind appropriation of traditions; this critical appropriation would validate only traditions that "stand up to the suspicious gaze made wise by the moral catastrophe" (p. 166; translation modified). Instead of a particularistic nationalism or even a policy of limited national alliances or regional unifications, Habermas called for a "postconventional identity" based on universal norms and a constitutional patriotism. In themselves these ideals may seem rather ineffective and overly indebted to the abstract aspirations of the Enlightenment and German Idealism. But one may argue that the larger project is to join these ideals to the selective appropriation of traditions, including those of the Enlightenment, which in their own way also carry historical sedimentation and concrete commitments. Indeed, present trends toward globalization in the economy and culture raise in a forceful manner the issue of the relation between the particular and universalization.

In a further intervention in the debate, an address delivered in Denmark,[23] Habermas stressed the postconventional implications of Kierkegaard's notion of a conversionlike existential choice that consciously and responsibly transforms one's life-history. This choice puts the individual in the ethical position of an editor deciding what should be considered essential and worth passing on in his or her past. The counterpart in the life of a people would be a decision that remains attentive to the ambivalence in every tradition and that publicly and critically determines which traditions or aspects of traditions deserve to be continued and which do not. The reference to Kierkegaard might itself be read to indicate that, with respect to the tense conjunction of universalizing constitutional principles and more specific, often nonreflective bonds, there is a need for continual rethinking and reworking rather than speculative synthesis, or *Aufhebung*.

Habermas strongly criticized the kind of uncritical, customary identity that seeks an affirmative conception of the past and self-confirming normalization or national identity even at the price of denial and distortion. The power of the following questions is enhanced when

[23] "Historical Consciousness and Post-Traditional Identity: The Federal Republic's Orientation to the West" in *The New Conservatism: Cultural Criticism and the Historians' Debate*, ed. and trans. Shierry Weber Nichols (Cambridge: MIT Press, 1989), pp. 249–67. Habermas's other interventions in the Historians' Debate may also be found in this volume.

they are contrasted with the questions I quoted earlier from Ernst Nolte:

> Can one continue the tradition of German culture without taking over the historical liability for the way of life in which Auschwitz was possible? Can one be liable for the context of the origins of such crimes, with which one's own existence is historically woven, in any other way than through common remembrance of that for which one cannot atone other than in a reflective, testing attitude toward one's own identity-endowing traditions? Can it not be generally said that the less commonality a collective life-context has afforded, and the more it has maintained itself outwardly by usurpation and destruction of alien life, the greater will be the burden of repentance imposed on the mourning and self-critical examination of the following generations? And does not precisely this sentence prohibit downplaying the weight of the burden with which we are saddled by making leveling comparisons? This is the question of the singularity of the Nazi crimes. ("On the Public Use of History" in *Forever in the Shadow of Hitler?*, p. 167)

Habermas saw no simple dichotomy between memory and history. Indeed, insofar as history is not seen in narrowly positivistic terms that make it irrelevant for processes of mourning and working-through, it has a complex relation to memory that cannot be resolved into a binary opposition or sheer dichotomy. Habermas's arguments indicate that a historical consciousness ideally performs critical work on memory in order to undo repression, counteract ideological lures, and determine what aspects of the past justifiably merit being passed on as a living heritage. Conversely, the workings of memory, including its significant lapses or repressions, help to delineate significant problems for historical research and criticism. Here I would further note that it would be mistaken to identify Habermas's specific and limited notions of historical liability and solidarity of memory with a perniciously indiscriminate conception of German guilt that is visited on each and every German as irrational fate or secularized original sin, even though those born later at times may unjustifiably feel guilty about the past or bear within themselves an unresolved, phantomlike residue of the past acquired through often unconscious, transferential processes of identification with loved ones and their encrypted experiences.

There were questionable aspects of Habermas's argument. Like

Nolte, Habermas did not distinguish between and pose the problem of relating what I have termed structural and historical trauma. In Nolte, a generalizing and normalizing tendency implied a conflation of the two and an occlusion of the specificity of Nazi atrocities. In Habermas, a focus on historical trauma and the distinctiveness of the Holocaust seemed to preclude inquiry into structural trauma. This absence or at least downplaying of structural trauma coincided with Habermas's general tendency not to thematize the problem of the unconscious or to view it only in the reduced terms of ego psychology and the "excommunication" of public discourse into a private sphere. Yet without a less restricted, more problematic understanding of the unconscious, one could not do justice to such issues as denial, repression, the return of the repressed, and belated temporality on which Habermas did touch. And one could neither sufficiently indicate the difficulty and the limitations of the attempt to work through problems nor signal the temptation to collapse structural and historical trauma when trying to come to terms with extreme or limit-events.

Still, it would be a mistake simply to interpret all of Habermas's arguments in the Historians' Debate in terms of a preset conception of his politics or philosophy. As I noted earlier, such a response to Habermas is itself rather leveling and leads one to miss or underplay significant, contextually important features of his interventions, not least of which was his role in triggering the Historians' Debate itself. Indeed, without Habermas's intervention, there probably would not have been a Historians' Debate. And there is no reason why that debate cannot stimulate other debates that bear more directly on the policies of other nations, including the questionable attitude of the United States government and large segments of the American population toward Holocaust victims during the Second World War, which warrants a prominent place in any Holocaust museum in this country and has received one in the museum in Washington.[24] Moreover, one need not

[24] On these issues see David B. Wyman, *Paper Walls: America and the Refugee Crisis, 1938–41* (1968; New York: Pantheon, 1985), and Arthur D. Morse, *While Six Million Died: A Chronicle of American Apathy* (1968; Woodstock, N.Y.: Overlook Press, 1983). As Leni Yahil notes, public opinion polls in the United States after 1937 "continued to show that over 80 percent of the population was opposed to any change in [a very restrictive] immigration policy." *The Holocaust: The Fate of European Jewry* (New York: Oxford University Press, 1990), p. 93. Targets for Allied bombing were military and strategic, and railroad lines to Auschwitz were not considered to be among them. See, however, Henry L. Feingold, *Bearing Witness: How America and its Jews Responded to the*

place concern for victims of the Shoah in some gruesome, idiotic zero-sum game implying lack of concern for other victims, such as those affected by slavery or by policies toward Native Americans. Similarly, within the German context, the attention given to the aftermath of the Holocaust does not necessarily function as a screen to divert one from more recent problems involving oppressed minorities, such as the status of *Gastarbeiter,* so-called guest workers, although the possibility of such a function should be an insistent concern.

"I think that the debate initiated by Habermas is unfortunate," asserted Thomas Nipperdey. Writing as a professional historian and perhaps as a conservative thinker, Nipperdey warned that "the areas under discussion are highly sensitive, the moral and political commitment of the participants is strong, [and] the difficult distinctions and differentiations will get lost in the fray." (*Forever in the Shadow of Hitler?,* p. 146). In retrospect other professional historians (for example, Ian Kershaw and Richard Evans) noted that the Historians' Debate unearthed no new facts about the Nazi period and provided no genuinely revised interpretation of it; they therefore tended to downplay its significance and saw it as generating more heat than light. Nipperdey himself impatiently called for a return to "real" history and objectivity: "We must historicize National Socialism. . . . Beyond apologetics and criticism, beyond conservative and progressive partisanship, there is objective history, which we, despite the limitations of our—transnational—scholarly endeavor, are closing in on. Everyone knows it: There simply is, beyond our bickering about values, history writing that is more or less valuable, outmoded or merely provisionally valid" (p. 145). I think many historians would like to believe what Nipperdey maintains, although they might hesitate to assert it with such blocklike authority. Moreover, they might tend to agree with the exclusively "professional" criteria of relevance enunciated by Kershaw and Evans,

---

Holocaust (Syracuse: Syracuse University Press, 1995). Taking issue with the conclusions of Wyman and Morse, Feingold argues that a realistic appraisal of options available to both the American government and American Jews indicates that they could not have done much more to assist the Jews of Europe. He also maintains that prevalent anti-Semitism and secularizing processes that weakened corporate solidarity among Jews help to explain why American Jews did relatively little to help European victims of the Holocaust. Whether or not one agrees with Feingold's argument, one may note that the minimal assistance given to European Jews during the Holocaust may be related to certain postwar tendencies toward overcompensation in the United States, at times including an identity-forming cult of the Holocaust in segments of American Jewry.

which fail to do justice to the significance of the debate, particularly in its bearing on the relation between professional historiography and a larger public.

Even Habermas, whom Nipperdey took to task, seemed at times to defend the ability to debate public issues in the press in terms that tended to confirm and reveal the prevalence of Nipperdey's assumptions, for Habermas sharply divided if not dichotomized between the public "arena" involving a "public use of history" which he characterized as an "arena" in which "there can be no impartial ones among us," and "the discussion of scholars who in their work must assume the perspective of an outside observer." ("On the Public Use of History" in *Forever in the Shadow of Hitler?*, pp. 167–68.) Yet two broader questions raised by the Historians' Debate itself were whether one could neatly separate between arenas or spheres in modern life (the professional and the public spheres, for example) and whether one could define history in purely professional, objective, third-person terms under the aegis of a strictly differentiated or even autonomized paradigm of research. The Historians' Debate itself pointed to the problematic nature of boundaries, the possibly valid status of hybridized roles (such as historian-public intellectual), and the need to argue for the relative strength or weakness of problematic but crucial distinctions that could not simply be conflated with comfortable dichotomies or binary oppositions. Here I would note that the critique of binaries, which has been so pronounced in deconstruction, need not lead to the collapse of all distinctions (as Habermas feared in *The Philosophical Discourse of Modernity*[25]). It may—and should—lead to the need to elaborate problematic distinctions and their actual as well as desirable articulations, a task that becomes more, not less, important because of the critique of pure binary oppositions. Habermas's own arguments in the Historians' Debate implied that only a narrowly positivistic self-definition could wall professional historiography off from such problems as the public role of memory and mourning.

The Historians' Debate may also be taken to indicate the need for a psychoanalytically informed approach, which does not assume that objectivity is a mere given or taken-for-granted professional stance and that biased deviations from it can always be corrected for, allowing a return to third-person objectivity. This limited notion of bias as-

[25] Cambridge: MIT Press, 1987.

sumes the given or normal status of objectivity, in relation to which bias is merely a correctable deviation. In contrast to this simplistic view, objectivity could be seen as a difficult, never fully achievable objective that is not even desirable in its imaginary total state and that in its justifiable, desirable forms (related to accuracy, meticulous empirical research, and rigorous argumentation) has to be elaborated by working through transferential relations, resistances, denials, and repressions. Also significant in this respect is the need for an explicit acknowledgement and possible transformation of subject-positions as one engages problems in historical research and self-understanding.

The Historians' Debate, which delivered relatively little in terms of new facts or particular interpretations of events, might contribute a great deal to historical self-understanding by disclosing the importance of the problem of one's relation to the past and its implications for the present and future. In this light it might also indirectly stimulate questions for research and interpretation: the positionality of the historian, the bearing of present contexts on the activity of research, the nature of the language used by the historian in his or her accounts, the limits and possibilities of historical discourse, and the relation of historical discourse to such processes as transference, acting-out, and working-through, including the role of mourning. The problem the debate posed was how to negotiate the relation between the specific demands of representing the Nazi period and the Shoah, on the one hand, and, on the other, the more general questions raised by one's differential implication in a controversial, traumatizing past. One crucial question in this respect is whether historiography may combine its modes of empirical research and analysis with a more dialogic engagement with the past that furthers the attempt to work through problems that remain alive as forces in the present.

I shall add a few more comments in the form of generalizations that would have to be nuanced and qualified in any more extensive treatment of the problems I address. In the more immediate post–World War II context, there was the danger that the events of the Nazi period would be seen as demonically inspired and that their predominant cause would be found in the personality of Hitler and the manipulations of his regime. The Nuremberg trials also intensified the temptation to emphasize the criminality of a diabolical elite and to use it as a stereotypical counter-image to the virtues of "our side." These simplifying responses were to some extent understandable as immediate reactions to extremely traumatic events, but their deficiencies became readily apparent. The German "economic miracle" furthered avoidance, denial, or repression of the Nazi past and provided manic outlets for those marked by an "inability to mourn." Indeed, arrested mourning was almost inevitable, since it was often unclear, at least for certain segments of the population, whether the cause of malaise was the lost "glories" of Hitler and his regime or the Jewish and other victims of the Nazis. Mourning is a social, even a ritual practice that requires the specification or naming of deserving victims. Without such specification, chances are that mourning will be arrested and one will be locked in melancholy, compulsive repetition, and acting out the past. One aspect of public debate and education should be the attempt to define what is indeed a genuine loss worthy of mourning and what should be not mourned but vigorously criticized and given the emotional response it deserves. In Hitler's case, mourning would not be appropriate; working-through might involve a critique that attempted to dislodge the affective investment and fantasy of those who remained tied to Hitler and his lost "glories". In this sense, mourning should be understood *and* felt to be an obligation as well as a gift of which not everyone deserves to be the recipient. On the other hand, in postwar Germany it has been difficult for Germans to express their own sense of loss and trauma, for example over Allied bombing or the displacement of people in the wake of the Russian invasion, without having it tendentiously tied to an argument that used it to balance books with respect to the Holocaust.

The events culminating in 1968 provided an opportunity to confront the past, especially for younger Germans who had no direct acquaintance with the Nazi period but who might not experience their position as altogether fortunate because of displaced guilt feelings and distrust of their parents' generation's silences, evasions, and impatient dismissals concerning the past. But 1968 and its aftermath were at best ambivalent in their bearing on the attempt to work through the past. For example, certain utopian tendencies demanded a total break with the past and a more or less blind leap into the future, which could generate its own variant of the *Stunde null,* or zero point in history. The emergence of conservative forces in the seventies, provisionally culminating in the political victory of the *Tendenzwende* (the turn toward the right) in the eighties, often seemed to bring a renewed avoidance of the past. The broadcast in 1979 of the TV series *Holocaust* is itself an almost case-book illustration of displacement in the classical Freudian sense, for a minor media event that was broadly recognized as a commercialized, offensively Hollywood-type production was nonetheless able to trigger a traumatizing return of the past that might function either as a transitory catharsis or, in the best of circumstances, as the occasion for critical reflection. The return of the repressed during the *Historikerstreit* in 1986 was expectably heated and disorienting, and some of its participants (notably Nolte) threatened to overreact against the earlier tendency (for example, in Friedrich Meinecke's *German Catastrophe*[26] or even in Thomas Mann's *Doctor Faustus*[27]) to represent the Nazi past as singular, demonic, and centered on Hitler. Such overreaction led to the opposite but complementary extreme of normalizing a traumatizing, disconcerting past through potentially leveling comparisons and modes of contextualization. Unfortunately, the debate's potential for a more effective and valid reckoning with the past is easily lost.

Aside from narrowly professional or neopositivistic attempts to downplay the significance of the debate, since 1989 the *Historikerstreit* has been eclipsed by the uncertainties as well as the promise of German reunification in the wider context of the movement for European integration. Habermas and other prominent left-liberal intellectuals opposed reunification and had relatively little to offer in the way of constructive responses to it once it unexpectedly arrived. Yet the debate over the so-called failure of the intellectuals in responding to the challenge of reunification (and especially the controversy centering around Christa Wolf) indicate that problems rehearsed in the Historians' Debate have not been transcended.[28]

The East German past has arisen to create difficulties, not only through the heretofore avoided issue of complicity in the Nazi regime and the role of postwar anti-Semitism concealed under the banner of official antifascism, but also through the more clear and present dan-

---

[26] 1946; Boston: Beacon Press, 1963.

[27] Trans. H. T. Lowe-Porter (1947; New York: Vintage Books, 1971).

[28] Christa Wolf wrote *Was bleibt?* ["What Remains?"] (Frankfurt am Main: Luchterhand, 1990) in 1979 but published it more than ten years later. It discusses her unsettling if not traumatizing experience in the late 1970s of being observed by the East German secret police (*Stasi*). Responses to the book ranged from sympathetic appreciations to accusations that Wolf, who had been lionized under the communist regime, was falsely assuming the role of victim. Reactions became even more complicated when, in January 1993, Wolf revealed that, for a relatively brief period early in her career (between 1959 and 1962), she herself had collaborated with the *Stasi*.

gers to stability created by disclosure of the shocking extent of spying, informing, and intimidation under the former communist government. These difficulties are of course compounded by the role of unemployment, decay of the economic infrastructure, and environmental hazards in eastern Germany. Andreas Huyssen has argued that the ultimate goal of both the *Historikerstreit* and the debate over the "failure of the intellectuals" is similar: "one wants to get away from a past that is considered either a burden or an embarrassment in order to construct an alternative agenda for the future. While the attempt to overcome the German past in the name of 'normalization' was not successful in the Historians' Debate, it may very well end up successful in its more removed and diluted form in the current culture debate."[29]

One may extend Huyssen's argument to the point of suggesting that the Historians' Debate prepared the way for the "failure of the intellectuals" insofar as it provided the liberal left with a pyrrhic victory and a false sense of security. There seemed to be little reason for anxiety about the future or readiness for the unexpected. Moreover, the "better arguments" of Habermas and others did not dislodge conservatives from positions of institutional power in the academy and government, and the debate did not change their views except perhaps by unintentionally provoking them to become more obdurate. The apparent discursive superiority of the liberal left even threatened to conceal the fact—however ironically counterpoised to the intentions of Habermas and the significant value of his interventions—that the Historians' Debate allowed for the entry into a broader public arena of reactive if not reactionary feelings, thoughts, and attitudes that earlier had been kept private or confined to small circles. Nolte expressed in public the types of things that others generally had kept to themselves or shared only with intimates. "After the wall" these sentiments could be circulated more freely and with fewer inhibitions, and they might have currency in politics.

One may nonetheless maintain that not only are predictions of success risky, but the very meaning of success is moot when one refers to an attempt to "overcome" the past through normalization involving blatantly ideological views. Whatever the future may hold in store for

[29] Andreas Huyssen, "After the Wall: The Failure of German Intellectuals," *New German Critique* 52 (1991), p. 126.

a reunified Germany, recent developments do not eliminate the significance of basic issues raised in the Historians' Debate. These issues must return in a different way in the new context of a unified German nation-state insofar as the manner in which one engages the past affects the attempt to construct the present and future. Among the most crucial of these issues is the very nature of a legitimate mode of coming to terms with the past in the interest, not of "normalizing" what is found to be disorienting, but of both critically confronting unresolved traumas and mourning what deserves to be mourned.

CHAPTER THREE

Rereading Camus's *The Fall* after Auschwitz and with Algeria

During the last generation, interest in Camus has declined precipi-
tously, at least among critical theorists and literary critics. A primary
reason for this decline in interest is his absence from the canon of writers favored in structuralism and poststructuralism. I doubt we shall
ever return to the time when the debate between Camus and Sartre after the publication of *The Rebel* (*L'Homme révolté* 1951) seemed to have
intellectual immediacy and to be indicative of political options for left-
of-center intellectuals. But, as has already happened with Sartre, attitudes toward Camus may undergo a reversal in the near future that to
some extent reinstates the status he achieved in the post–World War II
period.

One reason for renewed interest in Camus is the recent turn of critical theorists and literary critics to history and politics. More circum-
stantially, Camus is one of the few major writers who addressed the
problem of the Holocaust, which until recently has played an allusive,
indirect role in the work of major structuralists and poststructuralists.
Still, it should be observed that Camus's turn to the Holocaust in *The
Fall*, as well as one's own tendency to follow his lead, may function to
obscure or displace interest in a more recent series of events: the Algerian war and its troubled aftermath in Franco-Algerian relations.
This may be an instance of a more general phenomenon, to wit, the tendency of an earlier traumatic series of historical events to be remarked
upon belatedly after the occurrence of a more recent series of events.
The movement of historical notice and knowlege may thus repeat in

its own way the disconcertingly belated (*nachträglich*) temporality of trauma itself. Indeed the attention paid to earlier events may even serve as a screen to conceal both the significance of recent and, in certain respects, more pressing events and the limitations or inadequacy of one's response to them. As we shall see, Camus at most alluded very indirectly to Algeria in *The Fall*. Around the time he was writing *The Fall*, he addressed problems related to Algeria, however restrictedly and contestably, only in other, nonfictional, quasi-journalistic texts that frame *The Fall* and suggest another way to read it.[1]

Paradoxically enough, a recent sign of renewed interest in Camus comes from an appeal to him to elucidate and defend the silence of Paul de Man vis-à-vis his own World War II journalistic writings—a silence that has proven to be provocative in stimulating others in their turn to history and politics, however questionable the precise nature of that turn sometimes is. In *Testimony*, Shoshana Felman makes a commendable attempt to rehabilitate Camus in part because he made a significant effort to address the Holocaust and its attendant traumas.[2] But she more questionably looks to Camus to allegorize Paul de Man's plight and his manner of responding to it. Her chapter on Camus's *The Fall* (*La chute* 1956) is a counterpart to her earlier chapter on *The Plague* (*La peste* 1947), and her treatment of de Man is positioned between the two. (Her notable discussion of Claude Lanzmann's *Shoah* concludes the volume.) In her account *The Plague* is analogized to de Man's early World War II journalism while *The Fall* is related to de Man's later "withdrawal into silence, . . . his consequent retreat into a prose profoundly questioning the very possibility of representation, and into . . . ascetic self-denying and uncompromising rigor" (*Testimony*, p. xviii). In keeping with this reading, *The Plague* for Felman is a traditional narrative that attempts, despite its own explicitly allegorical structure, to provide too direct and literal a commentary on the Holocaust, while *The Fall* offers a more authentic encounter with the unrepresentable.

Hence Felman identifies the narrator in *The Fall*, Jean-Baptiste Cla-

---

[1] Any fuller discussion of Camus on Algeria would now have to include the posthumously published, largely autobiographical novel *Le premier homme* (Paris: Gallimard, 1994). Indeed, one way of reading it is in terms of Camus's complex, intensely felt conception of Arab-French relations in Algeria. It provides insight into the plight or double bind of Camus as a French Algerian of humble origins who genuinely sympathizes with the Arab population but nonetheless has a strong if internally divided identity as a French Algerian.

[2] Shoshana Felman and Dori Laub, M.D., *Testimony: Crises of Witnessing in Literature, Psychoanalysis, and History* (New York: Routledge, 1992).

mence, not only with Camus as author but with Paul de Man as silent interlocutor. At times these identifications take the form of unmediated, even imperceptible shifts in reference, during Felman's discussion, from the narrator of *The Fall* to its author or to de Man. At other times identifications are direct and altogether explicit.[3] Whatever their form, these identifications are especially interesting psychoanalytically because they seem so implausible. They would seem to be motivated by a desire to offer an apology for de Man, with whom Felman herself remains bound or even identified in a process of arrested mourning. The apology misfires, however, in that the identification of Clamence and de Man may in important respects excessively incriminate, even be unfair to, de Man.[4]

In any case, to identify Clamence with Camus is a wildly daring

[3] "The failed confession of *The Fall* could thus stand in the place of de Man's missing confession: insofar as it belatedly accounts for the aftermath of trauma—and for the belated transformation—occasioned by the war, *The Fall* indeed can be read as de Man's unspoken autobiographical story." *Testimony*, p. xviii.

[4] In addition to the conflation or simple identification of Camus with Clamence, Felman's allegorical interpretation, in substituting *The Fall* for de Man's missing confession, has many dubious consequences: (1) it gratuitously fills in a silence through a purely speculative leap of the imagination; (2) it relies on a truncated understanding of confession as self-exculpating private or personal expression and, assuming that confession must fail, sees the failure in *The Fall* as paradigmatic of all confession; (3) it tends to conflate failed confession with any attempt to break silence and, in particular, with the discourse of more traditional narrative; (4) it assumes without argument that the very significant differences between the early de Man and the early Camus, notably with respect to resistance and collaboration, are outweighed by the putative similarities, thereby establishing an outlandish, normalizing, purely formal correspondence between de Man's early journalism and narration in *The Plague*; (5) it relies on unargued, depth hermeneutics to elicit the putative relationships, including largely unexplicated similarities, between the later de Man and the later Camus of *The Fall*; (6) it assumes that *The Plague* embodies "a naive faith in witnessing" rather than a problematic, self-conscious appeal to traditional narrative as a healing device in a time of disorientation, trauma, and crisis. (One may support the last contention by noting that a crucial moment in *The Plague* comes with the explicit revelation that the troubled and only partially effective doctor Rieux is the narrator. In this sense, one might see the transformative relation between *The Plague* and *The Fall* not as a more or less teleological progression from naive blindness to sophisticated insight but as the exploration of two supplementary ways of coming to terms with traumatic events, each of which may in limited ways be valid.) Finally, one may note that identifying de Man with Clamence places de Man in an extremely (even excessively) questionable position. This point, combined with the general dubiousness of Felman's allegorical interpretation of *The Fall* as de Man's missing confession, raises the question of whether her apologetic desire masks ambivalence, including unacknowledged or unconscious aggression towards de Man. One cannot provide a simple answer to this question, for one may also argue that the very dubiousness of the interpretation functions to offer up the self and divert attention from the loved or cathected other. One in effect says: criticize me but not him. Through the constitution of the self as a quasi-sacrificial victim, one preserves the other as an ideal object, empowering totem, or Hidden God.

move if only because introductory literature classes warn against conflating a fictional narrator with an author. This identification is doubly surprising in that Camus elsewhere takes his distance (at times quite decisively) from the positions and the stylistic stratagems of a Clamence. In addition, the notion that Clamence's narration in *The Fall* bears paradoxical witness to a general collapse of witnessing makes Clamence a victim of a larger constraining process construed in insufficiently differentiated terms, for Clamence himself plays upon this collapse and the equivocations that ensue in a self-serving and manipulative, even victimizing manner. Clamence, I would suggest, does little to explore more defensible ambivalences that non-invidiously implicate self and other and counteract manipulative forms of interaction. He seeks, not partners in a dialogic exchange in which all are equally at risk, but accomplices in a game whose telos is victimization, domination, and slavery.

The notion of a collapse of witnessing not only obscures the distinction between defensible ambivalence and self-serving, oppressive equivocation. It also tends misleadingly to generalize the status of victim (as does the analysis of de Man in the chapter that intervenes between the discussions of *The Plague* and *The Fall*, in which de Man's silence is conflated with that of Primo Levi and other manifest victims of the Holocaust). Moreover, the idea that *The Fall* attests to a collapse of witnessing obscures the possibility that the text may be read more pointedly as a critique of the position of the bystander, a position that Clamence occupies when he fails to come to the assistance of the woman who falls into the Seine. Indeed Clamence as persona and as narrator is the exemplar of what might be termed the posttraumatic cynicism of the implicated bystander: the cynicism of one who has belatedly been unsettled by events to which he or she responded evasively at the time of their occurrence, yet who refuses to let trauma register and to work through it, maintaining instead a false, ironic facade and a discourse of suspect indirection.

In *The Rhetoric of Fiction* Wayne Booth argued that Clamence is the prototypical unreliable narrator who readily leads the reader astray and whose words provide little evidence of the moral position of the author.[5] For Booth *The Fall* represents a world of unrelieved extremism and nihilism: it is a document of the worst in modernity. Indeed, in ex-

[5] *The Rhetoric of Fiction* (Chicago: University of Chicago Press, 1961), pp. 294–96.

tending Booth's argument, I would note that *The Fall* might be seen as embodying precisely what Camus attacked in *The Rebel*: an unmediated combination of nihilism in condemning what exists and blind utopianism (or dystopianism) in seeking a quasi-religious, redemptive alternative or total solution. In this light Clamence is a secular evil demon who dominates the story. For Booth the signs that *The Fall* does not express the world-view of Camus himself are so buried in the text as to be indecipherable, and one can elicit the massive difference between Camus and Clamence only by looking to Camus's other works where, for Booth, Camus definitively puts Clamence in his place. Booth in effect postulates a decisive binary opposition between Clamence as the quintessential embodiment of modern equivocation, unreliability, and radical evil and Camus as a shining exemplar of secular value in a godless world.

In comparison with Booth, Felman may be seen as transvaluing and even reversing valuations by identifying Clamence with Camus and presenting him as the exemplar of modern authenticity and insight, particularly in his recognition of the "historical narrative impossibility" (p. 193) of any direct representation or witnessing of the Holocaust and comparable traumas or limit-events in history. In this view, all significant representation or recognition threatens to become *nachträglich* (belated) and to be reduced to silence. *The Fall* presumably reveals how "the contemporary witness has become, by definition, no longer the Socratic spokesman for the truth but on the contrary, *the bearer of the silence [Geheimnisträger], the secret sharer in a muted execution*" (p. 193). (The term *Geheimnisträger* is elsewhere used by Felman with reference to the *Sonderkommando*, the special detail of Jews in the death camps charged with burning and disposing of the bodies of victims. She takes the term from the commentary of Filip Müller, ex-*Sonderkommando*, in Claude Lanzmann's film *Shoah*.) Camus's novel thus, for Felman, provides telling insight into de Man as a necessarily silent witness, and it reveals to us that, with respect to the Holocaust, "we can only contemplate its trace, acknowledge that we are living, in its absence, on its *site*: 'the site of one of the greatest crimes in history' [quoting *The Fall*]" (p. 195).

In contrast to both Booth and Felman, I shall argue that there is a subtle interplay of proximity and distance between Camus as author/writer and Clamence as narrator, an interplay that varies in the course of the text and undergoes nuanced modulations. The Holocaust indeed receives a complex inscription in the text, but the silence that surrounds it cannot be rashly generalized, hypostatized, or absolutized to culminate in the sublime and paralyzing figure of all history as holocaust or as trauma. In one very important sense, silence concerning the Holocaust is the effect of the Nazi policy of silencing, evacuation, and extermination; repetition of this silence in one's own approach is at best an extremely problematic gesture that should never be made to serve apologetic functions (as it does in Felman). I shall also argue that even in *The Fall* there are markers of difference between the narrator and the author/writer but that the difference between the two is far from total. What Booth obliterates and Felman misappropriates are the critical elements in *The Fall*, including the way Camus may (whether intentionally or not) be placing himself in question, especially with respect to his public persona as the exemplary liberal humanist and lucid secular saint, the figure whom Sartre saw as always equipped with a portable pedestal.

In elaborating a reading of *The Fall* that differs in significant ways from both Booth's and Felman's, I shall begin with a set of questions that are either dubiously answered or not raised by Felman.[6] I have already alluded to the first question: the relation of Camus to Clamence as narrator. Second, there is the question of the mode of narration in *The Fall*, which could be described as a monologue that divides into a complex, skewed non- or pseudo-dialogue, or could be called an internally split, even projective monologue with polemical as well as self-serving effects, including polemic directed at Camus's own public image or persona. The mode of narration involves the issue of the position of the reader both in the text and outside it. The obvious question is: to whom does Clamence address himself? For whom does he toll? What is the relation between self and other in the text and beyond it? Third, there is the question of excess and limits, including problems of equivocation and ambivalence.

[6] My references, which are included in the text, are to *The Fall* (1956), trans. Justin O'Brien (New York: Vintage Books, 1991). Both Booth and Felman assert with no textual evidence that the woman in *The Fall* jumped into the Seine and committed suicide. This assertion itself lends to the woman's "act" and to the woman herself an importance that the text may not support. The "act" of the woman remains unclear in the text: she may have jumped, she may have fallen, or something else may have happened. Clamence himself was too far from her to know precisely what occurred. The lack of clarity attests, I think, to the occasional, even marginal, position of the woman and her fall in the novel. This position is emblematic of the position of women in general in the text, and what is crucial in the text's self-presentation is the nature of Clamence's response to her "act," whatever it may have been.

The relation between Camus and Clamence is, I think, an intricate displacement involving participatory proximity and critical distance. The initial sign of distance is the epigraph from Lermontov on the hero of our time, which functions in part as an alienation or distancing effect. The epigraph reads: "Some were dreadfully insulted, and quite seriously, to have held up as a model such an immoral character as A Hero of Our Time; others shrewdly noticed that the author had portrayed himself and his acquaintances. . . . A Hero of Our Time, gentlemen, is in fact a portrait, but not of an individual; it is the aggregate of the vices of our whole generation in their fullest expression. LERMONTOV." In the words Camus chose as an epigraph, Lermontov thus claimed that he was providing à la Galton a composite image of an entire generation.[7] Camus himself even said that he wanted to entitle his book "A Hero of Our Time." Moreover, his use of the epigraph is similar to that in Dostoevsky's *Notes From Underground,* and it may, as in that text, create the misleading impression that the text is to be read merely as a morbid, collective case history or representational, even symptomatic document of a vicious time. Camus in his public pronouncements about *The Fall* also stressed his distance from Clamence and emphasized the role of Clamence as a representative of a troubled era. With no doubt a touch of irony, he said that the only common point between him and his fictional narrator was a certain admiration for Christ.[8] Yet his self-interpretation is open to question and should not be taken at face value.

The epigraph also recalls Camus's argument in *The Myth of Sisyphus.* There the absurd is presented as an invitation to pathology, and the problem is how to confront it: whether through evasion, such as suicide, or through resistance, which Camus commends. Yet *The Fall* is more complex in the way it approaches problems. I think it suggests that extremism or excess in the wake of trauma cannot simply be denied. It is part and parcel of a posttraumatic condition, and the attempt to work through it may be required for coming to terms with that con-

[7] My reference to Galton may signal the dubious aspects of Lermontov's statement and, by implication, Camus's appropriation of it. Galton was used in the development of racialized biology, and the questionable, ideologically loaded notion of degeneration is very active in Lermontov's reference to a portrait embodying the aggregate vices of a generation.

[8] From *Le Monde,* 31 August 1956, as quoted in Albert Camus, *Théâtre, Récits, Nouvelles, préface par Jean Grenier, textes établis et annotés par Roger Quilliot* (Paris: Gallimard [Pléiade], 1962), p. 2011.

dition. Resistance to excess requires the recognition that it affects one at least as an inner temptation that tests necessary normative limits. But to some extent excess may have to be undergone and, in certain ways, even acted out in order to be worked through. Critical distance itself implies, not total exteriority, but the attempt to acquire perspective and to generate different possibilities in and through a confrontation with excess.

The notion of a fall itself places events within a displaced, secularized Christian problematic that is important in hegemonic dimensions of Western culture and colors possibilities in a particular way. In the text, there is of course the fall of a woman into the Seine, the fall of Clamence given his response (or non-response) to this event, and the fall of a generation. Yet excess, the more extreme side of temptation, is not simply presented as pure, external evil or abstract negativity. It is given a very strong and wily voice in Clamence the narrator. And Camus cannot be entirely dissociated from the devil's advocate within the self, although he certainly cannot be fully identified with his narrative envoy in fiction.

In other words, the epigraph from Lermontov does not simply dominate *The Fall* and convert it into a quasi-documentary case history or collective-cum-personal biography. It does mark a significant distance between Camus and Clamence. But total distance is questioned in the text, and any partial distance must be an achievement of textual work both within and without the covers of the book. I think that Sartre's assertion that Camus carried around a portable pedestal hit home. Clamence refers to people who mount a cross and seek crucifixion so that they may be seen from a greater distance. To some extent this reference applies to Clamence as well as to Camus himself, especially to the Camus persona or public image that Camus at times liked to indulge: Camus the secular saint as well as the Bogey-like, macho, hard-on-the-outside-soft-on-the-inside intellectual, activist, and ladies' man. As Felman intimates, *The Fall* also contains a concealed polemic against Sartre, not total agreement with him. Clamence refers quite tellingly to those who always talked of freedom and used it as a bludgeon to beat others into submission—what might be called the tactic of fanatics for freedom. These two possible references indicate how Clamence himself is at least in part a critical force who raises pointed questions about recent tendencies and is not merely symptomatic of them.

With regard to the second question, the mode or style of narration, we are told that at one point in the past Clamence the narrator had a stable identity as a do-good lawyer who specialized in noble causes. Yet this proved to be a false identity. Clamence's nobility was narcissistic, vain, and self-serving, like that of the pseudo-Christ for whom a cross is a billboard. There were signs of this falseness before his existential trial and the subsequent "fall." The fall in this sense was not an absolutely unique event, even though it marked a traumatic turning point in his life.

Here one may note the complex quality and position of the haunting laughter that pursues Clamence. In Clamence's life, the laughter *follows* his existential trial when he fails to respond to the cries of the woman who fell (jumped?) from the bridge. In the text, however, the laughter is mentioned *before* the incident at the bridge, and it is described as "good, hearty, almost friendly" ["*un bon rire, naturel, presque amical*] (p. 39). This positioning has multiple functions. It creates suspense in the narrative about the meaning of the laughter, and it relates it to a belated recognition or *nachträglich* effect for the reader. Once Clamence has himself fallen or failed his existential trial, the reader can say with narrative satisfaction: "Aha, now I know what the laughter was all about." But the textual positioning of the laughter may also be read to indicate that perhaps the laughter was there in repressed or concealed form in Clamence even before the explicit fall and the conversion from do-good lawyer to judge-penitent. Clamence may never have had a fully unified or stable identity, and the laughter may arise in the clefts or gaps within himself. This analysis certainly suggests itself in retrospect (or *nachträglich*). Moreover, after the fall, laughter tends to function in a rather one-dimensional way as a form of degradation or self-defeating equivocation deprived of regenerative personal and social value. It is not a carnivalesque source of renewal or a ribald force that turns the world upside-down, but rather a plaguing, mocking, disconcerting reminder of weakness and failure. The description of the laughter at the bridge as "good, hearty, almost friendly" nonetheless serves to bring out the ambivalent potential of laughter, which may be reduced but not entirely eliminated through self-serving equivocation or unilateral mockery. It also gestures toward the idea that weakness, disempowerment, or abjection may be constitutive of the human being in ways that may be abusively indulged or manipulated as well as explored in a more legitimate manner. Thus the laughter that appears in the text before the actual fall seems to point both towards the potential (even propensity) for a fall and to possibilities that may be foreclosed or avoided once a particular, empirical fall has taken place (or even been fantasized).

In his pointed reading of *The Fall*, Steven Ungar raises a thought-provoking doubt concerning the occurrence of the woman's fall into the Seine. He writes:

> Quite possibly, the whole incident never happened. After he seemingly heard the splash, Clamence did not turn back to verify whether the sound he heard was real or unreal. Nor did he read the newspapers the following days to check for reports of the drowning. In both instances, Clamence's refusal to confirm the status of the incident as real or imaginary was explicit, almost as though his refusal to resolve the situation extended a wider refusal to engage the truth of a previous—and presumably originary—incident.[9]

Ungar's comments point to the importance of *nachträglich* effects and raise the question of the relation between empirical reality and fantasy in trauma. He does, however, seem to see within the novel a potentially traumatizing "empirical" incident in relation to which the fall into the Seine served as a screen, an incident pointing to the significance of France's colonialist role: "The true objective of Clamence's elaborate confession was disclosure, not of the incident on the Pont Royal, but of the incident in the detention camp in North Africa that he let slip at the beginning of the novel's last chapter when he referred with understatement to the malaria he thought he had first caught at the time he was pope" (p. 30). This observation is in line with Ungar's general insistence that "acts of exclusion and violence perpetrated under Vichy toward internal minorities brought home to France practices that had been instituted abroad through colonial rule" (pp. xv–xvi). Thus for Ungar domestic forms of exclusion and violence repeated and made evident what was concealed, ignored, or perhaps deemed less consequential in its more distant colonial forms.[10]

[9] *Scandal & Aftereffect: Blanchot and France since 1930* (Minneapolis: University of Minnesota Press, 1995), p. 29.

[10] One may further conjecture, in line with Ungar's reading, that the woman's fall, in its very marginality, functions associatively to recall an earlier event and thus to trigger a traumatic reaction in Clamence. I would also note that Ungar's own insistence on the suppression of Maurice Blanchot's early rightist writings in the recent critical and theoretical appropriation of his work is not complemented by an examination of

The incident involving the detention camp is very obscure in the novel. Why Clamence or others at the camp are being detained remains enshrouded in night and fog, and there is no direct discussion of France's colonial rule. Here the novel would seem symptomatic of the tendency, prevalent in France until relatively recently, to resist distinctions between Jews and political prisoners or other detainees in the Nazi camps as well as to remain obscure about the treatment of internal and colonial minorities. The use of the term *déportés* to refer to all those sent from France under Vichy has itself had an assimilationist, homogenizing effect.

In *The Fall* Clamence's narrative is a split monologue or an invidiously skewed and manipulative non- or pseudo-dialogue, a shifting and shifty "conversation" with a depersonalized, silent other who is also within the self. It might also be interpreted as a genteel, cultivated form of terrorism that preempts the voice of the other and serves to dominate him or her. The narrative is in certain ways similar to that in Dostoevsky's *Notes From Underground* and to the scene in *The Brothers Karamazov* in which Ivan confronts the devil. (One may also mention comparable narratives in Diderot's *Rameau's Nephew* and the central chapter in Mann's *Doctor Faustus*.) Clamence speaks with another who is in a sense the other in himself—a resident alien. And Clamence is simultaneously the other in the reader—an other who may be effective in eliciting projective readings that say more about the reader than about himself. But Clamence does not accept the other as a distinct but equal interlocutor. He tries to dominate the other by anticipating questions, ironically undercutting counterarguments, and leading the other in the direction (or non-direction) he wants to take. The other—including the reader—is thus easily disempowered by the virtuoso-like, at times brilliant discursive feats of Clamence, which are internally dialogized or split yet resist any fuller, mutually challenging, transformative dialogue with the reader or within the self. The internal (pseudo-) dialogue thus threatens to fall into a fascinating repetition-compulsion that generates a com-

---

the apologetic dimensions of Shoshana Felman's reading of *The Fall*, which he renders in predominantly favorable terms. He does not, for example, see Felman's intensely transferential relation to de Man to be as questionable and question-worthy as that between Hannah Arendt and Heidegger (pp. 45–48). To this extent, he tends to split off and insulate the case of de Man from that of other figures such as Heidegger and Blanchot and to refrain from posing comparably probing questions concerning it and, especially, its reception in contemporary contexts.

plicitous specular relation between the divided narcissism of the narrator and that of the reader.

The reader or other is, however, assumed to be as cultured and self-reflexive as Clamence and to understand his subtleties and allusions, notably his religious allusions and their secular displacements. Clamence is a divided, equivocal Socrates who indiscriminately mingles telling criticism with deceptive, self-serving, and confusing movements of thought. There is indeed much slippage in his mode of thinking, which at times approximates a discursive glissando. Parodying Descartes, he tells us that "it's very hard to disentangle the true from the false in what I'm saying" (p. 119). And his identity, like that of his silent (or silenced) interlocutor, seems always in doubt. Here it is interesting to note that the second and third versions of the manuscript had an epigraph from Socrates. (The first had no epigraph, and the quotation from Lermontov is from the fourth version.) The Socratic epigraph read: "Young Athenians, vanity oozes out from all your pores."[11]

As Felman notes, Clamence is a connoisseur of empty spaces. He points out the empty space above the bar—a bar named Mexico City and located in Amsterdam—where the painting "The Just Judges" was positioned after its theft and before it found sanctuary hidden away in his cupboard. He also fills in a space cleared by the Nazis. Early in the text (p. 11), we are told that Clamence lives in the quarter of town from which the Jews were deported by the Nazis. In one sense, he represents the post-Holocaust consciousness of the false liberal, and he settles uneasily into a void created by the Shoah. This position is his little-ease or torture chamber. This early reference evokes a question that hangs like a cloud over the text: what has all this to do with the Holocaust and the need to come to terms with it? Does Clamence both evade an explicit, discriminating, sustained coming to terms with this question and provide one dubious answer to it, that of the judge-penitent? There also are later allusions to the Holocaust, including the suggestion that Christ was a not altogether innocent survivor of the slaughter of Innocents (p. 112)—an allusion that situates Christ belatedly with reference to the large-scale ineffectiveness or complicity of Christianity in the events of the Shoah. Clamence himself tells us that, in a prison camp where he happened to find himself, he was gratuitously elected pope (p.125).

[11] *Théâtre, Récits, Nouvelles*, p. 2015 (my translation).

Of the incident at the bridge, Felman writes: "Some years ago, the narrator was the chance witness of a suicide: a woman he had just passed by suddenly jumped into the Seine. Stunned, the narrator froze for a brief moment, then continued his itinerary: this involuntary witnessing was not part of his life" (p. 165). She then goes on to interpret the incident in terms of a "missed encounter with reality" (p. 167), a "non-recording" and "non-documenting of an event" (p. 168), a "missing of the fall" (p. 169), and, more generally, of a failure and betrayal of witnessing. What is not discussed is the problematic relation between the failure and the betrayal, as well as between passive and active subject-positions, insofar as the dominant tendency in Felman's interpretation is to present Clamence as a witness who is the victim of a traumatic incident.

There would seem to be a traumatic element in Clamence's reaction to the "fall" of the woman, even if one would want to question its use to justify a homogenized view of victimhood. (The general problem here is to resist, on ethical, social, and political grounds, the simple elision or conflation of subject-positions—those, for example, of victim, perpetrator, collaborator, and bystander—even though trauma in their cases may bring similar psychological effects or symptoms.) In a passage Felman herself quotes (pp. 165–66), Clamence notes that when he hears the sound, he had already gone "some fifty yards," thus providing a significant distance between himself and the immediacy of the event. He also observed that, "despite the distance," the sound "seemed dreadfully loud in the midnight silence." He further remarks: "I was trembling, I believe from cold or shock. I told myself that I had to be quick and I felt an irresistible weakness steal over me. I have forgotten what I thought then. 'Too late, too far . . .' or something of the sort."

The text thus registers the complexity of Clamence's response, including the way he alludes to the confusing temporal ("too late") and spatial ("too far") gaps involved in trauma. Felman herself notes that Clamence was a bystander (*un passant*) who failed to bear witness (pp. 189, 199), but she curiously makes this observation only in passing (*en passant*). Indeed she moves precipitately past the problem of the bystander and rapidly identifies Clamence's specific failure with a general collapse of witnessing that somewhat plausibly includes the Allies, less plausibly allows for an excessive stress on Sartre's failures (even a use of him as whipping boy), and implausibly involves manifest victims of the Shoah. Nor does Felman observe that Clamence's inability to help the woman is reinscribed and repeated through more lucid and explicit decisions in later life insofar as he trades manipulatively in equivocation and avoids any possibility of a different kind of response. In this way, he more actively and deliberately takes up the role of the far-from-innocent bystander and even moves from bystander to victimizer.

At the end of the text Clamence evokes the possibility of a second chance to save the woman who "jumped" into the Seine: "A second time, eh, what a risky suggestion! Just suppose, cher maître, that we should be taken literally? We'd have to go through with it. Br. . . ! The water's so cold! But let's not worry! It's too late now. It will always be too late. Fortunately!" The text ends with *Heureusement!*—fortunately it's too late. In an obvious sense it is always too late after something has happened. Yet Clamence seems to relish the fact in a way that denies the significance of recurrent existential trials. He does not want a second chance and lives without hope—but in a dubious manner. For he resists not only redemption or salvation (which Camus also resists and indeed envisions as a dangerous, murderous lure); Clamence resists any kind of renewal or working-through. In some devious, equivocating, destructive, and self-destructive way, he wants to be stymied and to fail. He desires to remain within an aporia or impasse, to bring others into it, and to do everything he can to intensify its fascination, ineluctability, and force.

After his "fall," Clamence becomes a judge-penitent. His new profession, his vicious parody of a calling, has an affinity with his narrative technique. One element of suspense in *The Fall* is the continual delay in offering the reader a definition of the judge-penitent, and when it comes it is too intricate and uncertain for narrative satisfaction or straightforward summary. As a false penitent, Clamence ironically and even nihilistically judges himself. He thus avoids being judged by others and arrogates to himself the right to judge them (p. 138). He also judges himself in a seductive and witty way that elicits the interest if not the admiration of his interlocutor. His narrative technique is geared both to victimizing and to making an accomplice of the reader. This device evokes a sense of complicity, and enables him to play on the shock of recognition and to judge the interlocutor who is not so different from himself. Clamence is thus both false penitent and wily judge, and his penitence seems largely instrumental in creating a basis for judging and victimizing the other.

The text of course positions the reader in the role of interlocutor. And the simple dismissal of Clamence may lead the reader to deny or repress the way Clamence is also within him- or herself. In fact Clamence's own identity as a lawyer may not be essential. He possibly changes his identity not only to protect himself from attack but also to suit the profession of the other, the interlocutor, and to facilitate complicity and mimetic involvement. In any case the interlocutor faces comparable trials and temptations to those of the chameleon-like Clamence.

In terms of religious allusions, Clamence is obviously like an Elijah or a John the Baptist crying or clamoring in the desert. But no redeemer is announced to follow him. He is a terminal false prophet and has no saving aftermath. In the words of the text, he is "an empty prophet for shabby times" (p. 117).

The concentric canals of Amsterdam are a manifest allegory of the circles of hell in Dante. And the novel situates Clamence in the last circle (p. 14). The reader is assumed to know that in Dante the last circle is for traitors. And the crime in *The Fall*—Clamence's crime—seems to be a form of secular treason. In a radical misprision of the allusion to Dante, Felman, pursuing her tendency to conflate the silences and indirections of Clamence, de Man, and Jewish victims, sees the Nazi concentration camps as the innermost circle of hell and goes on to provide this puzzling and easily misconstrued gloss : "The last circle of hell is inhabited by those who are no longer there, those who, from within the very center of the circle, have precisely been obliterated. The Jewish quarter—or the ultimate concentric circle—is inhabited by silence, a silence we can no longer dispel, denounce, deplore or simply understand" (p. 189). The notion of the camps as hell (or the last circle) has become a cliché, but there is a vast distance between this cliché and the figuration of the last circle in either *The Fall* or Felman's convoluted construction of it.

Clamence often equivocates instrumentally to victimize others and even himself. He tells us that judge-penitency is a provisional solution until one can achieve the "definitive" (he does not explicitly say "final") solution of slavery. This is another way he fills the space left empty by the Holocaust. Yet it is also significant that Clamence is not a secure and self-confident prophet of anything. His assertions are not made with an apodictic sense of authority, and he is filled with self-doubt. Toward the end of the text, he explicitly calls himself "a false prophet crying in the wilderness and refusing to come forth" (p. 147). In a manner that renders himself vulnerable to ridicule, he also fleetingly evokes youthful dreams of Greek isles, a sort of pastoral, sentimental utopia. This appeal to lost innocence has a disconcerting, disjunctive relation to the fact that Clamence's concern with penitence is not accompanied by any expression of guilt, which may be read either as a sign of repression and denial or as an indication of the irrelevance of guilt for him. In any case, he insistently turns away from the possibility of a second chance. He resists or refuses even the attempt to change in ways that would expose him to different and perhaps riskier possibilities, but he at times explicitly notes his own limitations and the manner in which he is prone to act problems out or compulsively repeat them.

Camus's other writings do help in gaining perspective on *The Fall*. But *The Fall* is exceptional in Camus in that it does not gravitate toward a temptation Camus at times gives in to, which might be called the temptation of excessive moderation or the unearned assertion of limits as if they were simply there for the taking. This facile judiciousness is not the alternative to, but the enemy brother of, a penchant for excess. And facile judiciousness easily leads to a misreading of those who address the problem of excess and limits in more nuanced terms, including the tendency to lump them all together as proponents of the putatively postmodern view that anything goes. *The Fall* explores extreme temptation, including the equivocal allures of the proliferating impasse as well as the fascination of nihilistic wit and posttraumatic cynicism. And it does so with the power to challenge the reader. The reader may be provoked not to identify with, or be the abject victim of, Clamence but rather to rethink the question of what in the modern world constitutes moderation from strength—moderation that understands and even undergoes the temptations of excess but comes with the question of when to resist it and how to work through it. (Camus himself approached this issue, for example, in *The Rebel*, in his own terms.) The reader may also be moved to pose the difficult question of the relation between self-serving equivocation and desirable forms of ambivalence.

In *The Fall* itself, Clamence's narrative does not exhaust the text because of the spaces or silences in it: pauses between statements where the reader, silenced in the literal text of *The Fall*, may nonetheless respond to Clamence. These gaps not only make oblique reference to the devastation and trauma of the Holocaust. They also leave room for the reader to think of other historical cases or to contest the complicities Clamence generates and to raise alternative possibilities. And Clamence himself points out limitations in his approach. One cannot look to his narrative for a moral message or for simple guidance, an inclination that would, in any case, be jejune. One can nonetheless read the text as exploring the problem of extreme temptation with a power of provocation that both has the reader undergo this temptation and incites him or her to argue with it, with Clamence and with certain clamoring voices within him- or herself. In this sense the text may actually bring one closer to the problem of moderation through strength than Camus's other texts.

I noted at the outset that Camus's turn to the Holocaust may be read as functioning to displace or even obscure the problem of the Algerian war and his response to it. In concluding, I would like to explore this issue and make a few preliminary, tentative points bearing on it.

As a person who thought of himself as a French Algerian, Camus explicitly wanted neither French withdrawal nor colonial domination, neither Algerian independence nor colonial dependence. He desired a just and democratic living arrangement that would articulate relations between equal but different peoples. He clearly opposed terrorism directed against civilians, whether Arab or French Algerian. After commenting on events in the early-to-mid-1950s, Camus decided, in 1956 and 1957, to keep silent for fear that any statements on his part might simply worsen things and contribute to positions or actions he found unacceptable. He insistently opposed French repression in Algeria both before and during the course of the war, and even during his period of public silence he intervened in favor of Algerian militants who were condemned to death by the French. But, unlike Sartre and others he disparaged as Parisian intellectuals who took up facile postures, Camus could agree with no existing, decisive position on Algeria, for all appeared to him extreme; he could defend only what he found to be a reasonable compromise solution but in the circumstances seemed to others a utopian dream or worse. Emerging from silence in 1958, he published *Actuelles* III that added to already known texts a memoir entitled *Algérie 58*. The book was coldly received on all sides, and the nature of its reception or non-reception helped foster the legend that Camus had simply remained silent about Algeria.[12]

---

[12] See the useful commentary of Raymond Quilliot in *Albert Camus Essais,* intro. R. Quilliot, annotations R. Quilliot and L. Faucon (Paris: Gallimard [Pléiade], 1965), pp. 1837–47. I would note that, along with the colonial context, another issue worth exploring is the gendering of relations in *The Fall*. Its world is very much a man's world, in which woman is absent as interlocutor, subject, or agent. The woman who falls into the Seine serves both to confirm this image and to undermine it by bringing out its self-

In *Algérie* 58 Camus proposed a settlement involving reparations for eight million oppressed Arabs, the right to exist for one million, two-hundred thousand native French Algerians, and a federal parliament for France and Algeria with roughly proportional representation for metropolitan French, Algerian French, and Algerian Arabs. (In this parliament of six hundred that would decide on issues of common concern to the federation, there would be approximately one hundred Arab Algerian and fifteen French Algerian deputies.) Camus envisaged a federation that united and respected the ways of life of different peoples. He saw this proposal as a revolution against the centralization and abstract individualism inherited from the French Revolution insofar as political representation would be based on equal but distinct groups of citizens. He also saw the cost of such an arrangement as requiring an austerity program in metropolitan France whose weight was to be born by well-off metropolitan French. In the absence of such a compromise solution, he envisioned disastrous consequences for Arabs as well as for the French.

In a related earlier text, *L'Avenir Algérien*, published in 1955, Camus provided the cultural background and larger vision for the political proposals he put forward in *Algérie* 58. In a move of symbolic importance, he proposed that Algiers, not Paris, be the seat of a federal parliament. Moreover, he tried to imagine how colonialism might give way to association in which the envisaged relation between the French and the Algerians might prefigure a transformation of relations that would take them beyond a narrow nationalism (but not all patriotism or even localism) and toward a larger idea of civilization. He argued that the "Algerian drama is in effect only a particular case of a vaster historical drama that marks our century even more than the conflict between capitalism and communism." He was referring to "the great movement that pushes the Eastern masses [*les masses orientales*] toward the conquest of their personality"—personality in the sense of "tradition, language, culture."[13] Colonialism depersonalized Arabs and de-

---

defeating effects. One also tends to assume that Clamence's interlocutor is a man. It would be interesting to speculate how *The Fall* and one's reading of it would be transformed if one imagined the interlocutor to be a woman.

[13] *Albert Camus Essais*, pp. 1873–75. Further page references are included in the text, and translations are mine. I would note that the Algerian leader whose position was closest to Camus's was Ferhat Abbas—at least until mid-1955 when Abbas, frustrated by the intransigence of the French government, rallied to the FLN (National Liberation Front) and the cause of Algerian independence. On Abbas, see Benjamin Stora and Zakya Daoud, *Ferhat Abbas: une utopie algérienne* (Paris: Editions Denoël, 1995).

prived them of an effective voice, subjecting them to oppression, evasiveness, and deceit. Association was possible only "between persons" (p. 1873), and only fundamental economic, social, and political change could provide the bases of "a true dialogue between qualified interlocutors" (p. 1874). For Camus "the dozen or so uprisings that punctuated the hundred years of colonization prove that [the Arab people] had something to say." The problem was to find a way beyond terrorism and armed conflict, provoked in good part by the history of deceptions marking French colonization, for them to say it. "If on one point of the globe we could find a formula that avoids the stage of despotism, bourgeois or totalitarian, we would have done more for the future than thirty revolutions destined to devour themselves." The goal was thus to bring about a French-Arab association that might become the ferment for a larger transformation realizing on a global scale the truth that "French culture and Arab culture have been complementary contributions to a larger civilization in time and space" (p. 1875). The untimely nature of these idealistic thoughts should not, I think, eliminate their force or conceal the extent to which they may be seen to inform much contemporary work in cultural studies. One significant difference, however, is that Camus did not move beyond the idea of association between distinct peoples to an affirmative conception of hybridization, creolization, or *métissage* in the relation of peoples and cultures.

L'Avenir Algérien (1955) and *Algérie* 58 frame *The Fall* (1956) and provide some sense of how it might be read as Camus's portrait of the colonized, preceded by the portrait of the colonizer (to adopt the title of Albert Memmi's work of 1957). At the very least Camus might be read as offering a portrait of intellectual and cultural elites in the colonial context. One might at first be tempted to see in Clamence a critical portrait of the colonizer, particularly the cynical, ironic, evasive, cultured individual who relied on the authorities to do the dirty work, while in his interlocutor one could see either another dimension of the colonizer or, alternatively, an internalized profile of the colonized as complicitous, acculturated *évolué* rather than as partner in critical dialogue or as *homme révolté*. The relation between the two would be non- or pseudo-dialogical, a form of failed communication in a negative and dire mode of hybridization that would stymie alternatives and have to be worked through to allow for more desirable possibilities. In his one allusion to *The Fall* with reference to Algeria, however, Camus did not propose this seemingly obvious interpretation. Because this interpretation seems so blatantly obvious, the very fact that Camus himself did not suggest it is both shocking and informative. One might even be inclined to see this glaring absence as indicative of repression or even of denial.

In his rather polemical and defensive "Avant-Propos" to *Actuelles* III, Camus noted that the texts gathered in it "stretch over a period of twenty years, since 1939, when almost no one in France was interested in [Algeria], to 1958, when everyone talks about it" (p. 892). He went on explicitly to apply the term "judge-penitent" to what was, in his judgment, a holier-than-thou segment of metropolitan French opinion (no doubt intended to include Sartre) that went to extremes in blaming the French for colonialism, supporting even the terror of the F.L.N. and indiscriminately condemning French Algerians. In the paragraph in which he used the term, he was especially upset by "a French partisan of the F.L.N. [who] dared to write that the French Algerians always considered France as a prostitute to exploit." Here Camus recalled the patriotic sacrifices of French Algerians, including his own ancestors, in wars in which France was involved and insisted that "three quarters of French Algerians resemble them." Reiterating that most French Algerians were little people who struggled to make a living and considered Algeria their home, he added that "there were undoubtedly exploiters in Algeria but rather fewer than in metropolitan France, and the first beneficiary of the colonial system is the French nation in its entirety" (p. 897). Earlier he objected to seeing "the Arabs of Algeria *en bloc* as a people of massacrers" and insisted that "the great mass of them, exposed to blows from all sides, suffer with a sorrow that no one expresses for them," whether in Algiers or in Cairo (p. 896). His position throughout was opposed to terrorism, torture, indiscriminate action or thought, and scapegoating, from whatever quarter they came. He adamantly opposed the use of French Algerians as "expiatory victims" by a segment of metropolitan France and saw the gesture as involving a displacement and projection of all guilt onto French Algerians. An extended quotation is apposite here:

It strikes me as disgusting to beat out one's guilt, as do our judge-penitents, on the breast of another, vain to condemn several centuries of European expansion, absurd to include in the same curse Columbus and Lyautey. The time of colonialism has passed; one must simply acknowledge the fact and draw the consequences. And the West which, in ten years, has given autonomy to a dozen colonies merits in this regard more respect and, especially, more patience than Russia which, during the same time, has colonized or placed under an implacable protectorate a dozen countries of great and ancient civilization. It is good for a nation to be strong enough in tradition and honor to find the courage to denounce its own errors. But it ought not forget the reasons it may have still to respect itself. In any case it is dangerous to ask it to recognize itself as the only guilty party and to dedicate itself to perpetual penitence. I believe that Algeria needs a politics of reparation, not a politics of expiation. It is in function of the future that problems must be posed, without eternally ruminating over the faults of the past. And there will be no future that does not give justice to the two communities in Algeria. (pp. 897–98)

Camus is here writing and thinking at a fever pitch, and, given his deep investment in immediate problems, is unable to sustain the critical and self-critical distance necessary to counteract, without simply denying or transcending, the excesses he explicitly deplores. As in *The Rebel*, he tends to get caught up in the dynamic he criticizes in the very process of criticizing it. Still, I do not think one can take his words as amounting to a general indictment of memory or a dissociation between memory and action in the present and future. Much else in *Actuelles* III would go against such an inference. Camus nonetheless indulges in indiscriminately dichotomizing thought when he refers to "the two communities in Algeria," thereby obscuring the distinctions and complexities on which he himself has insisted. He also tends to be excessive in condemning excess and pleading for moderation, going in the direction of what might anachronistically be termed anti-PC ("political correctness") rhetoric. And he invokes the cold-war context to bolster his position, as he does elsewhere in his writings on Algeria, as if the pronounced excesses of Russia mitigated those of the West. Here certain movements in *The Fall* may be more convincing than those in the nonfictional prose that appeals to it. In any case, these inadequate comments at least serve to indicate that the entire Algerian dimension of Camus's work and life may be ready for reexamination and constitute another reason for renewed interest in him.

In the present context, it is also useful to observe that the widespread concern with the Holocaust and the Vichy regime in France, especially among intellectuals and historians, has itself arrived belatedly, and for some observers it has recently reached obsessive proportions.[14] Indeed, the tone in which commentators such as Charles Maier or Henry Rousso make this point recalls the views of Camus I have just rehearsed, including their more dubious sides. (They even at times threaten to echo the plaints of certain hard-nosed, generally conservative or liberal-conservative German historians during the 1986 *Historikerstreit* who insisted almost obsessively on the need to turn to the future and get beyond, rather than "obsess" about, a "past that will not pass away.") I do not agree with the view that pathologizes concern with the unworked-through past as symptomatic of neurosis or obsession and assumes that one can have a quantitative excess or "surfeit" of memory with respect to traumatic limit-events. The significant question with respect to such events is the qualitative nature of memory, its effectiveness in working through the past in ethically and politically desirable ways, its relation to a critical historiography, and its functions in the present. In this light, it is indeed important to insist that the concern for the Holocaust and Vichy, however belated, inevitable, or desirable it may be, should be manifested without functioning as a diversionary screen to obscure or split off the need to come to terms with such more recent and pressing problems as France's role in Algeria.

[14] See especially Charles Maier, "A Surfeit of Memory? Reflections on History, Melancholy and Denial," *History & Memory* 5 (1993), pp. 137–52, and Eric Conan and Henry Rousso, *Vichy, un passé qui ne passe pas* (Paris: Fayard, 1994).

CHAPTER FOUR

Lanzmann's *Shoah:*
"Here There Is No Why"

"Un pur chef-d'oeuvre." With these words Simone de Beauvoir concludes her preface to the French edition of the text of the film *Shoah*
(1985) by Claude Lanzmann.[1] Any discussion of the film must begin
with an affirmation of its importance and of Lanzmann's achievement
in making it. It is a *chef-d'oeuvre.* But no *chef-d'oeuvre* is pure. Its status
is both confirmed and tested to the extent that it can withstand the closest scrutiny and the most sustained criticism. However, discussion of
Shoah has been marked by an understandable inclination to ritualize
the film and to regard its viewing as a ceremonial event with respect
to which criticism pales or even seems irreverent. Indeed the tendency to sacralize the Shoah itself and to surround it with a taboo may be
transferred to Lanzmann's remarkable film. Without denying other
possible readings or receptions of the film, I shall try to address critically the nature of Lanzmann's self-understanding as filmmaker and
the way it informs at least some aspects of *Shoah.* This approach in no
way exhausts the nature of the film or even provides a dominant manner of viewing it, but it does allow one to see things in it that are often
ignored or obscured in other interpretations.

---

[1] Simone de Beauvoir, "La Mémoire de l'horreur," preface to Claude Lanzmann,
Shoah (Paris: Fayard, 1985). The revised English edition, from which I shall quote, is
Lanzmann, *Shoah: The Complete Text of the Acclaimed Holocaust Film* (New York: Da Capo
Press, 1995), hereafter abbreviated as *S.* According to the back cover, this edition has
been "newly revised and corrected by Lanzmann in order to more accurately present
the actual testimony of those interviewed." Lanzmann disavowed the 1985 Pantheon
Books edition.

Although I shall attribute much importance to what Lanzmann says about his film, I shall resist one of his major inclinations in discussing it. Lanzmann insists that his film is not a documentary, that it is not primarily historical, and that it should not be viewed as first and foremost about the Shoah itself. In one limited sense, he is right. *Shoah* is not strictly a documentary film in that scenes in it are carefully constructed. The role of *mise-en-scène* in the film is indeed crucial. For example, one of the most salient scenes, to which I shall later return, is staged in a particular manner. It involves Abraham Bomba discussing his role as a barber in Treblinka as he cuts someone's hair on screen. The viewer is, I think, shocked to learn that the barber shop was rented and that the men in it are simply extras who do not understand the language (English) in which the exchange between Lanzmann and Bomba is conducted. Moreover, the manner in which the historical dimensions of *Shoah* are open to question is one of my principal concerns. The viewer expects *Shoah* to be historical and even to be a documentary. Indeed, this expectation is invited by the narrative prologue, which introduces the film by discussing in fact-laden terms the death camp at Chelmno. Hence the subtitle of the 1985 English edition of the work, *An Oral History of the Holocaust*, conforms to plausible viewer or reader expectations. One is, I think, taken aback when Lanzmann insists: "What interests me is the film. One has been able to discuss Nazism for forty years. One doesn't need the film for that."[2] Or again: "*Shoah* is not a documentary. . . . The film is not at all representational."[3] Most provocatively, Lanzmann has said that *Shoah* is "a fiction of the real."[4] Lanzmann's self-understanding and commentary give priority to his personal vision of the film as a work of art. Here a central question is what one means by "a fiction of the real" and where one sets limits or establishes priorities insofar as they must be set or established.

[2] Lanzmann, "Les Non-lieux de la mémoire," in *Au sujet de Shoah: le Film de Claude Lanzmann,* ed. Michel Deguy (Paris: Belin, 1990), p. 282; hereafter abbreviated as "NM." This book contains a series of articles on *Shoah* as well as interviews and contributions by Lanzmann himself. Unless otherwise indicated, all translations are my own.

[3] Lanzmann, "Seminar with Claude Lanzmann, 11 April 1990," *Yale French Studies* no. 79 (1991), pp. 96, 97; hereafter abbreviated as "SCL." This special issue, edited by Claire Nouvet, is entitled *Literature and the Ethical Question.*

[4] Lanzmann, "Le Lieu et la parole," in *Au sujet de Shoah,* p. 301; hereafter abbreviated as "LP."

One need not always agree with Lanzmann's interpretations concerning the nature of his film, and one may even see his own role in it as at times exceeding his self-understanding. In fact, one of my goals is to disengage the film from his view of it in order to make other readings more possible. Yet his interpretation is compelling and casts a particular light on the film. Indeed, the degree to which his views are taken to inform the film may perhaps be indicated by the prevalent critical practice of using them to initiate, substantiate, or illustrate the critic's own conception of the film without subjecting them to critical scrutiny. Lanzmann's views resonate, moreover, with forceful postmodern and poststructural tendencies in reading and interpretation, as evidenced, for example, in Shoshana Felman's noteworthy article on *Shoah*—an article Lanzmann himself obviously saw as crucial since he helped translate it into French for the important volume, *Au sujet de Shoah: Le Film de Claude Lanzmann*.[5] In certain respects, these tenden-

[5] See Shoshana Felman, "The Return of the Voice: Claude Lanzmann's *Shoah*" in Felman and Dori Laub, M.D., *Testimony: Crises of Witnessing in Literature, Psychoanalysis, and History* (New York: Routledge, 1992), pp. 204–83, hereafter abbreviated "RV"; trans. Lanzmann and Judith Ertel, under the title *"A L'âge du témoignage: Shoah de Claude Lanzmann,"* in *Au sujet de Shoah*, pp. 55–145. For an idea of the currency of views similar to Lanzmann's, see their role in Ron Rosenbaum, "Explaining Hitler," *The New Yorker* 1 May 1995, 50–70. Gertrud Koch, "Transformations esthétiques dans la représentation de l'inimaginable," trans. Catherine Weinzorn, in *Au sujet de Shoah*, pp. 157–66, offers a strongly aesthetic interpretation of the film that in certain respects coincides with Lanzmann's self-interpretation. Referring to what she terms Lawrence L. Langer's "option for an aesthetic of modern times," she appeals to "the (irresolvable) aporias of autonomous art" (pp. 160, 161). Autonomous art, for her, "draws its force from the theorem of the imagination, from the affirmation that art is not representation, but presentation, not reproduction, but expression. One accords to the imagination a proper autonomy; it is capable of conceiving, capable of annihilating being-in-society, of transcending it towards the radically other, capable of making arise in the mute body the natural substratum, however hidden, however dispossessed of expression, it may be" (p. 161). Quoting Samuel Beckett, on whom Theodor Adorno also relied for his conception of autonomous art, Koch asserts, "modern art has stopped talking and transformed itself into an enigma—the proof of its reflection on this [Beckettian] limit" (p. 161). *Shoah* for her brings about "an aesthetic transformation of the experience of extermination" (p. 166). In what almost amounts to a begrudging concession, Koch notes in passing: "That the film brings, in addition, enough material and contributes to necessary historical and political debates cannot be denied." But she stresses that "the fascination it exerts, its somber beauty, is assuredly an aesthetic quality" (p. 166). My own approach to *Shoah* insists on consistently relating aesthetic qualities and historical-political issues and conceives differently the priorities Koch postulates between them. Moreover, I would be wary of aestheticized renderings of the Shoah, including the unqualified inclination to validate certain tendencies (notably the desire to have the past relived or acted out) by viewing them in exclusively aesthetic terms.

cies connect as well with a long tradition in French thought that emphasizes tragic, self-rendingly ecstatic experience—a complex tradition often drawing from Nietzsche and Heidegger and passing through Georges Bataille and Maurice Blanchot to reach recent thinkers such as Michel Foucault, Gilles Deleuze, Jacques Lacan, and Jacques Derrida. This tradition has also played a pivotal role in post-structural and postmodern approaches in general.

In Lanzmann, art poses provocative questions to history. To some extent, I shall reverse the procedure and have history pose questions to art. I would suggest that the very limits of art's autonomy are tested not only on historical but also on ethical grounds insofar as art addresses limit-cases that still present live, emotion-laden, at times intractable issues. In this sense, not everything is possible in art when one asserts its autonomy, or even when one postulates a more disturbing sense of its enigmatic and abyssal nature as a "writing of disaster" in the face of the impossible and unspeakable.[6] Still, *Shoah* is probably best viewed as neither representational nor autonomous art but as a disturbingly mixed generic performance that traces and tracks the traumatic effects of limit-experiences, particularly in the lives (or afterlives) of victims. It is a film of endless lamentation or grieving that is tensely suspended between acting out a traumatic past and attempting to work through it. In Lanzmann's influential self-understanding, reliving the past tends to outweigh efforts to work through it. The historical shortfalls of the film may be related to this self-understanding; a more thorough memory of the past might conceivably further efforts to work through it. Moreover, there may be a sense in which the greatest challenges to art include—but of course are not reducible to—the attempt at historically valid reconstruction and understanding, particularly with respect to limit-events of the magnitude of the Holocaust.

Here one may turn for guidance to Pierre Vidal-Naquet.[7] Vidal-Naquet's statements initially seem contradictory, perhaps sympto-

[6] Lanzmann himself uses the phrase "writing of disaster" in his "Introduction" to the text of *Shoah* (*S*, p. viii). The phrase is taken from the title of a book by Maurice Blanchot (*The Writing of Disaster*, 1980; Lincoln: University of Nebraska Press, 1986, trans. Ann Smock).

[7] See Pierre Vidal-Naquet, "The Holocaust's Challenge to History," in *Auschwitz and After: Race, Culture, and "the Jewish Question" in France*, ed. Lawrence Kritzman (New York: Routledge, 1995), pp. 25–34; hereafter abbreviated as "HC." The French version, "L'Epreuve de l'historien: réflexions d'un généraliste," is in *Au sujet de Shoah*, pp. 198–208.

matic of his divided reaction to the film. On the one hand, he asserts in no uncertain terms that "the only great French historical work on the theme of Hitler's genocide is the film of Claude Lanzmann, *Shoah*" ("HC," p. 31).[8] On the other hand, he states, "if it is true that historical research demands 'rectification without end', fiction, especially when it is deliberate, and true history nonetheless form two extremes which never meet" ("HC," p. 30). The mediation between these contradictory statements is provided by his analysis of the way history and art pose questions to each other without ever becoming identical. "How," asks Vidal-Naquet, "does this film question the historian?" ("HC," p. 31). His first answer is that the film is not chronological or concerned with causes and effects. Vidal-Naquet asks: "In effect, how can one avoid moving backward from the gas chambers to the *Einsatzgruppen* and, step by step, to the laws of exclusion, to German anti-Semitism, to that which distinguishes and opposes Hitler's anti-Semitism and that of Wilhelm II, and so on *ad infinitum*? Raul Hilberg, for instance, proceeded in such a way in his admirable volume" ("HC," pp. 31–32). As we shall see, however, Lanzmann himself is not altogether consistent on these points, for in his extrafilmic commentary he both stresses the radically disjunctive nature and uniqueness of the Holocaust on the one hand and presents it as the culmination of Western history, especially with respect to anti-Semitism, on the other.

For Vidal-Naquet, "the second question Lanzmann's film asks the historian is perhaps even more fundamental. His attempt contains an element of folly: to have made a work of history at a juncture where memory alone, a present-day memory, is called upon to bear witness" ("HC," p. 32). Here Vidal-Naquet refers to Lanzmann's emphatic exclusion of archival material, especially documentary footage, from the Nazi period and the Holocaust and to his insistence on discovering the past in and through the present alone, through testimonies or acts of witnessing. Yet there is an important sense in which Lanzmann relies on an antimemory or on the silences and indirections of memory in ar-

[8] This comment is made not only to confer genuine praise on Lanzmann but to criticize French historiography, notably the *Annales* school, for its tendency to avoid recent history and emphasize *la longue durée*. One consequence has been that, in France, basic work on the Holocaust and related issues such as the Vichy regime has, until the relatively recent past, often been done by figures who are not professionally trained historians.

riving at what I take to be the object of his quest: the incarnation, actual reliving, or compulsive acting out of the past—particularly its traumatic suffering —in the present.

Vidal-Naquet draws on Thucydides in eliciting three characteristics of history, but does not make their bearing on Lanzmann's *Shoah* explicit. First, "a history of the present is indeed possible." Second, "any history, including that of the present, presupposes a distancing of the historian from the events." And "finally, and perhaps essentially, any history is comparative, even when it believes it is not" ("HC," p. 26). Here one may note that Lanzmann often seems to remove any distance between the present and the past and that he adamantly rejects comparisons as invariably normalizing attempts to deny the absolute uniqueness and disjunctiveness of the Shoah. Moreover, what is meant by *history*, including a history of the present, with respect to Lanzmann's understanding of *Shoah*—indeed, his very understanding of understanding—is open to question.

A key document in these respects is Lanzmann's one-page manifesto, "Hier ist kein Warum." It is written in an apodictic, almost prophetic mode. Like much of Lanzmann's writing and commentary, it trades in absolutes. It begins with the hyperbolic statement, "All one has to do is perhaps formulate the question in the simplest form, to ask: 'Why were the Jews killed?' The question immediately reveals its obscenity. There is indeed an absolute obscenity in the project of understanding."[9] "Absolute obscenity": the use of such a phrase and the entire cast of this and comparable statements in Lanzmann raise a question. To what extent do references to art, fiction, personal obsession or vision, and even ethics serve in good part as a screen for the role of displaced, disguised, and often denied religious elements in Lanzmann's approach? I would suggest that Lanzmann returns to what he explicitly denies, represses, or suppresses: a tendency to sacralize the Holocaust and to surround it with taboos. He especially affirms a *Bilderverbot*, or prohibition on images, with respect to representation, notably representation relying on archival documentation or footage, and he also insists on what might be called a *Warumverbot*, or a prohibition on the question *why*. The most pronounced manifestation of a displaced secular religiosity may well be

[9] Lanzmann, "Hier ist kein Warum," in *Au sujet de Shoah*, p. 279; hereafter abbreviated as "HKW."

Lanzmann's tendency to grant the highest, perhaps the sole legitimate, status to the witness who not only provides testimony but who self-rendingly relives the traumatic suffering of the past—a status with which Lanzmann as filmmaker would like to identify. A further question that agitates my own inquiry is whether this "tragic" identification or rather uncontrolled transferential relation has something problematic about it both in its attempt to provoke repetition of trauma in the other and in its desire to relive that suffering in the shattered self.

For Lanzmann, on the contrary, his "blindness" to the *why* question is identical with his insight and constitutes "the vital condition of creation." Without mitigating its shock effect, he elaborates his absolute, unmediated paradox in this way:

> Blindness should be understood here as the purest mode of looking, the only way not to turn away from a reality that is literally blinding: clairvoyance itself. To direct a frontal look at horror requires that one renounce distractions and escape-hatches, first the primary among them, the most falsely central, the question why, with the indefinite retinue of academic frivolities and dirty tricks (*canailleries*) that it ceaselessly induces. ("HKW," p. 279)

It may again seem paradoxical that Lanzmann refers to "a frontal look at horror" insofar as he rejects direct representation, notably in the familiar but still disconcerting form of archival film and photographs. But here the paradox may be dissipated, or at least transformed, when one understands the frontal look in terms of the actual reliving or acting out of a traumatic past.

Still, Lanzmann proceeds to make a series of statements whose shock may not be dissipated but only increased through exegesis. He concludes his manifesto thus:

> "Hier ist kein Warum" ("Here there is no why"): Primo Levi tells us that the rule of Auschwitz was thus taught from his arrival in the camp by an SS guard. "There is no why": this law is also valid for whoever assumes the charge of such a transmission. Because the act of transmitting alone is important and no intelligibility, that is, no true knowledge, preexists the transmission. It is the transmission that is knowledge itself. Radicality cannot be divided: no why, but also no re-

sponse to the refusal of why under the penalty of instantly reinscribing oneself in the aforementioned obscenity. ("HKW," p. 279)

What is the process of "transmission" that Lanzmann contrasts with the *why* question and equates with knowledge? A first answer is that it is testimony or witnessing: that of the primary witness, particularly the survivor or victim, and that of the secondary witness empathetically attentive to the voice, silences, and gestures of the primary witness. We shall return to this answer, which in turn raises many questions, notably: Granting the crucial importance of witnessing and testimony, can one simply equate them with knowledge? Do they radically exclude all other modes of representation and understanding? What is the relationship between the primary and the secondary witness? Is it—or ought it be—one of full identification or total "empathy"? The force of these questions is increased when one realizes that by *transmission* Lanzmann means not only testimony but also, and more insistently, incarnation, actual reliving, or what would in psychoanalytic terminology be called acting-out.

Before returning to these questions and documenting further my assertions about Lanzmann's self-understanding, I shall pause over Lanzmann's use of Levi and then make some preliminary theoretical remarks about the problems of representation and understanding, the attempts to pose and address the *why* question. What is surprising is that Lanzmann takes up in his own voice, without adequate qualification and exegesis, the statement of an SS guard to Levi. He postulates this statement as constituting a valid law for one charged with transmission of . . . what precisely remains unclear: the testimony of witnesses, traumatic suffering, the horror of the Shoah, the unspeakable or impossible itself? Here one may refer to the context of the statement Lanzmann quotes in Levi's *Survival in Auschwitz:*

> In fact, the whole process of introduction to what was for us a new order took place in a grotesque and sarcastic manner. . . . Driven by thirst, I eyed a fine icicle outside the window, within hand's reach. I opened the window and broke off the icicle but at once a large, heavy guard prowling outside brutally snatched it away from me. "*Warum?*" I asked in my poor German. "*Hier ist kein warum*" (there is no why here), he replied, pushing me inside with a shove.
>
> This explanation is repugnant but simple, not for hidden reasons,

but because the camp has been created for that purpose. If one wants to live one must learn this quickly and well: "No Sacred Face will help them here! it's not a Serchio bathing party. . . ."[10]

Levi does not present the guard's "explanation" as a mere lesson in survival; he qualifies it as repugnant but simple while situating it as a grotesque and sarcastic aspect of the concentration camp context. Does it change its basic character in Lanzmann's use of it? Is its postulation as a general law valid only if one accepts the concentration camp and its "new order" as a model for the world as a whole? Is the danger in this acceptance the possibility that one's outlook or "law" may become a self-fulfilling prophecy?

A great deal—perhaps everything—depends not on whether one poses the *why* question but on how and why one poses it. Nor can one escape the dilemmas and opportunities of critical self-reflection. Levi himself wanted an answer, however partial and inadequate. He did not take up the words of the SS guard in his own voice and he attempted in his own work to address the *why* question with humility and in the belief that even partial understanding might prove of some use in the attempt to resist tendencies that led to, or were manifest in, the Nazi genocide. This belief may be naive or at least based on a kind of faith. But the question is whether Lanzmann's view is preferable. Here one may attempt to elaborate a set of difficult distinctions indicating orientations toward which Lanzmann has significantly different reactions.

One may distinguish among at least three ways of approaching the *why* question. The first involves the expectation of a totally satisfying answer on the level of representation and understanding. A prominent variant of this first approach, the attempt at totalization, has been the object of deconstructive criticism and is generally the butt of post-structural and postmodern attacks. Jean-François Lyotard detects totalization in master narratives and theories of liberation. For Derrida, it is embodied in the metaphysical idea of representation as the reproduction or mimetic re-creation of a putative full presence. A basic point in these critiques is that there is no full presence that may be represented. Instead there is a mutual marking of past, present, and future, and the past itself is an object of reconstruction on the basis of

---

[10] Primo Levi, *Survival in Auschwitz*, in *"Survival in Auschwitz" and "The Reawakening": Two Memoirs*, trans. Stuart Woolf (1958; New York: Macmillan, 1968), pp. 28, 29.

traces and traces of traces. Interestingly, Lanzmann himself describes his effort in terms of working with traces of traces in a present that is marked by its relation to the past and future, although one may contest some of the denials and inferences he draws from his description. "When I say that I constructed the film with what I had, it means that the film is not a product of the Holocaust, that it is not a historical film: it's a sort of originary event since I made it in the present. I was obligated to construct it with traces of traces, with what was strong in what I had made" ("LP," pp. 303–4). But, as we shall see, Lanzmann also, and even more insistently, employs language that would seem to involve him in a quest for full presence in the attempt to erase or fully instantiate traces by incarnating and reliving a past not marked by distance from the present.

One may detect a quest for full presence in a number of tendencies still current in contemporary thought. On a religious level, there is the idea of full incarnation of divinity in the world, an idea that may also be seen as idolatrous. The *Bilderverbot* would apply most clearly to representations of divinity or of objects construed as immanently sacred or as incarnations of divinity. On an epistemological level, there is positivism in the idea that an objectifying notational system can ideally represent, transparently render, or capture the essence of an object. On a psychological level, there is what might be seen as the reversal of positivism in the reliving or reincarnation of a past that is experienced as fully present. I shall stress the last sense since it is so important in Lanzmann's self-understanding. Positivism and objectivism, which Lanzmann clearly rejects, deny or repress a transferential relation to the object whereby crucial aspects of it are repeated in the discourse or experience of the observer. In acting-out, on the contrary, one reincarnates or relives the past in an unmediated transferential process that subjects one to possession by haunting objects and to compulsively repeated incursions of traumatic residues (hallucinations, flashbacks, nightmares). Here the quest for full presence becomes phantasmic and entirely uncontrolled.

Another variant of fully satisfying representation and understanding is insistently rejected by Lanzmann. This is the harmonizing, normalizing account—whether narrative or theory—in which the past is seen to lead continuously up to a present or in which the present is derived from a past or from some general theory. Here knowledge would preexist its transmission because one would have a schema, developmental process, or general theory of causation that would explain the event before its "transmission" or even its investigation. An analogous procedure would be the kind of account or presentation that would give the reader or viewer a pleasure of the sort that would deny or repress the very existence of the trauma that called the account into being. Certain uses of archival footage or direct representations of the Holocaust, such as re-creations of scenes of mass death, might fall prey to this harmonizing, normalizing approach, although they might also traumatize the viewer.

Lanzmann indicts conventional historiography precisely because of its normalizing, harmonizing, idealizing proclivities. For example, he states:

> The worst crime, simultaneously moral and artistic, that can be committed when it is a question of realizing a work dedicated to the Holocaust is to consider the latter as *past*. The Holocaust is either legend or present. It is in no case of the order of memory. A film consecrated to the Holocaust can only be a countermyth, that is, an inquiry into the present of the Holocaust or at the very least into a past whose scars are still so freshly and vividly inscribed in places and consciences that it gives itself to be seen in a hallucinatory intemporality.[11]

Here Lanzmann indicts full objectification of the Holocaust that would relegate it to an inert past or assume that it has been thoroughly historicized and normalized. With implicit reference to a phrase of Pierre Nora, he also brings out how the sites that are so important in his film are "non-lieux de mémoire" in that they are traumatic sites that challenge or undermine the work of memory. And aspects of his comment, notably the reference to a "hallucinatory intemporality," raise the general issue of acting out or reliving the past.

Lanzmann's rejection of chronology is comparably insistent. "The six million assassinated Jews did not die in their own good time and that's why any work that today wants to do justice to the Holocaust must take as its first principle to break with chronology" ("HH," p. 316). Lanzmann would seem to be referring not to simple chronology but to the narrative integration of chronology in a developmental story having a satisfying beginning, middle, and end, a story dedicated to filling in

[11] Lanzmann, "De l'holocaust à *Holocaust*, ou comment s'en débarrasser," in *Au sujet de Shoah*, p. 316; herefter abbreviated as "HH."

gaps, reaching some sort of closure, providing the reader or viewer with pleasure, and perforce denying or remaining untroubled by trauma.

In *Shoah* the former *Sonderkommando* Filip Müller has a traditional narrative style that to some extent conveys his disconcerting story in a conciliatory, modulated form. He seems to have recounted his tale many times before and is able to proceed with the virtuosity of a seasoned narrator, almost becoming a bard of ultimate disaster. Lanzmann does nothing to disturb Müller's narrative and is a patient, attentive, and responsive listener. Müller's narration breaks down only when he himself comes to a breaking point as he tells of the way in which his compatriots on the verge of death in the "undressing room" began to sing the Czech national anthem and the "Hatikvah." With tears in his eyes, he says, "that was happening to my countrymen, and I realized that my life had become meaningless. Why go on living? For what? So I went into the gas chamber with them, resolved to die. With them" (*S*, pp. 151–52). Müller leaves the gas chamber only when one of the women about to die tells him his act is senseless: "You must get out of here alive, you must bear witness to our suffering, and to the injustice done to us" (*S*, p. 152). Lanzmann, as we shall see, makes comments concerning his own desire to die with victims that indicate how close he feels to Müller.

In art, the term for works that bring unearned, premature pleasure is *kitsch*: the harmonizing and sentimentalizing rendition of disconcerting, potentially traumatizing subjects. A good example of kitsch is George Segal's 1984 sculpture *The Holocaust,* which is on display in Lincoln Park, San Francisco. In it there are simulacra of dead bodies strewn casually on the ground in a contemplative scene that somehow soothes the onlooker. Another example is the 1979 American miniseries *Holocaust,* which, as Lanzmann notes, "shows the Jews entering gas chambers holding one another by the shoulder, stoic, like Romans. It's Socrates drinking the hemlock. These are idealist images that permit every sort of consoling identification. Well, *Shoah* is anything but consoling." As Lanzmann observes, harmonizing efforts in general, and the 1979 miniseries in particular, fail to recognize that in all transmissions of the traumatic, there is always a part "that is not transmissible" ("LP," p. 295).[12]

---

[12] A recent object of what might almost be called Lanzmann's spleen is Steven Spielberg's 1993 film *Schindler's List,* which Lanzmann sees as the epitome of kitsch. Although Lanzmann's response is extreme, this film is, to a significant extent, sentimentally harmonizing, particularly in its upbeat ending, which depicts the Schindler figure as a saint and martyr and presents a ritual in living color that seems to provide consolation that is too facile for the wounds of the past.

This last statement introduces a second approach to the *why* question that certain comments of Lanzmann seem to support and that provides one way to view or read *Shoah*. This approach requires the active recognition that any account—representation, narrative, understanding, explanation, form of knowledge—is *constitutively* limited, notably when it addresses certain phenomena. In historiography this recognition would require the elaboration of different ways of representing, narrating, and understanding the Holocaust that do not fall prey to harmonization, idealization, kitsch, and premature "pleasure in narration." Saul Friedlander has suggested two requirements of this kind of historiography: the interruption of the narrative of the historian by the voices of victims—precisely the kinds of testimony that form the basis of Lanzmann's film; and the further disruption of narration (or any continuous, harmonizing account) by the critical and self-critically reflective commentary of the historian. As Friedlander formulates the latter point:

> Whether . . . commentary is built into the narrative structure of a history or developed as a separate, superimposed text is a matter of choice, but the voice of the commentator must be clearly heard. The commentary should disrupt the facile linear progression of the narration, introduce alternative interpretations, question any partial conclusion, withstand the need for closure. Because of the necessity of some form of narrative sequence in the writing of history, such commentary may introduce splintered or constantly recurring refractions of a traumatic past by using any number of different vantage points.[13]

I would suggest that one function of these interruptions or disruptions is to introduce into the account a muted dosage or form of trauma that—at some degree of distance allowing for critical thought and working-through—reactivates, but does not simply reincarnate or

---

[13] Saul Friedlander, *Memory, History, and the Extermination of the Jews of Europe* (Bloomington: Indiana University Press, 1993), p. 132. Friedlander also writes: "The major difficulty of historians of the Shoah, when confronted with the echoes of the traumatic past, is to keep some measure of balance between the emotion recurrently breaking through the 'protective shield' and numbness that protects this very shield. In fact, the numbing or distancing effect of intellectual work on the Shoah is unavoidable and necessary; the recurrence of strong emotional impact is also often unforeseeable and necessary. 'Working through' means, first, being aware of both tendencies, allowing for a measure of balance between the two whenever possible. But neither the protective numbing nor the disruptive emotion is entirely accessible to consciousness" (p. 130).

make live again, the traumas of the past. I would also observe that Friedlander's view is not an invitation to narcissism or endless self-reflexivity but an insistence on inquiry into procedures of representation and understanding, particularly with respect to limit-cases that most forcefully bring out the constitutively limited nature of inquiry. Indeed, the avoidance of such critical self-reflection may invite narcissism and even involuted, aestheticizing self-reflexivity.

Lanzmann himself seems close to this second position on the *why* question when he writes:

> One must know and see, and one must see and know. Indissolubly. If you go to Auschwitz without knowing anything about Auschwitz and the history of this camp, you will not see anything, you will understand nothing. Similarly, if you know without having been, you will not understand anything either. There must therefore be a conjunction of the two. This is why the problem of places or sites is capital. It is not an idealist film that I made, not a film with grand metaphysical and theological reflections on why all this happened to the Jews, why one killed them. It's a film on the ground level, a film of topography, of geography. ("LP," p. 294)

At times, moreover, Lanzmann sees that his rejection of direct representation cannot itself be total and that there are no pure traces of traces. The archival documentary footage he excludes makes its presence felt, and his method of confining himself to present words and sites derives its effect from its relation to what is omitted. Indeed, the scenes of the present state of camp and ghetto sites will themselves be haunted by afterimages of films and photographs that almost everyone of a certain age (including Lanzmann's witnesses) has seen. He notes, for example: "It happens at times that I meet people who are convinced that they saw documents in the film: they hallucinated them. The film makes the imagination work. Someone wrote me, quite magnificently: 'It is the first time that I heard the cry of an infant in a gas chamber.' Here one has all the power of evocation and of the word" ("LP," p. 297). A question, however, is what will happen for viewers from a later generation, who may not be familiar with the images Lanzmann intentionally excludes. Will they take his beautiful pastoral landscapes at face value or simply as nostalgic, often chiaroscuro aestheticizations of ruins from a forgotten past rather than as a bitterly ironic commentary on the past these sites conceal and, for those with certain afterimages and knowledge, simultaneously reveal? Moreover, is it possible that archival documents, images, and footage would not have a merely banalizing effect but might serve to provide reality tests for an imagination that can otherwise run rampant to the point of obsession and hallucination? Indeed, might they even increase the challenge confronted by the artistic imagination in rendering the impossible?

One of Lanzmann's own most haunting and memorable statements about his film is apposite here. This statement teeters on the brink between a conception of understanding and representation as constitutively limited and one that goes beyond this recognition to a third position: the absolute refusal of the *why* question.

> I began precisely with the impossibility of recounting this story. I put this impossibility at the beginning. What there is at the beginning of this film is on the one hand the disappearance of traces: there is no longer anything. There is nothing [*le néant*], and I had to make a film starting with this nothing. On the other hand, there was the impossibility of telling this story for survivors themselves, the impossibility of speaking, the difficulty—which is seen throughout the film—of giving birth to the thing and the impossibility of naming it: its unnamable character. This is why I had such difficulty in finding a title. ("LP," p. 295)

Here I would succinctly interject that an account addressing the *why* question is constitutively limited by at least two sets of factors or forces: trauma and performativity, particularly performativity involving normative issues. I have already repeatedly invoked trauma, and it is indeed crucial for understanding Lanzmann's approach to understanding. Trauma is precisely the gap, the open wound, in the past that resists being entirely filled in, healed, or harmonized in the present. In a sense it is a nothing that remains unnamable. As Cathy Caruth has written:

> [In] Post-Traumatic Stress Disorder (PTSD) . . . the overwhelming events of the past repeatedly possess, in intrusive images and thoughts, the one who has lived through them. This singular possession by the past . . . extends beyond the bounds of a marginal pathology and has become a central characteristic of the survivor experience

of our time. Yet what is particularly striking in this singular experience is that its insistent reenactments of the past do not simply serve as testimony to an event, but may also, paradoxically enough, bear witness to a past that was never fully experienced as it occurred. Trauma, that is, does not simply serve as record of the past but precisely registers the force of an experience that is not yet fully owned.[14]

One may maintain that anyone severely traumatized cannot fully transcend trauma but must to some extent act it out or relive it. Moreover, one may insist that any attentive secondary witness to, or acceptable account of, traumatic experiences must in some significant way be marked by trauma or allow trauma to register in its own procedures. This is a crucial reason why certain conventional, harmonizing histories or works of art may indeed be unacceptable. But there is no single view of how trauma should be addressed in life, in history, and in art. Freud argued that the perhaps inevitable tendency to act out the past by reliving it compulsively should be countered by the effort to work it through in a manner that would, to whatever extent is possible, convert the past into memory and provide a measure of responsible control over one's behavior with respect to it and to the current demands of life. For example, the isolation and despair of melancholy and depression, bound up with the compulsively repeated reliving of trauma, may be engaged and to some extent countered by mourning in which there is a reinvestment in life, as some critical distance is achieved on the past and the lost other is no longer an object of unmediated identification.[15] It would be presumptuous—indeed, worse than *canaillerie*—to pass judgment on the lives of Holocaust victims. But one may argue that, at least with respect to secondary witnesses in art and in historiography, there should be interrelated but differentiated attempts to supplement acting-out with modes of working-through.

The problem of working-through brings up the question of how performativity goes beyond any restricted idea of representation or understanding. Performativity may be identified with acting-out or

---

[14] Cathy Caruth, "Introduction," *American Imago* 48 (1991), 417.

[15] See especially "Remembering, Repeating, and Working-Through" (1914), *The Standard Edition of the Complete Psychological Works of Sigmund Freud*, trans. James Strachey, vol. 12 (London: Hogarth Press, 1958), pp. 145–56, and "Mourning and Melancholia" (1917), *Standard Edition*, vol. 14 (1957), pp. 237–60.

reliving the past. But this is a truncated view, however prevalent it may be in post-Freudian analysis or criticism. Performativity in a larger sense may be argued to require the conjunction of necessary acting-out in the face of trauma with attempts to work through problems in a desirable manner—attempts that engage social and political problems and provide a measure of responsible control in action. The question is whether Lanzmann in his more absolutist gestures tends to confine performativity to acting-out and even tends to give way to a displaced, secular religiosity in which authenticity becomes tantamount to a movement beyond secondary witnessing to a full identification with the victim. This full identification would not only allow one to act out trauma vicariously in the self as surrogate victim but cause one to insist on having the victim relive traumatizing events, thus concealing one's own intrusiveness in asking questions that prod the victim to the point of breakdown.

Before returning to what I have termed Lanzmann's absolutist turn, his movement from an idea of the constitutively limited nature of an account to his absolute refusal of the *why* question and of understanding, I shall briefly turn to Shoshana Felman's important essay. Felman's extended discussion is perhaps the most famous and influential treatment of *Shoah,* and it is truly exceptional in that it has met with Lanzmann's favorable reception. Indeed it might almost be seen as the authorized reading of *Shoah.* One might say that there is a certain convergence if not identity between Felman and a certain Lanzmann, the Lanzmann who absolutely refuses the *why* question. In Felman, *Shoah* becomes a fiction of the Lacanian real rather than of the historically real, and the result is an absolutization of trauma and of the limits of representation and understanding. Trauma becomes a universal hole in "Being" or an unnamable "Thing," and history is marginalized in the interest of History as trauma indiscriminately writ large. More precisely, Felman's approach to *Shoah,* contains a distinctive combination of Paul de Man and Lacan, and it makes an unmediated transition from the status of the witness to that of the shattered, traumatized victim, not only in the object of discussion but in the subject-position of the narrator or writer. There is also a routinization of hyperbole or excess, and uncontrolled transference and acting-out—often justified through a restricted theory of performativity or enactment—seem to be the horizon of psychoanalysis and of Felman's own discourse. A symptomatic indication of the routinization of excess and the absolutization of trauma is Felman's repeated use of the phrase *paradoxically enough* or the word *paradoxically* which attests to the force of the repetition-compulsion but may also flatten paradox, evacuate its generative possibilities, and generalize the double bind as the well-nigh ubiquitous stumbling block in language and life.

Felman's discussion of *Shoah* is distinctive in that it is one significant place in her contributions to the book *Testimony* in which de Man is not present either in his own voice or as ventriloquized by others (such as Melville, Camus, or even Levi) whose words she turns to in order to fill in de Man's silences concerning the Holocaust and his relation to it. Indeed, de Man hallucinatingly haunts *Testimony,* and Felman's analysis tends to be apologetic with respect to him and his "silence" concerning his early World War II journalism.[16] Through conflation with Levi, de Man even emerges as a traumatized victim who can only, in admirable silence, bear witness to the collapse of witnessing. Felman's general arguments about silence, indirection, and the "paradoxical" witnessing of the breakdown of witnessing tend to be compromised by the specific purposes to which they are put with respect to de Man. Still, her turn to Lanzmann enables her to work through, or at least leave behind, her uncritical transferential relation to de Man. The disconcertingly moving consequence seems, however, to be a comparable relation to Lanzmann.

Felman's approach to *Shoah* is one of celebratory participation based on empathy or positive transference undisturbed by critical judgment. Her discourse resonates with a certain dimension of the film that is most pronounced in Lanzmann's *Warumverbot.* Her discursive strategy is to repeat themes or motifs of the film in a fragmented, often arresting series of comments whose dominant chord is the idea that *Shoah,* "paradoxically enough," bears witness to the breakdown and impossibility of witnessing in a world in which trauma is tantamount to History and true writing is necessarily a writing of disaster. "To understand *Shoah* is not to *know* the Holocaust, but to gain new insights into what *not knowing* means, to grasp the ways in which *erasure* is itself part of the functioning of our *history*" ("RV," p. 253).

Felman emphasizes the limits of understanding and knowledge and the importance of recognizing what escapes cognition and mastery.

---

[16] See my discussion of this issue in *Representing the Holocaust: History, Theory, Trauma* (Ithaca: Cornell University Press, 1994), pp. 116–25.

Yet, from her perspective, this emphasis becomes so prepossessing and pervasive that witnessing the impossibility of witnessing becomes an all-consuming process: trauma is so overwhelming that distinctions threaten to collapse and the world emerges as a *univers concentrationnaire*. The reliance on the rhetorical question (and the related use of emphasis) spreads throughout the text, and theory seems to consume itself and to confuse life with both self-reflexive art and self-dramatizing criticism.[17] Thus:

> *Shoah* addresses the spectator with a challenge. When we are made to witness this reenactment of the murder of the witness, this second Holocaust that appears spontaneously before the camera and on the screen, can we in our turn become *contemporaneous* with the meaning and with the significance of that enactment? Can we become contemporaneous with the shock, with the displacement, with the disorientation process that is triggered by such testimonial reenactment? Can we, in other words, assume in earnest, not the finite task of making sense out of the Holocaust, but the infinite task of encountering *Shoah?* ("RV," p. 268)

Here the "infinite task" of "encountering" a film seems bizarrely to displace the "finite task" of "making sense of the Holocaust." One might instead insist on the priority of making sense—and actively recognizing the limits of sense-making—with respect to the Holocaust and situate a film, however important, as an element in that attempt. In Felman, to become contemporaneous with the shock, displacement, and disorientation triggered by testimonial reenactment at times seems tantamount to reliving or acting out the past through self-rending identification with the victim, a process that attests to the futility of total mastery and the inescapability of compulsive mechanisms. Yet, in its unmediated form, this process not only has self-dramatizing implications but also forecloses the possibility of working through problems in however limited and differential a manner for both victim and

---

[17] Self-dramatization is most blatant in Felman, "Education and Crisis, Or the Vicissitudes of Teaching," chap. 1 of Felman and Laub, *Testimony,* in which Felman discusses her own and a class's reaction to viewing Holocaust testimonies. In one lengthy section of her discussion of Lanzmann (see "RV," pp. 242–57), Felman interprets *Shoah* in terms of Lanzmann's personal "journey" or saga, thereby threatening to subordinate the film to biographical or even narcissistic concerns.

secondary witness.[18] The "second Holocaust" to which Felman refers is the scene in *Shoah* outside the church in a Polish village near Chelmno where Simon Srebnik, one of the two survivors among 400,000 killed in the death camp, is indeed subjected to a process of revictimization.[19]

Shoah is a film very long on *hows* and *how preciselys* and very short on *whys*. In this scene, Lanzmann poses his only *why* question. He asks Polish peasants, outside the very church where Jews were incarcerated on their way to Chelmno, why the Jews were killed. He receives versions of the age-old blood-guilt story. First, a Mr. Kantorowski, organ player and singer in the church (a role with an ironic relation to Srebnik's role as boy singer during the Holocaust), steps forth and enacts a doubly displaced blaming of the victim. He states that his friend told him about a story presumably recounted by a rabbi: "The Jews there were gathered in a square. The rabbi asked an SS man: 'Can I talk to them?' The SS man said yes. So the rabbi said that around two thousand years ago the Jews condemned the innocent Christ to death. And when they did that, they cried out 'Let his blood fall on our heads and on our sons' heads.' Then the rabbi told them: 'Perhaps the time has come for that, so let us do nothing, let us go, let us do as we're asked.'" Lanzmann asks the translator, "He thinks the Jews expiated the death of Christ?" The translator answers, "He doesn't think so, or even that Christ sought revenge. . . . The rabbi said it. It was God's will, that's all!" (*S*, p. 89). But then, as if to contradict the translator and to express the collective *mentalité* of the crowd, a woman erupts in her own voice:

[18] When her class threatens to get out of control in the aftermath of viewing Holocaust testimonies, however, Felman assumes the authoritative role of the Lacanian "subject who is supposed to know " and presumably returns the class to the symbolic order: "After we discussed the turn of events, we concluded that what was called for was for me to reassume authority as the teacher of the class and bring the students back into significance" (Felman, "Education and Crisis, or the Vicissitudes of Teaching," p. 48). (In Lacan the notion of the "subject who is supposed to know" is of course meant to ironize the position of the analyst who claims such an untenable status.) Perhaps too rapidly, Felman reaches the conclusion that "the crisis, in effect, had been worked through and overcome and . . . a resolution had been reached, both on an intellectual and on a vital level" (p. 52). The question is whether one can construe as working-through the turn to an authoritative figure in order to bring closure to disorientation and acting-out.

[19] The exact number of those killed at Chelmno is debatable. Henry Friedlander places the *minimum* number at 152,000. See his *The Origins of Nazi Genocide: From Euthanasia to the Final Solution* (Chapel Hill: University of North Carolina Press, 1995), p. 287.

"So Pilate washed his hands and said: 'Christ is innocent,' and he sent Barrabas. But the Jews cried out: 'Let his blood fall on our heads!' That's all; now you know!" (*S*, p. 90). Here one indeed does seem to have an uncanny acting-out of the return of the seemingly repressed.

Lanzmann at times appears to think that any *why* question must elicit a response similar to that of the Polish peasants. This view indiscriminately conflates all modes of inquiry and approximates historical understanding to myth and prejudice. Felman herself not only tends to share this view but offers a marked overinterpretation of the scene in front of the church.

> What *speaks through him* [Mr. Kantorowski] (in such a way as to account for his role in the Holocaust) is, on the one hand, the (historic) silence of the church and, on the other hand, the silence of all given frames of explanation, the nonspeech of all preconceived interpretative schemes, which dispose of the event—and of the bodies—by reference to some other frame. The collapse of the materiality of history and of the seduction of a fable, the reduction of a threatening and incomprehensible event to a reassuring mythic, totalizing unity of explanation—is in effect what all interpretive schemes tend to do. Mr. Kantorowski's satisfied and vacuous interpretation stands, however, for the failure of all ready-made cultural discourses both to account for—and to bear witness to—the Holocaust. . . . What the church scene dramatizes is the only possible encounter with the Holocaust, in the only possible form of a *missed encounter*. ("RV," pp. 266, 267–68)

Here the "(historic) silence of the church" is closely associated with Lanzmann's belief, developed in a more qualified form by Felman, that Nazi anti-Semitism and genocide, while unique and radically disjunctive, were nonetheless continuous with traditional Christian anti-Semitism, a belief that may itself rely overmuch on a preconceived interpretive scheme insufficiently sensitive to the specificity of historical developments. But the more general point is that Felman confines options to the "preconceived interpretive scheme," "reassuring, totalizing unity of explanation," or "ready-made cultural discourses" on the one hand and the "threatening and incomprehensible event" or "missed encounter" on the other. The only discourse able to address the latter is indirect or paradoxical discourse that makes *"the silence speak* from within and around the false witness" ("RV," p. 266). The point, I would suggest, is not that indirect discourse and paradox are unimportant but rather that restriction of all valid discourse to them depends on an excessively truncated understanding of understanding that dismissively conflates history and myth (or confines History to a theoretically conceived, abstract "materiality"). Moreover, such a restriction tends to exclude the possibility of constitutively limited historical discourse that addresses the difficult issue of how to work through problems without discounting the significance of trauma and the intricate relation of direct and indirect discourse in addressing it.

Felman would seem to restrict herself to indirection and acting-out, and her own prose testifies or bears witness to an interminable repetition-compulsion as she makes and remakes her argument with obsessive intensity, turning and returning to scenes in *Shoah* that are read in its light. Felman's approach effectively brings out the film's compulsive power over the empathetic viewer in a manner that may not be fully conveyed in a more critical analysis. I would therefore urge the reader to examine Felman's essay closely and use it as a counterpoint to my own approach. But I would also suggest that the very length of her essay testifies to a melancholic mode of repetition that has a mimetic or emulatory relation to the length and movements of Lanzmann's film.

In the case of *Shoah*, the issue of length is nonetheless more problematic. On the one hand, one might argue that the very subject of the film (in significant contrast to the film as the subject of Felman's essay) is so vast and important that any length is small and inadequate—indeed, that the length, seeming repetitiveness, and empty stretches or silences of the film are necessary to transmit to the viewer a muted trauma required for empathetic "understanding." On the other hand, one might contend that the nine-and-one-half hours of *Shoah* indicate a mode of acting-out and that the repetitions of the film, while often bringing subtle modulations, also attest to the working of a melancholic repetition-compulsion in which trauma may at times be enacted or transmitted with insufficient attention to attempts (including survivors' attempts) to work through problems.[20] Both the first and

[20] As Felman remarks in a footnote: "Cf. Lacan's conception of 'the Real' as 'a missed encounter' and as 'what returns to the same place'" ("RV," p. 268 n. 44). One may argue that historical reality is a compromise formation that involves, or is repeatedly disrupted by, the Lacanian real (trauma?) but cannot simply be reduced to, or conflated with, it. One may also guardedly speculate (in line with the views of Nicolas Abraham and Maria Torok) that Lanzmann's own desire to identify with the victim is based on an encrypted or hidden wound caused by the fact that he was not in

the second parts of the film seem to end—or terminate without end-ing—in the same place: the first with the melancholic despair of Sreb-nik, who thought he would be the last person, and the rolling of a type of truck reminiscent of one used to gas Jews; the second with the des-peration of Simha Rottem, a surviving leader of the Warsaw Ghetto up-rising who thought he would be the last Jew, and the rolling of a train. Certainly and significantly, these scenes resist closure and attest to a past that will not and should not pass away, a past that must remain an open wound in the present, but they do so with a dominant tonal-ity of unrelieved melancholy and desperation.

These "endings" almost seem to set the stage for Lanzmann's next film, *Tsahal* (1994), where Israel in one sense seems to be the land of re-birth if not of redemption, and the opportunity for Jews to be agents stands in stark contrast to their role in the diaspora as victims. More-over, the army seems to be the problematic but nonetheless celebrat-ed, even sacred, exemplar of agency, and the tank or airplane contrasts with yet somehow recalls the truck or train in *Shoah*. This reading of *Tsahal* and its relation to *Shoah* is too simplistic but strongly suggests itself nonetheless. In *Tsahal* the Holocaust remains a crucial reference point and a haunting motif, and in the land of rebirth one still lives in constant fear and with the taste of death. There is, however, a marked contrast between the position of Jews in the two films, and in *Shoah* there is a limited construction of the role of Jewish agency and resis-tance in the Holocaust.

Rudolf Vrba, a resister who escaped from Auschwitz, appears in the film primarily to testify to the elimination of the deceived Jews in the Czech family camp and the suicide of Freddy Hirsch, their leader, who felt a special responsibility for the children and thus could not bring himself to lead a revolt.[21] These events are inserted into an editorially

reality a victim of the Shoah sharing the fate of his objects of study. Indeed his specif-ic "trauma" may itself be this missed encounter or disturbing absence, which he con-verts into a lack or loss in his experience. Lanzmann never explicitly acknowledges the wound or gap caused by his not participating in the unspeakable event—an acknowl-edgment that may be necessary for attempting to work through his relation to victims rather than endlessly and obsessively acting it out (or intrusively "incorporating" the other). See Nicolas Abraham and Maria Torok, *The Shell and the Kernel: Renewals of Psy-choanalysis*, trans. and ed. Nicolas T. Rand (Chicago: University of Chicago Press, 1994), esp. part 4.

[21] It is noteworthy that Lanzmann has little to say about Vrba in his commentaries and interviews. Vrba was not a member of the *Sonderkommando* and does not "relive" the past. If anything, his reliance on irony is sustained and perhaps overdone. It is also

orchestrated sequence involving Vrba, Müller, and Richard Glazar, which includes as subdued motifs the explosion of one of the Auschwitz crematoria and preparations for revolt at Treblinka. (It is during this sequence that Müller breaks down.) The Warsaw Ghetto uprising is presented with little sense of its genuinely heroic dimension—a dimension perhaps overly monumentalized in Nathan Rapoport's famous sculpture that serves primarily as ironic counterpoint in *Shoah*. The dominant view of the uprising is through the eyes of two surviving leaders in Israel who dwell on its devastation and hopelessness. The second-in-command of the Jewish Combat Organization, Itzhak Zuckermann ("Antek"), speaks offscreen as a ghostly voice-over to a ravaged face and body. He says, "I began drinking after the war. It was very difficult. Claude, you asked for my impression. If you could lick my heart, it would poison you" (*S*, p. 182). The longer testimony of Simha Rottem ("Kajik") is more composed but consonant with Zuckermann's words.

Let us return to Lanzmann's absolute refusal of the *why* question and examine more closely how it informs dimensions of his self-understanding and his desire as filmmaker. Lanzmann is frank about the role of his obsessions in making *Shoah*: "One also always asked me: 'What was your concept?' This was the most absurd question. *I had no concept*, I knew there would be no archives; I had some personal obsessions. . . . I have always asked the same questions. The circularity of the film is linked to the obsessional character of my questions, of my own obsessions" ("LP," pp. 294, 300). It is perhaps not irrelevant that these obsessions were those of a secular intellectual who was not raised as a practicing Jew but who assumed a certain Jewish identity in significant measure through the making of his trilogy of films (*Why Israel*, 1973; *Shoah*, 1985; and *Tsahal*, 1994). And in making *Shoah*, Lanzmann had the sense that "there was an absolute gap between the bookish knowledge I had acquired and what these people told me" ("LP," p. 294).

One thing Lanzmann apparently learned in making the film was the

---

interesting that Vrba is mentioned only briefly in passing in Felman's essay, and his name does not appear in the index of her book. Richard Glazar does appear in her index, but his self-possessed testimony receives relatively little attention in either her comments or in Lanzmann's. Indeed, a sustained analysis of Vrba's and Glazar's testimonies, along with their extrafilmic statements, might provide one basis for a reading of *Shoah* that diverges in significant ways from Lanzmann's seemingly dominant self-understanding.

absolute uniqueness and purely disjunctive nature of the Holocaust, which invalidated historical understanding in trying to account for it. "Between the conditions that permitted the extermination and the extermination itself—the *fact* of extermination—there is a break in continuity, there is a hiatus, there is a leap, there is an abyss" ("HH," pp. 314–15). Thus "there is for me an absolute specificity of anti-Semitism." Moreover, "the destiny and the history of the Jewish people cannot be compared to that of any other people" ("HH," p. 310). Similarly, "Auschwitz and Treblinka cannot be compared to anything, will never be compared to anything" ("HH," p. 307). And it is precisely "this certain absolute of horror that is not transmissible" ("HH," pp. 309–10).

Yet Lanzmann contradicts himself insofar as he believes that the Holocaust is "the monstrous but legitimate product of the entire history of the Western world" ("HH," p. 307). He mitigates the contradiction by asserting, "*The Holocaust is unique but not aberrant. It is not the work of a group of irresponsible, atypical criminals but must be regarded, on the contrary, as the expression of the most fundamental tendencies of Western civilization*" ("HH," pp. 311–12). But the mere qualification that the Holocaust is not aberrant does not eliminate the contradiction between asserting that it is absolutely unique and disjunctive and asserting that it is the "product of the entire history of the Western world" or "the expression of the most fundamental tendencies of Western civilization." Lanzmann never clarifies the specific sense in which he thinks the Holocaust is the product of the entire history or of the most fundamental tendencies of the West. He does not, for example, in the manner of Philippe Lacoue-Labarthe, rely on Heidegger's notion of the destiny of Being that assumes the modern form of a technological *Gestell*.[22]

Lanzmann probably relies most, here as elsewhere, on Hilberg's notion of the development of Christian anti-Semitism into Nazi anti-Semitism, although certain subtleties of Hilberg's analysis are lost in the absolutism and starkness of Lanzmann's formulations. Hilberg stated in *Shoah*:

They [the Nazis] had to become inventive with the "final solution." That was their great invention, and that is what made this entire

[22] See Philippe Lacoue-Labarthe, *Heidegger, Art and Politics*, trans. Chris Turner (Cambridge, Mass.: Basil Blackwell, 1990).

process different from all others that had preceded that event. In this respect, what transpired when the "final solution" was adopted—or, to be more precise, bureaucracy moved into it—was a turning point in history. Even here I would suggest a logical progression, one that came to fruition in what might be called closure, because from the earliest days, from the fourth century, the sixth century, the missionaries of Christianity had said in effect to the Jews: "You may not live among us as Jews." The secular rulers who followed them from the late Middle Ages then decided: "You may not live among us," and the Nazis finally decreed: "You may not live." (S, p. 60)

This passage hints that temporality involves displacement in the sense of repetition with change—at times disjunctive or traumatic change. But Hilberg's stress tends to be on incrementalism and anonymous, structural bureaucratic processes, which may not do full justice to the distinctiveness of the Nazi genocide and the complex role of biologistic racism, scapegoating, and distorted, displaced sacrificialism in the Holocaust.[23]

[23] There is also a sense in which Lanzmann's almost bureaucratic interest in details and seemingly endless, perhaps intentionally tedious panning and travelling shots—notably of railroads—attest to his film's presentation of the Shoah in terms of the industrialization of mass murder and the "machinery of destruction" (in Raul Hilberg's phrase) as well as to the way in which traces of the Nazi past have been covered over or absorbed by "normal" contemporary life. This partially accurate conception is not sufficiently counterbalanced by other considerations. Even ex-Nazis who are interviewed tend to be bland and complacent about their memories or to deny knowledge of and involvement in Nazi crimes. Little in the film suggests the less routine elements of Nazism: its at times "ecstatic" appeal for its proponents and followers, its power to fascinate in the contemporary setting, and the displaced ritualistic or crazed sacrificial components of its animus against victims. (It should be noted that it is simplistic to interpret these components as a regression to barbarism. Rather they pose the specific problem of the relation of certain forces, such as scapegoating and distorted sacrificialism—which may be repressed forms that return in Western history—to modern phenomena such as extreme bureaucratization and formal rationality. On these questions, see my Representing the Holocaust: History, Theory, Trauma, especially pp. 90–110.) I would also note that there is a crucial difference between arguing that displaced religious elements, notably a distorted sacrificialism involving victimization and scapegoating, are operative in aspects of the Holocaust (especially in the outlook and behavior of certain elite perpetrators) and affirming those elements in one's own voice. Indeed, detecting their possible role may be a basis for a critique of them as well as for vigilance with respect to their possible recurrence. By contrast, Elisabeth Huppert, "Voir (Shoah)," in Au sujet de Shoah, pp. 150–56, relies on negative theology to offer a rather indiscriminate religious interpretation of the Holocaust and transfers religious qualities to Lanzmann's film and even to Lanzmann himself. Thus she writes: "It is possible that something important happened in the concentration camps—the most important thing in the history of the world. It is possible that God showed himself

In Lanzmann, in contrast to Hilberg, the stress tends to be on absolute uniqueness and radical disjunction. Lanzmann also tends to insist on violence and death. "It is from naked violence that one must take one's beginning and not, as one always does, from campfires, songs, blond heads of the *Hitlerjugend.* Not even from the fanaticized German masses, the 'Heil Hitler!' and the millions of lifted arms" (*Au sujet de Shoah,* p. 315). Or again:

> For there to be tragedy, the end must already be known; it must be present from the very origin of the account [*récit*]; it must scan its every episode; it must be the unique measure of the words, of the silences, of the actions, of the refusals of action, of the blindnesses that make it possible. A chronological account . . . is essentially anti-tragic and death, when it comes, is always on time, that is to say, it comes as non-violence and non-scandal. ("HH," pp. 315–16)

The "tragic" preoccupation with death as originally known yet violent and scandalous has implications for the making of *Shoah.* "In my film, the Final Solution must not be the point of arrival of the account, but its point of departure" ("HH," p. 315). Lanzmann also observes:

> I have always been haunted by the last moments, the last instants that precede death. Well, for me "the first time" is the same thing. I always ask myself the question of the first time. I ask it to the Pole: "Does he remember the first convoy of Jews he saw arriving from Warsaw on

there" (p. 150). In the film, "the unnameable is not represented," but "we contemplate those who have gone to the brink of the abyss." Moreover, "the emptiness that we carry in ourselves is perhaps that through which we participate in the divine principle. In *Shoah* it is on the exterior of the film, but *it exists.*" Hence the film is prophetic. "To attach the term *prophet* to Claude Lanzmann is embarrassing but not to do so is a lie" (p. 151). Sami Naïr's, "*Shoah,* une leçon d'humanité," in *Au sujet de Shoah,* pp. 164–74, offers an existential humanist interpretation with religious overtones. He sees Abraham Bomba, when he breaks down, as finally being unable "to repress his martyrized humanity," and he characterizes the ensuing dialogue between Bomba and Lanzmann as "worthy of the greatest tragic works" (p. 172). "Precisely because he pursues, in spite of his tears, his relived martyrology," Bomba "gains entry to physical ascesis. He covers himself in bruises [*il se meurtrit*] as body and consciousness in order to be liberated as word. For there is no other way than this: *to relive in one's flesh the tragedy of tortured victims.*" Moreover, this "acceptance of ascesis . . . imposes itself not only on witnesses but also on Lanzmann himself" (p. 172). Naïr also sees Lanzmann as "rehabilitating and transfiguring" surviving Jewish members of the *Sonderkommando* "by showing their profound *sanctity*" (p. 175). Naïr thus unguardedly affirms and validates in his own voice the possible role of quasi-sacrificial processes in the film.

July 22, 1942? The first shock of Jews arriving. The first three hours in Treblinka. The first shock of the Nazis themselves: one day they too must arrive there. . . .

The first time is the unthinkable! It is acting-out (*le passage à l'acte*): how does one kill? ("NM," pp. 288–89)

These reflections provide Lanzmann with another opportunity to excoriate historians who try to understand: "These historians: I tell myself at times that they are going mad in wanting to understand. There are times when understanding is madness itself. All these presuppositions, all these conditions that they enumerate are true; but there is an abyss: to act out (*passer à l'acte*), to kill. Every idea of engendering death is an absurd dream of the nonviolent" ("NM," p. 289).

It would seem that the first time is, paradoxically, repeated in the last moments before death and in the reliving of a traumatic past. And the first, the last, and their compulsive repetition escape all understanding. Whether or not one agrees with this extreme position, one may observe that there is an important sense in which the traumatized victim has not lived the initial experience that comes to be compulsively relived. The initial "experience" was a gap in existence typically producing a state of numbness and disorientation. The victim will come to relive or act out what was not lived, in the best of circumstances in order to work through the experience in some viable form that allows a reengagement with life in the present. While Lanzmann has little to say about working-through and seems to absolutize acting-out, it is nonetheless the case that he wants to put himself in exactly the same position as the traumatized victim who relives what has not been lived. A questioner seizes on this point and presses Lanzmann when he refers to returning to the scene of the crime or of reliving what had occurred. "As if you had already lived, as if you had already been there" ("NM," p. 290). "Yes," says Lanzmann, " surely it is true. . . . One only knows (*connaît*) what one recognizes (*reconnaît*)" ("NM," p. 290). Then he adds:

At the same time I never lived that! I needed to pass through a certain mental experience, which has nothing to do with what has been lived, and yet . . . I needed to suffer in making this film with a suffering that is not that of filming in 25 degrees below zero at Auschwitz. A suffering . . . I had the feeling that in suffering myself, a compassion would pass into the film, permitting perhaps the spectator as well to pass through a sort of suffering. . . . ("NM," pp. 290–91; ellipses in original)

After Lanzmann affirms that he needed to suffer in making the film and to have the viewer go through a sort of suffering as well, the questioner astutely notes: "Something that had not been lived must nonetheless be relived" ("NM," p. 291).

An important consequence ensues for the very choice of "characters." Lanzmann prefers figures who are closest to death, who have an eschatological significance in that they bring together two ultimate singularities: the absolute beginning and the final end. Hence his avowed predilection among victims for members of the *Sonderkommando*, the special detail charged with the burning and elimination of bodies in the crematoria. Even more specifically, he wants people who relive the traumas of the past in front of the camera, people with whom he can identify in an unproblematically positive or negative way. He thinks, for example, that Bomba, the barber who cut women's hair before their entry into the gas chamber at Treblinka, was at first evasive, neutral, and flat. (From another perspective Bomba might seem relatively self-possessed but still shaken by his experiences.) For Lanzmann:

It becomes interesting at the moment when, in the second part of the interview, he repeats the same thing, but differently, when I place him back in the situation by saying to him: "What did you do? Imitate the gestures that you made." He takes the hair of his client (which he would already have cut long ago if he were really cutting his hair since the scene lasts twenty minutes!). And it is starting from this moment that the truth is incarnated and he relives the scene, that suddenly knowledge becomes incarnated. In truth it is a film about incarnation. ("LP," p. 298)

Here Lanzmann is satisfied only when he is able to induce the victim to become retraumatized and to relive the past. His idea both of the best acting and of truth itself amounts to acting-out, including the breakdown of the victim who cannot go on. The portion of the scene leading up to Bomba's "breakdown" demonstrates the intrusive, if not inquisitorial and violent, nature of Lanzmann's insistent questioning.

Lanzmann: But I asked you and you didn't answer: What was your impression the first time you saw these naked women arriving with children? What did you feel?

Bomba: I tell you something. To have a feeling about that . . . it was very hard to feel anything, because working there day and night between dead people, between bodies, your feeling disappeared, you were dead. You had no feeling at all. As a matter of fact, I want to tell you something that happened. At the gas chamber, when I was chosen to work there as a barber, some of the women that came in on a transport from my town of Czestochowa, I knew a lot of them. I knew them; I lived with them in my town. I lived with them in my street, and some of them were my close friends. And when they saw me, they started asking me, Abe this and Abe that—"What's going to happen to us?" What could you tell them? What could you tell?

A friend of mine worked as a barber—he was a good barber in my home town—when his wife and his sister came into the gas chamber. . . . I can't. It's too horrible. Please.

Lanzmann: We have to do it. You know it.

Bomba: I won't be able to do it.

Lanzmann: You have to do it. I know it's very hard. I know and I apologize.

Bomba: Don't make me go on please.

Lanzmann: Please. We must go on. (*S*, pp.107–8; ellipses in original)

It is impossible to render the long pause in Bomba's speech as he literally seems to relive the past. I think it would be wrong to see this scene simply in terms of Lanzmann's somewhat sadistic insistence on going on. More important in Lanzmann's subject-position as filmmaker is a desire to find people with whom he may identify and whose suffering he may take up as vicarious victim. Still, it is difficult to interpret the fact that the camera is nowhere visible in the barber shop even though one is surrounded entirely by mirrors. Is this a sign of the absence of critical self-reflection in Lanzmann's subject-position in the film or an alienation effect that prompts thought and questioning in the viewer?

In the film, Poles tend to be objects of strongly negative identification except in two cases: Jan Karski and the train conductor, Henrik Gawkowski. Karski, a university professor in the United States at the time of his interview, was the courier of the Polish government in exile who told of his experiences in visiting the Warsaw Ghetto and tried to impress upon the Allies the importance of what was happening to the Jews of Europe. He breaks down right at the beginning of his testimony. His initial words are: "Now . . . now I go back thirty-five years. No, I don't go back . . . [Precipitately, he leaves the room.] I come back. I am ready" (S, p. 154; ellipses in original). In the course of his statement, however, Karski makes a few dubious comments. Even in him there may be, mixed with undoubtedly genuine sympathy for the plight of the Jews, a refined form of the anti-Semitic prejudice that bursts forth in such populist abandon in the Polish peasants. He tells us that of the two Jewish leaders he encountered, he "took, so to say, to the Bund leader, probably because of his behavior—he looked like a Polish nobleman, a gentleman, with straight, beautiful gestures, dignified" (S, p. 158). In the Warsaw ghetto, however, "the Bund leader, the Polish nobleman . . . is broken down, like a Jew from the ghetto, as if he had lived there all the time. Apparently this was his nature. This was his world" (S, pp. 158–59). Moreover, concerning the Jews in the ghetto, Karski exclaims without sufficient qualification or explanation, "It was not a world. There was not humanity" (S, p. 159).

Gawkowski is, at least for Lanzmann, an exceptionally positive figure among the Polish peasants interviewed. He is the first in the film to make the famous throat-cutting gesture to Jews as they arrive at Treblinka, a gesture that other peasants try to rationalize as a sign of warning but that Lanzmann accurately sees as a threateningly sadistic form of *Schadenfreude*. Gawkowski's gesture was not rehearsed or anticipated, and it came as something of a shock to Lanzmann. Of Gawkowski, Lanzmann states: "I really liked him. He was different from the others. I have sympathy for him because he carries a truly open wound that does not heal. Among all the Polish peasants of Treblinka, he is the only one who has human behavior. He is a man who drinks, since 1942. . . ." ("NM," p. 282). One may of course wonder whether Lanzmann's liking for Gawkowski blinded him to more equivocal aspects of his character that one might detect in the film. For example, the expression on Gawkowski's face when he makes the throat-cutting gesture seems to be somewhat diabolical, and his sigh of sorrow for dead Jews seems feigned and histrionic, although it is difficult to account for one's subjective impression or the results of staging and rehearsal. Yet it is clear that Lanzmann's affective response to Gawkowski is colored by the train conductor's harrowing possession by the past.

Here Lanzmann's reason for excluding from the film another testimony from a Pole is significant. As Neal Ascherson writes:

> He [Lanzmann] wanted people he questioned to relive the past instead of simply describing it. He wanted them to be "characters" (*personnages*). Asked about why he did not keep the testimony of Wladisaw Bartoszewski, for example, who was quite ready to give him a firsthand account of the manner in which the Zegota group had heroically succeeded in saving Jews under the Occupation, he answered that he had met Bartoszewski whose discourse he found altogether boring. Bartoszewski was satisfied in simply recounting and was incapable of reliving the past.

Ascherson concludes:

> The fact of excluding Bartoszewski leads to not telling the public that there were Poles who, at times at the peril of their lives, tried to save Jews from extermination. . . . The truth is that those who see *Shoah* will understand it as an account of events, as a historical documentary of a particular type, and will get no further than an idea of the way the Poles behaved with respect to the Jews, an idea that is not substantially false but marked by omissions.[24]

In his contribution to *Au sujet de Shoah,* Timothy Garton Ash, while in no sense downplaying the prevalence of virulent anti-Semitism in Poland, especially among the peasantry, argues that, although Lanzmann tells the truth, it is not the whole truth about Poland; the German occupation of Poland was particularly harsh, and, in spite of severe sanctions, some Poles did help Jews.[25] I would add that Lanzmann's emphasis on Poland may be excessive, especially in contrast to the limited interviewing of ordinary Germans. Frau Michelsohn, the wife of the Nazi teacher at Chelmno, is the only German who did not serve in some official capacity during the Holocaust, although given her views she might just as well have done so.[26]

[24] Neal Ascherson, "La Controverse autour de *Shaoh,*" trans. Jean-Pierre Bardos, in *Au sujet de Shoah,* p. 231.

[25] See Timothy Garton Ash, "La Vie de la mort," trans. Nathalie Notari, in *Au sujet de Shoah,* pp. 236–55.

[26] In response to Lanzmann's question concerning how many Jews were "exterminated" at Chelmno, Frau Michelsohn gives one of her more memorable answers: "Four

Other significant, historically dubious omissions in *Shoah* are also prompted by Lanzmann's desire to have only characters who relive or act out the past, and who do so in ways that provide him with relatively unproblematic objects of transferential identification in either a positive or a negative sense. Among victims, there are only Jews, with no mention of "Gypsies" (Sinti and Roma), homosexuals, or Jehovah's Witnesses. Among Jews, there are no members of the Jewish councils. (There is only a limited use made of Adam Czerniakow's diary by Hilberg, largely as a counterpoint to the evasive testimony of the former Nazi and second-in-command of the Warsaw Ghetto, the supreme bureaucrat Franz Grassler.) Nor is there any sense of what Levi termed the "gray zone" created by the Nazis' attempt to generate complicity among victims.

Among perpetrators, there is scant indication of the role of fanatical commitment, elation, world-historical mission, *Führerbindung,* and a heroic cult of death, regeneration through violence, and, failing total victory, total annihilation—elements that are evident, for example, in Himmler's 1943 Posen speech to upper-level SS officers. (The one inkling comes in the glint in Franz Suchomel's eye as he sings the song celebrating Treblinka.) Here original footage or at least the testimony of a historian other than Hilberg would have been necessary. Lanzmann interviews lower-level SS (such as Suchomel) or Eichmann-like bureaucrats. Nazis after the war may have assumed an evasive, bureaucratic, "I-was-only-doing-my-job-and-obeying-orders-and-besides-I-didn't-know-anything" attitude. But this is hardly sufficient for understanding why they became Nazis or followed the leader in executing the "Final Solution." One may also observe that there are no French witnesses in *Shoah* and that the

---

something. Four hundred thousand, forty thousand." Lanzmann: "Four hundred thousand." Michelsohn: "Four hundred thousand, yes, I knew it had a four in it. Sad, sad, sad!" (p. 83). Whatever one's view of the general adequacy of Lanzmann's portrayal of the role of Poles in the Holocaust itself, it is arguable that, in the contemporary context, his emphases were instrumental in generating a controversy concerning, and a reexamination of, the nature of anti-Semitism in Poland. Indeed, a more qualified approach might have been less effective in helping to bring about such a reexamination (which was also furthered by groups in Poland itself, notably the younger generation prominent in the Solidarity movement). It is important to emphasize the point that anti-Semitism was pronounced and prevalent in Poland and remained so after the war. Moreover, before the appearance of *Shoah*, relatively little had been done in Poland to come to terms with the problem of anti-Semitism or the broader issue of the relation between Poles and Jews in the nation's history and contemporary life. On these issues, see the important essay of Jean-Charles Szurek, "Shoah: De la question juive à la question polonaise," in *Au sujet de Shoah*, pp. 258–75.

problems treated are kept at a safe distance from France.[27] Finally, the role of women, especially among victims, is very limited; they tend to appear only in cameo roles.[28]

This list of omissions is partial, but it suffices to raise the question of its basis. I have suggested that it may be understood in terms of Lanzmann's own subject-position and his desire for objects of transferential identification. Before trying further to substantiate this claim, I would also note that the same reason may be given for Lanzmann's refusal of the *why* question. In the case of victims, it is superfluous because the point is to identify empathetically and relive their reliving. In the case of perpetrators, understanding might mitigate condemnation. For Lanzmann the Holocaust was "an absolute crime" and its character was "incommensurable" ("HH," pp. 306, 308). Therefore the responsibility of those perpetrating it must be absolute. Any attempt to understand them psychologically or historically is "obscene."[29] Thus one has a linkage between an absolute refusal to understand and a belief in absolute responsibility. On the side of the victims, Lanzmann's predilection is for absolute innocence in closest proximity to death. Lanzmann states: "The Jews of Corfu have, in my opinion, a special function in *Shoah*. It is the reason why I say there are people who are more innocent than others. The Jews of Corfu are absolutely innocent, for me. I had a breaking point myself. I think this was the most difficult thing for me to do—to shoot and edit the sequence on the Corfu Jews" (*SCL*, p. 99). Lanzmann reaches his breaking point in contact with what he sees as the embodiment of absolute innocence.

I would certainly want to insist on the importance of the contrast be-

---

[27] On this question, see Nelly Furman, "The Languages of Pain in *Shoah*," in Lawrence Kritzman, ed., *Auschwitz and After*, pp. 299–312.

[28] In *Tsahal* the role of women is even more limited in spite of the fact that the Israeli army is known for their participation. By and large, women are either seen and not heard or (as translators) heard but not seen. In *Shoah*, aside from supporting cameo parts for victims, the primary role of women is as translators and technical assistants. And the problem of translation (as well as the role of the translator) is not thematized in the film despite its major importance. Unfortunately, the one truly memorable woman is Frau Michelsohn. For an excellent discussion of the problematic role of gender in *Shoah*, see Marianne Hirsch and Leo Spitzer, "Gendered Translations: Claude Lanzmann's *Shoah*", *Gendering War Talk*, ed. Miriam Cooke and Angela Woollacott (Princeton, N.J.: Princeton University Press, 1993), pp. 3–19.

[29] At Yale in 1990 Lanzmann created a sensation when he refused even to discuss a film he was invited to discuss because he believed it provided a tendentious, apologetic psychological account of a Nazi doctor. In good academic fashion, the event turned into a discussion of Lanzmann's decision not to discuss the film. See "The Obscenity of Understanding: An Evening with Claude Lanzmann," *American Imago* 48 (1991), 473–96; hereafter abbreviated as "OU."

tween perpetrators and victims. But the question is how to make distinctions and critical judgments in a world in which one does not have the bedrock security or the dogmatic dictates of simple absolutes. Even with respect to the Holocaust, an idea of absolute guilt and innocence, with only minor shading to impede the inclination to identify in unproblematically positive or negative ways, is much too simple to serve as one's sole guide. For one thing, it leads to too many unexplained omissions. At the very least, one would have wanted omissions thematized and justified in the film to enable a better appreciation of its limits and achievements. Such a procedure would have required a more critically self-reflective role for Lanzmann in the film itself. In touching on the question of his own subject-position as filmmaker, Lanzmann is at times unguarded in affirming his participatory desire to identify, relive, and trigger the imaginary, indeed his reliance on obsession, phantasm, and related affects. He refers to "this sort of urgency I had to relive that" ("NM," p. 282). Of his interviewees, he states: "Not characters of a reconstitution, because the film is not that but, in a certain fashion, it was necessary to transform these people into actors. It is their own history that they recount. But to recount is not sufficient. They must play it, that is to say, derealize. This is what defines the imaginary: to derealize. . . . Staging [*mise-en-scène*] is that through which they become characters [*personnages*]" ("LP," p. 301).

The next passage is particularly interesting, for in it there is a slippage from characters to Lanzmann himself, which testifies to the unchecked role of obsessions and transferential identifications as the *metteur-en-scène* becomes part of the *mise-en-scène*. "The film is not made with memories; I knew that immediately. Memory [*le souvenir*] horrifies me. Memory is weak. The film is the abolition of all distance between the past and the present; I relived this history in the present [*j'ai revécu cette histoire au présent*]" ("LP," p. 301).

The paramount role of details in *Shoah* is overdetermined, but it has a special relation to Lanzmann's unchecked transferential subject-position. It testifies to his affinity with Hilberg, whose *Destruction of the European Jews* was Lanzmann's avowed "Bible."[30] In certain statements Lanzmann echoes Hilberg's memorable words in *Shoah*:

In all of my work I have never begun by asking the big questions, because I was always afraid that I would come up with small answers;

[30] Raul Hilberg, *The Destruction of the European Jews*, rev. ed., 3 vols. (New York: Holmes and Meier, 1985).

and I have preferred to address these things which are minutiae or details in order that I might then be able to put together in a gestalt a picture which, if not an explanation, is at least a description, a more full description, of what transpired. And in that sense I look also at the bureaucratic destruction process—for this is what it was—as a series of minute steps taken in logical order and relying above all as much as possible on experience. . . . And this goes not only, incidentally, for the administrative steps that were taken, but also the psychological arguments, even the propaganda. Amazingly little was newly invented till of course the moment came when one had to go beyond that which had already been established by precedent, that one had to gas these people or in some sense annihilate them on a large scale. . . . But like all inventors of institutions they did not copyright or patent their achievements, and they prefer obscurity. (S, p. 59)

This passage is especially noteworthy because it enacts the manner in which what is presented as mere description actually tends covertly to include theory, interpretation, and even explanation. There is clearly a theory of logical incrementalism until one reaches a certain threshold at which invention becomes necessary. Moreover, the significance lies in impersonal, obscure processes that lend themselves to structural explanations. In Hilberg's famous book, the role of technological rationality and the bureaucratic machinery of destruction emerges as the interpretive center of the argument. Hilberg also downplays the importance of Jewish resistance and gives little sense of the impossible situation that often confronted members of Jewish councils.

Hilberg has a unique status in *Shoah* as "the" historian, the only nonparticipant or secondary witness.[31] And his views have the weight of authority for the viewer. Lanzmann never questions him critically. Hilberg is in the privileged position of the Lacanian "subject who is supposed to know," providing knowledge that seems incontestably objective. In fact Hilberg is not "the" but a historian—a very important one, but one whose views are at times open to question. (He was

---

[31] Felman somewhat misleadingly writes: "*Shoah* is a film made exclusively of testimonies: first-hand testimonies of participants in the historical experience of the Holocaust" ("RV," p. 205). She goes on to discuss Hilberg as "the" historian, yet she tries to construe his role as that of "yet another witness" ("RV," p. 213). She thus tends to obscure his unique position in the film.

trained as a political scientist, but his work measures up to the strictest standards of a certain type of history.) It is interesting that some of Lanzmann's extrafilmic comments do not conform to Hilberg's emphases, but there is little indication of this in the film itself. For example, Lanzmann responds to one questioner:

> I have the impression that you would like to take me toward the bureaucratic thesis. I am not entirely in agreement. One may always think that one has been caught in a chain! I am resolutely against the thesis of Hannah Arendt concerning the banality of evil. Each of these men, each of these consciences, knew what it was doing and in what it participated. The guard at Treblinka [Suchomel], the bureaucrat at the Railway System [Walter Stier], the administrator of the Warsaw ghetto [Grassler] knew. ("NM," pp. 291–92)

Lanzmann thus dissociates himself from the bureaucratic thesis which is typically linked with the banality of evil, notably through the paradigmatic figure of Adolf Eichmann. In good part because of Hilberg's commentary, the image of the Nazi regime with which *Shoah* leaves the viewer is nevertheless that of a machine made up entirely of cogs with no motor. The names of prime movers such as Hitler, Himmler, Heydrich, Göring, and Goebbels are not even mentioned. Of course these figures do not bear sole responsibility or exonerate all other Germans, but the regime, its policies, practices, and ideological motivation cannot be understood without them.

   In an even more thought-provoking remark, Lanzmann asserts: "The story of the banality of evil—peace to Hannah Arendt, she wrote some things that were better, no?—I think that all these people know perfectly that what they were doing was not banal at all. Maybe they were banal, but they knew that what they were achieving was not banal, surely not. . . ." ("OU", p. 489). Here one is reminded of Himmler's Posen speech, with its reference to the annihilation of Jews as an "unwritten, never to be written page of glory" in German history.[32] But, once again, there is little indication of this side of the story in *Shoah*. By contrast, Lanzmann's offscreen rejection of the "banality of evil" thesis is categorical and is clearly related to his rejection of the *why* ques-

---

[32] See Lucy Dawidowicz, *A Holocaust Reader* (West Orange, N.J.: Behrman House, 1976), p. 133.

tion and his desire for absolute responsibility in all perpetrators. But it has possibilities that are not exhausted by these traits, especially in the insight that banal people can do far from banal things.

Another basis for Lanzmann's insistence on details is philosophical. For him philosophy is descriptive phenomenology of experience in the sense of the early Sartre and a certain Husserl. Quite close to Hilberg's historiographical method is Husserl's famous phenomenological version (or inversion) of the dictum that God is to be found in details: "The small change, gentlemen, the small change!" Lanzmann began his intellectual career as a close friend, disciple, and collaborator of Sartre on *Les Temps modernes*, which Lanzmann has himself edited for a number of years. Lanzmann's insistence on details, however, comes with a resistance to theory (if not an anti-intellectualism) that differs from Sartre's own thought and is bound up with the *Warumverbot* and the desire to relive the past. "So why all these details? What more do they bring? In fact I believe that they are capital. It is what reactivates things, what gives them to be seen, to be experienced, and the entire film, for me, is precisely the passage from the abstract to the concrete. This, for me, is the entire philosophical process" ("NM," p. 282).

The obsession with details even at times seems to lead Lanzmann to repeat, in his own voice as interviewer, aspects of the bureaucratic mentality he is investigating. It leads as well to an expression by Hilberg of a kind of archival fetishism that attests to the extraordinary fascination of documents in establishing contact or continuity between past and present:

> Lanzmann: But why is this document so fascinating, as a matter of fact? Because I was in Treblinka, and to have the two things together . . .
> Hilberg: Well, you see, when I hold a document in my hand, particularly if it's an original document, then I hold something which is actually something that the original bureaucrat held in his hand. It's an artifact. It's a leftover. It's the only leftover there is. The dead are not around. (*S*, p. 131; ellipsis in original)

Yet the consuming interest in details also bears on the importance of sites and machines as incarnations of the lived and of concrete materiality. Sites and machines are among the principal characters of *Shoah*, and, at least in the film, machines do not break down. One of the indelible images in the film is created by mournfully elegiac yet melancholy shots of endlessly rolling trains. The presence of the past also persists in its ruins and material embodiments. "These disfigured places are what I call nonplaces of memory [*non-lieux de mémoire*]. At the same time it is nonetheless necessary that traces remain. I must hallucinate and think that nothing has changed. I was conscious of change but, at the same time, I had to think that time had not accomplished its work" ("NM," p. 290).

Fully empathetic identification with people and places enabled Lanzmann to feel that he was reliving—indeed suffering through—a past he had never in fact lived. He would even be phantasmically able to die others' deaths with them. "The idea that always has been the most painful for me is that all these people died alone. . . . A meaning for me that is simultaneously the most profound and the most incomprehensible in the film is in a certain way . . . to resuscitate these people, to kill them a second time, with me; by accompanying them ("NM," p. 291; second ellipsis in original).

I have intimated that Lanzmann seems to have been more interested in victims, especially dead or shattered victims, than in survivors—except for survivors who remained close to their experience as victims. His identification with victims was so complete that it could justify, for him, filming from their perspective, phantasmically seeing things through their eyes: "It was the middle of winter, and I said: 'We'll get into the train car and film the sign, Treblinka.' The distance between past and present was abolished; all became real for me. The real is opaque; it is the true configuration of the impossible. What did filming the real mean? To make images starting from the real is to make holes in reality. To enframe a scene is to excavate" ("LP," p. 298).

This crucial constellation links positive, fully empathetic, transferential identification with the victim; absolute, noncomprehending distance from the perpetrator; a general refusal of the *why* question; obsessive, imaginary acting-out or reliving of the traumatic past; the equation of the "real" with holes in reality; and a hallucinatory reincarnation of the past in details of the present without appeal to archives. One consequence was what Lanzmann is himself willing to call a lack of human respect for others. With particular reference to his interchange with Suchomel, Lanzmann states, "to lack human respect is to promise a Nazi that one will not disclose his name while it has already been given. And I did that with an absolute arrogance" ("NM," p. 287). More dubious, as I have intimated, is that Lanzmann's identification with victims allows him at times to be rather blindly intrusive in the manner in which he interrogates them. He asserts that there are no real encounters or dialogic relations between people in the film even when they are in the same place. "No one encounters anyone in the film" ("LP," p. 305). A major sign of this nondialogic situation is the fact that, in the film, victims for the most part do not speak in their mother tongue. The characters who speak in their own language are primarily perpetrators and more or less complicitous and collaborating bystanders. This relation or nonrelation to others and even to the self is conspicuous in the juxtaposition of Srebnik and the Polish peasants or, as Lanzmann adds, in Srebnik's alienated relation to himself.[33] But a major question is the extent to which it may also apply to Lanzmann's own role as interviewer. His exchanges often play out his own obsessions, affects, and phantasms and do not embody the tense interaction between proximity and distance required for critical dialogic exchange. Still, through inquisitorial rigor or specular projection, they do lead others to divulge what is in them—although one might question the desirability of the ways in which those revelations are prompted.

Lanzmann's personal, imaginary, or phantasmic apprehension of the nature of art itself emerges quite forcefully in a kind of death or destruction wish through which he envisions the annihilation of the 350 hours of footage not used in *Shoah*: "You want to know my deep wish? My wish would be to destroy it. I have not done it. I will probably not do it. But if I followed my inclination I would destroy it. This, at least, would prove that *Shoah* is not a documentary" ("SCL", p. 96). Art and destruction are here in the closest proximity. Still, what may be the most crucial dimension of Lanzmann's desire to be a vicarious victim is a displaced religious longing that is encrypted in his vision of art, a longing for which the term *masochism* may be too facile a designation.

One of the most disturbing scenes in *Shoah* is the almost Beckettian sequence in which Abraham Bomba breaks down and cannot go on but Lanzmann insists that he go on nonetheless. I would like to return

---

[33] Of Srebnik surrounded by Poles, Lanzmann observes: "At the church, he is there, silent; he understands everything, and he is terrorized by them just as he was as a child [*il est terrorisé par eux comme lorsqu'il était enfant*]. And then he is alone in the clearing; he is double: he does not encounter himself" ("LP," p. 305). The problem is whether the revictimization and internal splitting of Srebnik can be detached from the manner in which Lanzmann has actively arranged and staged his encounter with the Poles.

briefly to this scene and pose again the problem of trauma with respect to the survivor-victim, the secondary witness as filmmaker or historian, and the reader or viewer. One difficulty in discussing *Shoah* as a "fiction of the real" is that in it survivors *both* play *and* are themselves. Any boundary between art and life collapses at the point trauma is relived, for when a survivor-victim breaks down, the frame distinguishing art from life also breaks down and reality erupts on stage or film. The occurrence of trauma cannot be controlled, but one may to some extent control the settings that could facilitate or check its incidence. A survivor may willingly agree to tell his or her story and find that, in the course of recounting it or answering questions, the past is relived and the self is shatteringly (re)traumatized. The particular problem in *Shoah* is the motivation and insistence of Lanzmann in trying to bring this reliving about so that he may share or relive it himself. One may well believe that there is something awe-inspiring about Lanzmann's willingness to subject himself to traumatization or shattering of the self and to relive the extreme suffering of others. And at times Lanzmann realizes that his wish is impossible to fulfill and that he too can only go through a sort of suffering related, however indirectly, to the trauma of victimized survivors. But the sticking point is when as in his exchange with Bomba, he insists on going on in the face of the extreme disorientation or suffering of the other so that he may participate in it.[34]

With respect to the filmmaker or historian as secondary witness, I earlier stated that the goal should not be full empathy in the sense of an attempt to relive the trauma of the other but rather the registering of muted trauma and the transmission of it to the reader or viewer. Of

[34] In the exchange between Lanzmann and Bomba that precedes the latter's "breakdown," Lanzmann asks Bomba, "Can you describe [the gas chamber] precisely?" Bomba answers, "Describe precisely . . . We were waiting there until the transport came in. Women with children pushed in to that place. We the barbers started to cut their hair and some of them—I would say all of them—some of them knew already what was going to happen to them. We tried to do the best we could—" Lanzmann: "No, no, no . . ." Bomba: "—the most human we could." Lanzmann: "Excuse me. How did it happen when the women came in to the gas chamber? Were you yourself already in the gas chamber, or did you come afterwards?" (pp. 103–4; ellipses in original). What is happening at this point in the exchange between Lanzmann and Bomba? I would suggest that Bomba is going in directions Lanzmann rejects and with which he cannot identify. Lanzmann therefore becomes intrusive and insists on bringing the witness back in line with his own preoccupations and desires. This response to Bomba is in marked contrast with Lanzmann's attentive listening to Müller, with whom he can identify in an almost specular manner.

course one cannot prescribe that the secondary witness limit empathy at a certain degree or dosage, nor is it plausible to construe the situation in a voluntaristic manner that obscures the role of unconscious forces. At most one may argue that the setting or staging of an interview or the formulation of problems be such that the triggering of trauma is counteracted, for example, by the manner in which questions are posed or pursued. This argument is most compelling with respect to the survivor-victim, who should not be put in impossible situations or set up to relive the past, whatever the effects may be for the film, the filmmaker, or the viewer. Needless to say, this past may be relived even if all precautions are taken not to facilitate its recurrence.

If one objected to the notion of a muted trauma and maintained that the very term *trauma* should be reserved for limit-cases that pass a certain threshold, it would be more cogent to argue that the secondary witness should reactivate and transmit not trauma but an unsettlement, which Lanzmann terms "a sort of suffering," that manifests empathy (but not full identification) with the victim and is at most an index of trauma. One may also argue that this attempt, insofar as possible and without avoiding or denying the insistence of acting-out, should be related to the furtherance of working through problems, especially in terms of achieving a sense of agency that resists reenactment of, or helpless possession by, the past and makes ethical considerations involving responsibility and obligation not only relevant (which they always are) but also cogently applicable. Such ethical questions were often not applicable to the situation of victims in concentration or death camps, and they may not be for those (including secondary witnesses) who relive the traumas or bear the open wounds of the past. Of course, working-through would require different things of different people, depending on their subject-positions, and it is intimately related to the recurrent movement from the status of victim to that of survivor and agent. But in all cases—notably that of those born later, who will soon be the only ones left—it would necessitate not only remembering what happened in the past but actively recognizing the fundamental injustice done to victims as a premise of legitimate action in the present and future.

In this, I have treated Lanzmann both as a principal interlocutor or character in his film (a position that is often ignored when he is seen simply as a cipher or transparent secondary witness) and as an important viewer or interpreter of it whose self-understanding has either influenced or coincided with the views of notable commentators. I would like to conclude with a series of open questions concerning my argument. Is *Shoah* (perhaps disengaged from, or read against the grain of, Lanzmann's self-understanding) closer to mourning and working-through, or at least more effective in relating acting-out and working-through, than my argument allows? Can one provide a cogent reading of the film that answers this question in the affirmative? Would this answer be provided by an avowedly liturgical or ritual reading or reception of the film, which has in fact been active, implicitly or explicitly, in many readings or receptions?[35] On the other hand, should any film have a liturgical function? Is this a valid role for a commercially distributed film? Should *this* film have such a function, to the extent that my argument is convincing and Lanzmann's self-understanding is also active in liturgical receptions? What are the social, political, and

---

[35] See, for example, Michael S. Roth, "*Shoah* as Shivah," in *The Ironist's Cage* (New York: Columbia University Press, 1995), pp. 214–27, and, especially, Robert Brinkley and Steven Youra, "Tracing *Shoah*," *PMLA* 111 (1996), 108–27. Particularly in film studies, *Shoah* often has the special status of an icon, or at least a largely unquestioned standard with which one measures the accomplishments of other films on related topics. For an attempt to rehabilitate *Schindler's List* that simultaneously presupposes and tries to counter this tendency, see Miriam Bratu Hansen, "*Schindler's List* Is Not *Shoah*: The Second Commandment, Popular Modernism, and Public Memory," *Critical Inquiry* 22 (1996), 292–312. See also Geoffrey Hartman, *The Longest Shadow: In the Aftermath of the Holocaust* (Bloomington: Indiana University Press, 1996), for a discussion of *Schindler's List* (chap. 5) and for at times critical comments on *Shoah* (especially pp. 129–30). After completing this study, I read Tzvetan Todorov's *Facing the Extreme: Moral Life in the Concentration Camps*, trans. Arthur Denner and Abigail Pollak (New York: Henry Holt and Company, 1996), which contains certain analyses and criticisms of *Shoah* similar to those I offer. (See pp. 271–78.) Todorov's interpretive framework, however, differs in important ways from my own. For example, he does not employ psychoanalytic concepts or emphasize Lanzmann's desire to identify with and relive the experience of the victim. Rather, he relies on the concept of totalitarianism both to approximate Stalin's gulags and Nazi concentration camps and to explain the Holocaust as an effect of totalitarianism's positioning of the enemy other. He also attributes the excesses of the Nazi genocide to "the fragmentation of the world we live in and the depersonalization of our relations with others" (pp. 289–90). Todorov argues that "our industrial and technological civilization [is] responsible for the camps ... because a technological mentality invaded the human world as well" (p. 290). I would rather stress the conjunction of a technological framework and all that is associated with it in the Nazi context (including racial "science," eugenics, and medicalization based on purity of blood) with the return of a repressed (seemingly out of place or *unheimlich*) sacrificialism in the attempt to cleanse (or purify) and thereby redeem the *Volksgemeinschaft* and fulfill the leader's will by getting rid of Jews as polluting, dangerous, phobic (or ritually impure) objects. Perhaps only this disconcerting conjunction helps to explain the incredible excesses of brutality, cruelty, and at times carnivalesque or "sublime" elation in Nazi behavior toward Jews.

personal functions of a liturgical reception, for example, in constructing a certain kind of Jewish identity, and how valid are these functions? Does a liturgical reception attest to a protected core of the personality that is not questioned and that may indeed be the basis on which seemingly radical or experimental views may be deployed elsewhere? Is this a reason why criticisms of *Shoah* may provoke visceral and vitriolic responses in otherwise "open-minded" people? Is constitutively limited understanding, along with affective response, one desirable basis of working through the past, and is historical validity, even in a film subject to liturgical reception, a component of such understanding?

Although these questions could be extended further, they are meant to create a movement of self-criticism in my argument as well as in certain critical responses to it. In posing these questions, I would nonetheless insist that nothing in my discussion should be taken to lessen the importance of *Shoah* as a film or its role in resisting the trivialization or dubious relativization of the Holocaust. Rather, my argument should be seen as indicating and exploring the tensions among historical, aesthetic, and liturgical perspectives on the film. While the film seems to present itself in terms of the historical, and while Lanzmann's commentaries stress the aesthetic, the printed version of the text of the film seems to point primarily in a liturgical direction. The prose of the film is set as if it were blank verse, but this typographical positioning of the words creates the effect less of a collection of poems than of a series of prayers based on the principle of call and response. Perhaps the basic point of my argument is that, at least in a secular context, liturgy is not easy to come by and that any secular work, even when taken as liturgical, must be open to certain forms of questioning. Such questioning is related to the attempt to work through the past. Working-through, of which mourning is one prominent form, should not be conflated with utopian optimism or total liberation from the past and its melancholic burdens, but it should be seen as a supplement and counterforce to melancholia and acting-out. It should also be disengaged from discourses of pathology or medicalization and understood in an explicitly normative manner as a desirable process, however limited it may be in terms of actual success, especially in the face of trauma and limit-events.

'Twas the Night before Christmas:
Art Spiegelman's *Maus*

For memory to be effective on a collective level, it must reach large numbers of people. Hence the acts or works that convey it must be accessible. A difficult novel, such as Thomas Mann's *Doctor Faustus,* or a comparably demanding film, such as Claude Lanzmann's *Shoah,* will have a limited audience and will affect larger numbers, if at all, only through the mediation of teachers and commentators, particularly if it becomes a "media event." A novel such as Camus's *The Fall* may reach larger numbers, but its intricacy creates extreme indeterminacy about the way it may—or should—be read. But there is no greater icon of popular culture and mass diffusion than the comic book, and its messages may seem simple and straightforward enough to reach everyone in a relatively transparent way. One grows up with it as one grows up with TV, and one may be inclined to find it interesting or even captivating without knowing or perhaps caring why. (The taboo on images in certain religions has an obvious relation to the fascination of images and to the feeling that they truly capture the thing itself, however transcendent or sacred the *Ding an sich* may be.)

Those of us of a certain age had Sunday comics as part of our weekly routine, and a younger generation has a more differentiated set of tastes and probably a more educated palate. There has even been a proliferation of subgenres of the comic, more or less high-brow and low-brow forms, and entire stores cater to fans and collectors. Still, the greatest initial shock in encountering Art Spiegelman's *Maus* is its risky, even foolhardy attempt to bring Auschwitz to the comics.[1] Baudelaire wrote that Flaubert's *gageure* in *Madame Bovary* was to take the banal theme of adultery in the provinces and make it the basis of a great novel.[2] Spiegelman's corresponding but inverse venture was to take Auschwitz, which Spiegelman terms "the central trauma of the Twentieth Century," and make it a topic for the comics.[3]

The very idea of treating Auschwitz in the comics seems shockingly inappropriate. This shock is not only aesthetic or vaguely cultural. It may also be ritual and religious, even for those who believe themselves to be thoroughly secularized. I think we do—and ought to—retain the sense that certain things are simply inappropriate. They create a dissonance or malaise that indicates their *prima facie* unacceptability. This is not to say that they are absolutely taboo. But it is to say that they have an uphill fight and have to prove themselves against formidable odds before they pass muster. The achievement of *Maus* is that one is tempted to argue that it does prove itself acceptable, and even that it accomplishes considerably more by addressing certain impossible issues and topics. Precisely how much more is the moot issue *par excellence*.

Maus has been both a critical and a commercial success. Introducing one of the many interviews attesting to and reaffirming its acclaim, Susan Jacobowitz (writing in 1994) notes: "*Maus* has currently been translated into sixteen languages and there are almost 400,000 copies in print."[4] *Maus* also exists in CD-ROM, selling (in January 1997) for $50. Commercial success usually raises the suspicion if not the hackles of intellectuals, but *Maus*'s success has not in fact met with this response,

[1] Art Spiegelman's two volumes are entitled *Maus: A Survivor's Tale* (subtitled *My Father Bleeds History (Mid-1930s to Winter 1944)* (New York: Pantheon Books, 1986) and *Maus II: A Survivor's Tale and Here My Troubles Began* (New York: Pantheon Books, 1991). Page references, which are included in the text, are to M and M II.

[2] Charles Baudelaire, "*Madame Bovary* by Gustave Flaubert," in Flaubert, *Madame Bovary*, ed. with a substantially new translation by Paul de Man (New York: W. W. Norton, 1965), p. 339.

[3] The phrase, "the central trauma of the Twentieth Century," appears in "Art Spiegelman, 'If there can be no art about the Holocaust, there may at least be comic strips'," an interview with Claudia Dreifus, *The Progressive Review* 53 (1989), p. 34. For a broad-ranging survey of the comic book, see Joseph Witek, *Comic Books as History: The Narrative Art of Jack Jackson, Art Spiegelman and Harvey Pekar* (Jackson: University of Mississippi Press, 1989).

[4] "'Words and Pictures Together': An Interview with Art Spiegelman," Susan Jacobowitz, *Writing on the Edge* 6 (1994), p. 49. See also the interview conducted by Gary Groth, "Art Spiegelman and Françoise Mouly," in *The New Comics*, ed. Gary Groth and Robert Fiore (New York: A Berkley Book, 1988).

in large part for good reasons.[5] There are two rather bad reasons for defending *Maus*'s success. One is the desire to be shocked at least superficially, and the other is general ignorance or avoidance concerning the events of the Holocaust. We have tended to become shock- or scandal-friendly, at least in matters of art and aesthetic culture—a tendency in which modernism and postmodernism join forces. In a postmodern context, we are even ready to be deliriously laudatory when a work shocks us and at the same time blurs distinctions, especially the distinction between popular and elite culture. And the prevalent level of ignorance and avoidance concerning the Shoah has not been lessened but, if anything, intensified by its recent use as a media allusion or kitsch background element, which Spiegelman terms Holokitsch. Such use normalizes it or even reduces it to a throw-away commodity, assuming knowledge about it that does not really exist and thereby relying only on a vague, titillating shock-effect when the Shoah bell is rung.

One of the artistic challenges *Maus* confronts is how to figure the Holocaust in a way that does not conform to its use as a mere convention or titillating background element, particularly in mass culture. Its skillful and thought-provoking manner of interweaving the historical (the Holocaust), the ethnographic (contemporary Jewish, especially survivor, culture), and the autobiographical (the collectively and the personally traumatic) may be seen as one way in which it meets this challenge. On a historical level, *Maus* successfully brings to the attention of people who might not otherwise be exposed to them certain crucial events and problems related to the Holocaust. It takes certain issues to the street and simultaneously inserts them into the happy home. It probably does not tell a knowledgeable person anything new about the events it treats. And it is a shame that its role in public education is still necessary. But it definitely is. More important, *Maus* by

[5] Spiegelman himself senses the danger of commercial success both in his interviews and in *Maus* itself. In a scene I later discuss, Artie is reduced to a whimpering child calling for his mother and goes to see his analyst after an encounter with various impresarios who want to cash in on *Maus*'s success (M II, pp. 42–43). In the interview with Susan Jacobowitz, Spiegelman notes: "At this point I'm carrying a 500-pound mouse on my back, which might even become my tombstone. Success and popularity are drugs, and it's difficult to arrange myself in a way to stay free of the desire for another fix. That's one of the more pernicious aspects of success. On a more minor level, my time is more fragmented because there are more demands made on me than when nobody gave a shit about what I was doing" (p. 58).

and large presents material without resorting to misplaced sentimentality or a Hollywood format, and it is able to render certain complexities simply, without unduly distorting them. Despite, or perhaps because of, its sustained level of metaphor or allegory, it is soberly exact, committedly ironic, and insistently exacting in its approach to the most difficult questions.[6]

Indeed, there is little that is funny about this comic book. Humor (at least gallows humor) most obviously emerges from certain contexts that are worthy of the sitcom, notably the plight of the intellectual, sensitive, vaguely inept and overwhelmed son confronting an impossible but necessarily iconic survivor-father. More encompassing, carnivalesque (yet still gallows) humor comes from the scandalous premise of presenting Auschwitz and its aftermath in the comic-book genre, thus in some sense bringing what is imposingly high to the level of the putatively low genre without implying disrespect. But otherwise there is little in these books that is comic in the sense of provoking either nonironic laughter or conciliatory good feeling. The humor remains muted, infused with sadness, and very close to tears. Still, one does acquire a greater tolerance for, and ability to accept or at least critically appreciate, things that might otherwise be laughable in an invidious sense, particularly the characteristics of Vladek, the Holocaust survivor as paradigmatic impossible person and burdensome father. *Maus* brings this problematic figure to the forefront of consciousness without diminishing its complexity or its demands on our careful attention and empathetic yet critical understanding.

Perhaps the most pronounced impetus of *Maus* is to problematize identity in multiple and strenuous ways but to do so without simply obliterating the self as responsible agent or the group as locus of belonging and commitment—particularly the oppressed group for which nonessentialized identity plays important moral and political roles. Moreover, the problematization of identity, while at times compulsively undergone by characters possessed by the past (notably Vladek), does not become the inverted telos of the tale, for in the work and play of the text there is at least a generative straining toward new-

[6] In this context, Adam Gopnik asserts: "*Maus* manages to give dignity to the sufferers without suggesting that their suffering had any 'meaning' in a sense that in some way ennobled the sufferers, or that their agony has a transcendent element because it provides some catharsis for those of us who are told about, or are shown, their suffering." *The New Republic* 196 (1987), p. 33.

er articulations of an in-between or hybridized form that is definitely not to be seen in terms of a *juste milieu* or a middling complacency. The problematization of identity takes place in at least four interacting and partially overlapping areas: (1) in Art Spiegelman as well as in his relation to his text; (2) in the genre of the text; (3) in the relation of the text to its readership; and (4) in the text's work and play, including the role of its animal characters (one of whom is Artie, the Spiegelman-narrator-character). Since these areas interact, I shall not treat them in a strictly serial manner but attempt to bring out their interconnectedness.

The question of how to see or classify Spiegelman, the genre of *Maus,* and its readership has preoccupied critics and interviewers. Lawrence L. Langer in his review for the *New York Times* states that *Maus* II "is a serious form of pictorial literature, sustaining and even intensifying the power of the first volume. It resists defining labels."[7] Joshua Brown adds: "*Maus* is an oral history account and also an account of an oral history. Vladek's history is framed and often disrupted by the relationship between the teller and the interviewer."[8] In Miles Orvell's view, "part biography, part autobiography, part history, part novel, *Maus* straddles genres; yet in dramatizing self-reflexively the act of its own composition, it also claims formal kinship with modernists like Gide, Joyce, Nabokov, and Faulkner. Above all, *Maus* is committed to its function as an authentic, factual record of the Holocaust and thus immerses the reader in the banal particularities of the story of sur-

[7] *New York Times Book Review,* 3 November 1991, p. 3. The problematization of identity is briefly but pointedly treated in Michael E. Staub, "The Shoah Goes On and On: Remembrance and Representation in Art Spiegelman's *Maus,*" *Melus: The Journal of the Society for the Study of Multi-Ethnic Literature of the United States* 20 (1995), 32–46. For Staub, "*Maus* itself is constantly preoccupied with the utter lack of self-evidence in ethnic identities and deconstructs essentialist assumptions at every turn" (p. 39). Staub nonetheless asserts: "Yet at the same time, and held in tension with this point, *Maus* takes seriously the way marginalized peoples not only often rely on group identity to survive, but also have every right to celebrate their specialness and differences from the dominant culture. But—and this is the key issue—*Maus* clearly suggests that identity can never be understood as self-evident; *Maus* works continually to disrupt comfortable assumptions about where the differences between people lie" (p. 38).

[8] *Journal of American History* 79 (1993), p. 1669. It is of course significant that *Maus* was reviewed in such a mainstream professional journal as the *Journal of American History.* In an earlier review of the first volume of *Maus,* Brown is even more insistent: "*Maus* is not a fictional comic-strip, nor is it an illustrated novel: however unusual the form, it is an important historical work that offers historians, and oral historians in particular, a unique approach to narrative construction and interpretation." *Oral History Review* 16 (1988), p. 91.

vival."[9] For Adam Gopnik "*Maus* is an act not of invention, but of restoration. And in rediscovering the serious and even tragic possibilities of the comic strip and the cartoon, Spiegelman has found another way to do what all artists who have made the Holocaust their subject have tried to do: to stylize horror without aestheticizing it."[10] Rick Iadonisi, framing his argument as a problematization of Philippe Lejeune's idea of autobiography, argues that *Maus* suggests a more interactive model of collaborative autobiography in which the Spiegelman-figure as interviewer not only collaborates with his father but, in a forensic twist to Oedipal rivalry and the family romance, actually struggles for control of the account. "Spiegelman demonstrates his obligation (as collaborator) to provide a 'true' narrative while simultaneously placing himself in the privileged position of attorney to his father's witness or defendant, in a sense 'owning' the narrative rather than merely serving as 'surface to his [father's] story'."[11]

[9] Miles Orvell, "Writing Posthistorically: *Krazy Kat, Maus,* and the Contemporary Fiction Cartoon," *American Literary History* 4 (1992), p. 118. Given his emphasis, it is curious that "fiction" appears in the title of Orvell's article. In her comparison of Spiegelman and Klaus Theweleit, Alice Yaeger Kaplan asserts: "*Maus* is both an autobiography, a biography, and a novel of testimony, for it is Spiegelman's father Vladek who supplies the narration, the survivor's tale, while Spiegelman himself elaborates the frame." "Theweleit and Spiegelman: Of Mice and Men," in *Remaking History,* ed. Barbara Kruger and Phil Mariani (Seattle: Bay Press, 1989), p. 153. Kaplan notes that Theweleit introduced Spiegelman's work to the German public and asks whether "Spiegelman's brilliant formal invention—the rendering of a high tragic story in comic strip form" may be "incomprehensible in a society so troubled by its racist past" (p. 168). One convergence she finds between Theweleit and Spiegelman is in the concern with the "fascism within": the manner in which fascism lives on in often concealed or encrypted ways that are not subjected to critical scrutiny and may even be screened by preoccupation with the past. She may herself go too far and embody some of the excess and propensity for vague or rash generalization she finds in Theweleit when she claims that "the fascism within, the way Spiegelman shows it to us, is the fascism visited upon his father in the camps, a fascism his father has come to embody and project even as he has triumphed in his survival" (p. 171). Kaplan appeals to the need for context in her criticisms of Theweleit, yet context is also important in understanding Vladek, who is indeed prejudiced and may incorporate tendencies that in certain contexts foster fascism but could not himself be called fascist.

[10] *The New Republic* 196 (1987), p. 31. Paul Buhle echoes this sentiment by drawing a paradoxical correspondence between caricature and an unrepresentable or unrealistic referent: "More than a few readers have described it as the most compelling of any depiction, perhaps because only the caricatured quality of comic art is equal to the seeming unreality of an experience beyond all reason." "Mice and Menschen: Jewish Comics Come of Age," *Tikkun* 7 (1992), p. 16.

[11] "Bleeding History and Owning His [Father's] Story: *Maus* and Collaborative Autobiography," *CEA Critic: An Official Journal of the College English Association* 57 (1994), p. 53.

These references give only a partial idea of Spiegelman as artist, writer, cartoonist, novelist, historian, biographer, autobiographer, ethnographer, secondary witness, memory-worker, modernist, postmodernist, interviewer, and interviewee, and of *Maus* as documentary art, pictorial literature, novelized comic or cartoon, graphic novel, oral history, biography, autobiography, ethnography, vehicle for testimony, and medium for memory-work. Spiegelman himself observed: "I don't know how to refer to myself—author, artist, cartoonist, historian. They are all words trying to surround actuality. I think of comics as co-mix, to mix together words and pictures."[12] Here the stress on multiplicity is supplemented by that on hybridity or mixture, comics or comix (in the diacritical underground and avant-garde spelling) as co-mix. A letter Spiegelman wrote to *The New York Times Book Review* is especially interesting on the question of genre. After indicating his thanks for recognition and his delight that *Maus* appeared on the bestseller list, he added: "Delight blurred into surprise, however, when I noted that it appeared on the fiction side of your ledger."

If your list were divided into literature and nonliterature, I could gracefully accept the compliment as intended, but to the extent that "fiction" indicates that a work isn't factual, I feel a bit queasy. As an author I believe I might have lopped several years off the 13 I devoted to my two-volume project if I could only have taken a novelist's license while searching for a novelistic structure.

The borderland between fiction and nonfiction has been fertile territory for some of the most potent contemporary writing, and it's not as though my passages on how to build a bunker and repair concentration camp boots got the book onto your advice, how-to and miscellaneous list. It's just that I shudder to think how David Duke—if he could read—would respond to seeing a carefully researched work based closely on my father's memories of life in Hitler's Europe and in the death camps classified as fiction.

I know that by delineating people with animal heads I've raised problems of taxonomy for you. Could you consider adding a special "nonfiction/mice" category to your list?[13]

---

[12] Quoted in Esther B. Fein, "Holocaust as a Cartoonist's Way of Getting to Know His Father," *New York Times*, 10 December 1991, p. C 15.
[13] *The New York Times Book Review*, 29 December 1991, p. 4. Writing of *Maus* in *The New York Times* a few days earlier, Esther B. Fein noted: "The Times lists it under fic-

It is significant that Spiegelman protests the categorization of *Maus* as fiction while only jokingly suggesting its categorization as nonfiction. *Maus* is not made up, although it is obviously made or shaped. Spiegelman's search for a novelistic structure did not imply novelistic license and was related to careful, indeed painstaking research as well as to the accurate recreation of a contemporary context. It is also important that Spiegelman points to the dubious political implications of categorizing *Maus* as fiction insofar as it may play into the hands of negationists and the far right. A basic point here is that binary ledgers in general, and the binary between fiction and nonfiction in particular, are inadequate to designate *Maus*. Its in-between or hybridized status resists dichotomous labeling, and the very notion of hybridity should not be made to imply a form of comprehensive explanation or masterful understanding that is not warranted by the nature of the text.[14] Still, Spiegelman, while appreciating the "fertile territory" for "potent contemporary writing" furnished by the "borderland between fiction and nonfiction," would like to resist some of the legerdemain that has also occurred in that bewildering area. Moreover, as we shall see, the delineation of people with animal heads raises problems for my own account but not in exactly the same way it did for the editor of the *Times Book Review*.

A pronounced form of hybridity in *Maus* is that created by the relation between forceful, memorable images and the discursiveness of the text. It is significant that Spiegelman made use of interviews with his father in a kind of oral history or auto-ethnography. These interviews, as well as Spiegelman's experience growing up as the child of sur-

---

tion, reasoning that the events, though real, did not happen to animals" (10 December 1991, p. C 19). The *Times Book Review* editor's response to Spiegelman (29 December 1991, p. 4) is also worth recording: "The publisher of 'Maus II,' Pantheon Books, lists it as 'history; memoir.' The Library of Congress also places it in the nonfiction category. '1. Spiegelman, Vladek—Comic books, strips, etc. 2. Holocaust, Jewish (1939–1945)—Poland—Biography. . . . 3. Holocaust survivors—United States—Biography. . . .' Accordingly, this week we have moved 'Maus II' to the hard-cover nonfiction list, where it is number 13."

[14] One may also note that blurring and hybridization should not be conflated although they may at times be very close and one may be mistaken for the other. Hybridization generates newer forms of articulation that have to be carefully examined, and these forms may create more or less durable double binds as they pull the reader or viewer in different directions. Hybridization appears as blurring from the interior of securely defined, if not monological, disciplinary or generic lines. Yet mixtures without articulation may indeed be blurred, and this condition may lead to confusion as well as to newer articulations.

vivors, became the basis for the drawings and the discourse of *Maus*.[15] The actual inclusion of tapes comprising about sixty percent of the interviews (others were not recorded) in the CD-ROM version intensifies the text's hybridity and multivoiced character. Spiegelman himself saw the insertion of Vladek's tapes into the CD-ROM version as a way of giving his father a voice that does not appear in the same form or with the same force in the printed version. The ability to "find Vladek's version of an anecdote," Spiegelman observes, means that "rather than having me always *win* in my discussion with Vladek of how something should be presented," his father would have "the last word."[16] Even if Spiegelman's voice is also heard on the tapes, the tapes do give Vladek a fuller opportunity to answer back. At the very least they disrupt the narrative with the voice of the survivor and provide the possibility of readings that may diverge from those prompted by the printed version of the text.[17]

The movement from tape to word and image in the printed version is an important phenomenon in its own right, bearing not only on the process of production but on the artifact itself. *Maus* is not a comic in which the words merely punctuate, gloss, or float unmotivatedly above the images. Nor does language become condensed into one-liners that bring comic relief. Words are a crucial component of the text. They may even compete with the images for the reader's attention and create a

---

[15] The circuit is in a sense completed in the CD-ROM version of *Maus* which includes the various materials—the "field notes" of the auto-ethnographer or oral historian—that went into its making.

[16] Quotation from "page one" of the CD-ROM version of *Maus*. See also Roy Rosenzweig's review of the CD-ROM version, *Journal of American History* 81 (1995), esp. p. 1639.

[17] In discussing the problem of working-through the past in a manner that is respectful of the experiences and voices of victims, including the ways in which they may have to repeat trauma in a modified form in order to work it through, Saul Friedlander notes: "The dimension added by the [historian's] commentary may allow for an integration of the so-called mythic memory of the victims within the overall representation of this past without its becoming an obstacle to rational historiography. For instance, whereas the historical narrative may have to stress the ordinary aspects of everday life during most of the twelve years of the Nazi epoch, the 'voice-over' of the victims' memories may puncture such normality, at least at the level of commentary. The reintroduction of individual memory into the overall representation of the epoch implies the use of the contemporaries' direct or indirect expressions of their experience. Working through means confronting the individual voice in a field dominated by political decisions and administrative decrees which neutralize the concreteness of despair and death. The *Alltagsgeschichte* [history of everyday life] of German society has its necessary shadow: the *Alltagsgeschichte* of the victims." *Memory, History, and the Extermination of the Jews of Europe* (Bloomington: Indiana University Press, 1993), p. 132.

state of divided consciousness.[18] They signal the role of "novelization" in the text and attest to its high degree of self-reflexivity. Here one may note *Maus*'s own self-reflexive judgment concerning the success of its venture. Toward the beginning of *Maus* II, Artie, the Spiegelman-figure, justly observes: "There's so much I'll never be able to understand or visualize. I mean, reality is too complex for comics. . . . So much has to be left out or distorted" (M II, p. 16). On the other hand, Mala, Artie's stepmother, seems equally right when she says: "It's an important book. People who don't actually read such stories will be interested" (M, p. 133). In yet another instance of its in-between status, *Maus* exists in the tensely dialogic space created by these different judgments. These equally plausible and cogent judgments might even be taken as an initial way in which the hybridity in *Maus* tends at times to put the reader in a double bind. One continually wants to say "yes" but "no" or "no" but "yes" to what *Maus* does and how it does it. In creating a small-scale, anxiety-producing analogue of the impossible situation facing victims of the Shoah itself, this double bind may be useful and provocative in sensitizing readers to their catastrophic, traumatic experience. It may thus assist in creating an initial basis, however limited, for empathy and understanding with respect to the plight of the Jews of Europe and other victims of Nazi genocide.

In reading *Maus* one has a sense of its complexity, its inscription of uncanny ruptures, and its insistent problematization of identity but one does not, I think, find the text poorly composed or incoherent. One

[18] Spiegelman's resistance to the impression of mastery and to the dominance of the image is related to his departure from a standard practice in cartooning. As Joshua Brown notes: "The standard approach is to draw a page twice the size of the published version, permitting the artist to tackle detail more easily. The reduced finished product appears tighter and sharper to the reader's eye (and practically obscures mistakes). An illusion, in effect, is produced for the reader, a 'naturalized' image divorced from its production. Spiegelman decided, instead, to draw *Maus* in the constricted format in which it would be finally published." (Brown, *Oral History Review*, p. 102.) Spiegelman himself said of his attempt to avoid harmonizing trompe-l'oeil effects and the erasure of traces of the productive process: "I wanted it to be more vulnerable as drawing so that it wouldn't be the master talking down to whoever was reading." (Quoted in Brown, *Oral History Review*, p. 102.) Speaking of the avoidance of virtuosity and the role of simplicity, even uniformity, in the drawings of animal figures, he commented: "I didn't want people to get too interested in the drawings. I wanted them to be there, but the story operates somewhere else. It operates somewhere between the words and the idea that's in the pictures and in the movement between the pictures, which is the essence of what happens in a comic. So by not focusing you too hard on these people you're forced back into your role as reader rather than looker." (Quoted in Brown, *Oral History Review*, pp. 103–4.)

may even be inclined to overinterpret it and to provide a meaning, motivation, or intention for features that could be argued to be unintentional or even aleatory.[19] This inclination bespeaks the way in which *Maus* is well articulated and largely successful as a hybridized form even if one cannot fit it comfortably within an existing genre or fully explain its hybridity. In this sense, its characters (notably Vladek and, to some extent, Artie) may be possessed by the past, unable to supplement melancholy with successful forms of mourning and working-through, and caught up in endless repetition. Still, the text's orchestration, which does not offer total mastery but allows for the unsettling reinscription of trauma, may enable the reader to see how the tensely interactive processes of acting-out and working-through might be engaged. One of Spiegelman's comments regarding his earlier work indicates his own perspective on such problems. The question posed to him was: "Why was RAW # 1 'The Graphix Magazine of Postponed Suicides'? A postponed suicide is just a stall till suicide, isn't it? That doesn't sound very hopeful at all. . . . " Spiegelman's answer should be interpreted in relation to the pressure or heavy weight (which Nietzsche termed the *Schwergewicht*) created by his own mother's suicide:

> Let me answer that with a quote from Nietzsche. "The thought of suicide is a great consolation: with the help of it one has got through many a bad night." To think about suicide isn't necessarily to commit suicide. It's to acknowledge the possibility and to acknowledge the precariousness of being alive and to affirm it. Every moment that you don't commit suicide is an affirmation. It's deciding to live some more. The reason I think it's actually an optimistic notion is the fact that . . . well, that quote that's in the inside front cover by Cioran, "A book is a postponed suicide," to me implies an act of faith has been committed. Which is, to create a work of art, a book, a painting, a poem, a magazine, a comic strip, whatever, and that the work is in itself a justification for remaining alive. In that sense, at least, I felt it was provisionally optimistic. . . . (Groth, *The New Comics*, p. 197)

This type of "provisional optimism" would be necessary not only for writing or art but for forms of political and social activity as well, and

---

[19] Spiegelman's intentionality is especially important in Rick Iadonisi, "Bleeding History and Owning His [Father's] Story: *Maus* and Collaborative Autobiography."

Spiegelman often indicates his concern for such activity. Yet his attitude, while allowing for desirable social change may not sit well with utopianism. Here the comparison and contrast Miles Orvell draws between Jay Cantor and Spiegelman is of interest:

> Where they differ from each other most tellingly is in their psychoanalytic orientation: Cantor, writing out of a utopian political orientation inherited from the teachers of the sixties generation (Nietzsche, Herbert Marcuse, Norman O. Brown), creates a tale about the perpetual remaking of the self and about the need to encompass the fullest definition of wholeness—the complexities of sexual identity, of love and renewal, along with the impulse toward destructiveness and death. Spiegelman, more pessimistic in a classic Freudian sense (and more classically modernist as well), writes out of compulsion to understand the heavy weight of the past as both a public and a private burden. There is no joy of renewal in Spiegelman's universe: there is understanding and at best acceptance. Cantor's revolutionary utopianism is, in this respect, the opposite of Spiegelman's conservative pessimism. (Orvell, p. 126)[20]

The comparison is noteworthy, but the contrast is overdrawn. Spiegelman's problem might well be seen as that of working through problems, as a condition of sociopolitical action and ethical responsibility, in the very face of a past that cannot be entirely transcended in utopian directions, notably directions that imply a forgetting or eradication of that past or at best a paradoxical recall of a revolutionary tra-

---

[20] Michael Rothberg ends his analysis with a stress on the melancholic dimension of *Maus:* "Simultaneously reproducing and recasting Holocaust history, *Maus* partakes of the melancholy pleasures of reading, writing, and talking 'Jewish'." "'We Were Talking Jewish': Art Spiegelman's *Maus* as 'Holocaust' Production," *Contemporary Literature* 35 (1994), p. 685. In keeping with his analysis in *Holocaust Testimonies: The Ruins of Memory* (New Haven: Yale University Press, 1991), Lawrence L. Langer strikes a similar note: "As if to confirm his doubts about making any sense out of Auschwitz, Mr. Spiegelman ends his tale with the same melancholy answer that nearly every Holocaust testimony, written or oral, provides: the dead, those who did not return, have the last word, How could it be otherwise? . . . We are offered a whisper of hope for the future, since the book is also dedicated to his daughter, Nadja (born in 1987), but we are left wondering what kind of shadow her father's narrative will cast over her life, when she grows old enough to read it. Like the other questions raised in 'Maus II,' the answer remains shrouded in uncertainty. Perhaps no Holocaust narrative will ever contain the whole experience. But Art Spiegelman has found an original and authentic form to draw us closer to its bleak heart." *New York Times Book Review,* 3 November 1991, pp. 35–36. I later repeat Langer's question about Nadja in a somewhat different way.

dition (for example, the Jacobin or the radical modernist tradition) itself devoted to burying or erasing the past and beginning anew *ex nihilo*. Spiegelman points to the necessity of memory-work and play in coming to terms with the burdens of the past that cannot simply be cast off. Orvell's discussion of this issue has an important implication for the readership of *Maus:*

> Yet both writers, drawing upon and expanding the limits of graphic comic literature, are working outside the boundaries of the suspensive irony defined by Alan Wilde as characteristic of postmodern fiction, an irony in which "an indecision about the meanings or relations of things is matched by a willingness to live with uncertainty, to tolerate and, in some cases, to welcome a world seen as random and multiple." With their hybridized inventions, Cantor and Spiegelman are attempting to occupy a cultural middle zone in which the reader is brought back into the catastrophes of twentieth-century history in a way that calls for a healthy self-interrogation and self-renewal along with a reckoning of guilt and that takes us finally well beyond the usual pastiches of postmodernism and the forever disappearing self. (Orvell, p. 126)

It is difficult to define the nature of this "middle zone" occupied by Cantor and Spiegelman and related to a readership, whether implied, intended, or ideal. It would presumably be neither high-cultural (the "art" and gallery world or the traditional canon fodder) nor popular and mass cultural. Nor would the tensely fraught "middle zone" be simply a "middling" accommodation among existing options; it would somehow bridge a gap and create a new readership with different conceptions, expectations, and practices concerning the relation of the putatively "high" and "low," the elite and the popular. It would itself be disarticulated and rearticulated in terms of challenging and thought-provoking hybrids such as *Maus* itself. The underground comic when it comes aboveground and attains a popular success would thus still have a mission that might not be utopian but nonetheless would be committed and even combative.

With *Raw* Spiegelman intended an audience that numbered 5000; with *Maus* he found an audience of 400,000.[21] This is a quantum leap,

21 An audience of 5000 for *Raw* is mentioned in "Art Spiegelman and Françoise Mouly," the interview conducted by Gary Groth in *The New Comics*, p. 202, where Spiegelman asserts: "A unique object, yet not a unique object. There's 5000 of them."

but not one of revolutionary proportions. I do not know of empirical studies of the readership or reception of *Maus*, but my impression is that the audience, although mixed, is largely middle class and relatively well educated (even, at times, academic). But this does not imply that all of its readers are well informed about *Maus*'s object of figuration, the Holocaust.[22] It does, however, indicate the difficulty of creating a sociological, political, and philosophical "middle zone" that responds to the kind of "middle zone" or no-man's-land of hybridization that *Maus* intimates and Spiegelman seems to intend. Spiegelman and his wife and coworker Françoise Mouly are well aware of this problem. Interviewed along with Spiegelman, Mouly stated:

> We're in touch with a certain number of artists in New York, who are trying to work the "gallery circuit." And are stuck in that. For us, that seems to be almost a certain dead end. In working for galleries, in being elitist, in doing an original work of art that can't be accurately reproduced. And that group of well-meaning doctors and lawyers on Fifty-seventh Street going to see it in a gallery. Somehow it is so perverted. Artists have tried everything for the past fifty years or more to come out of that ghetto. They have not succeeded.
>
> A number of things have been tried out—doing multiple works of art, and so on—and none has really gotten the artist out of the vicious circle, the elitist market of art. (Groth, *The New Comics*, p. 201)

Mouly and Spiegelman apparently feel they are making the effort to forge a different form of art with an appeal to a different audience, but it is unclear to what extent they are succeeding. For example, is the fact that I am writing about *Maus* within an elitist academic market a sign of my "descent" into popular culture, my contribution to the attempt to "elevate" the comix to "serious" thought or high art, or my own modest effort at hybridization and the creation of a different audience that is cross-disciplinary and possessed of some potential for social

---

One of the techniques to prevent *Raw* from being stacked with more conventional comics was to use a large, glossy format which at least got it placed with other large magazines. On Spiegelman's work in general, see his far-ranging interviews with Gary Groth in *The Comics Journal* 180 (1995), pp. 52–114, and 181 (1995), pp. 97–139.

[22] I have, for example, been told by a former student at Boston University that, while on line for a book-signing of *Maus II*, she heard students expressing unconscious revisionist awe that the author of *Raw* had come up with a wild, incredible story about mice, a story whose invention they could hardly believe.

and political practice? I might prefer the third option, but how clear is it that I have a right to it or can, in any significant way, attain it?

It is important that Spiegelman is himself sensitive to the transference problem as it involves the reader and the narrator. Commenting on the ending of *Maus I* and his own relation to Artie as character and narrator, Spiegelman observed: "Well, I think people were very troubled by the ending of *Maus,* and this was good. 'Why is he calling his father a murderer—his father who went through all that horrible stuff.' It catches people up short because there's a tendency to see through the eyes of the narrator in any work you read. I wanted to provide some kind of blockage to that kind of transference." Here Spiegelman marks his distance from the Artie-figure and indicates ways in which the critical framing or ironic treatment of that figure is intended to function in the text. He also notes: "I don't know if it's clear from my drawings. But in the frames where I am talking to my shrink, I have him wear this little mask of my father. It's not just that he's the father I might have chosen. It's a little observation about the psychoanalytic process. It's all about transference, which is being able to work out the problems one has with one's parents in a safer setting" (Dreifus, p. 35). Art in its own way provides a relatively "safe haven" for the exploration of certain problems, including extreme problems and problems of excess, while nonetheless having more or less indirect relations to forms of social and political practice in which the safety nets of aesthetic distance are not available (despite the illusions of "aetheticized" politics).

Perhaps the most difficult questions for inquiry, including inquiry into the relation of Spiegelman to his characters, are raised by the work and play of *Maus* as a text. It is important to insist that Spiegelman and the Artie-figure cannot simply be conflated; there is a complex relation of proximity and distance between the two. In this sense it would be misleading to see the text as simply autobiographical or even as a form of cooperative autobiography. It is clear from comments in interviews that Spiegelman did not fully identify with Artie and intentionally created ways in which Artie would not appear as a fully sympathetic character or object of transferential identification for the reader.

Active in *Maus* is at least a fourfold network of interacting relations involving problems of transference. First, there is the relation of the (hybridized) Spiegelman to his (hybridized) text, a complex problem which I have already touched on and do not intend to belabor. Second, there is the relation of the survivor, especially Vladek, to his or her own past, which is inhabited by the ghosts of dead loved ones and by experiences he would prefer to forget. For Vladek and even for those close to him, these ghosts are more real or present than people in the contemporary world. Third, there is the relation of the son, Artie, to his father and his mother Anja. The son is the crypt for the parents' traumatic residues, the ghosts and obsessions that are transmitted across generations, often in seemingly unconscious and distorted ways. The question that may haunt both Artie and the reader is whether and to what extent Artie is coming to repeat or reincarnate precisely what he criticizes or even execrates in his father, notably obsessiveness, peevishness, and imperviousness to the needs of others. Fourth, there is the relation of the reader to Spiegelman, to the text with its characters, and to the entire network of problems or relationships they signify. The reader's access to the events and issues of the Holocaust is thus multiply mediated, first through the reluctant memories of Vladek and then through the specific way in which those memories are represented in a comic-book rendition of them (as well as addressed in paratexts such as interviews). Moreover, the Holocaust past constantly interacts with the present of Artie's world (prominently including his father) as well as with the difficulties he encounters in putting together and coming to terms with his book. Here the very notion of the present serving as a narrative frame with the Holocaust as an inner or framed story may well be too simple or even misleading, for the past returns to create uneven developments in the present and to pose the problem of the intricate relation between acting-out and working-through for survivors, for children of survivors, and for others born later.

Through *Maus* Spiegelman works out a multifaceted and layered memory of the past that is continually questioned and riven by contemporary concerns, thus raising the question of the extent to which past and present are inextricably interwoven through belated effects and partial recognitions—notably the insistent quest of the son for knowledge of the father's traumatic experience of a lost world. The father may himself not fully possess this knowledge, and he is reluctant to try to evoke that past or reconstruct missing knowledge. The son who wants to become the heir of a nonpossessed experience, who wants in a sense to incarnate a ghost or become his own dispossessed father, may be inclined to push the father into awareness that may be destructive or at least hurtful to him in order to assume a memorial task, particularly toward the mother, that the father has not been able to perform. And both father and son are constrained to try to relate past and present without letting the former simply become the performative or projective effect of desires, demands, or avoidances marking the present, most prominently including the son's quest for some kind of satisfying or even redemptive meaning through memory and commemoration. Through this quest, the Holocaust, which for the father was a source of traumatic disorientation in a past that will not "pass away," seems to be transfigured into a founding trauma holding the elusive (perhaps illusory) promise of meaning and identity for the son in the present.[23]

The present takes place in Rego Park (Queens, New York), the Catskills, and Florida, in a Jewish world that contrasts sharply with, yet is uncannily reminiscent of, the central European past. These shifting scenes include their share of contemporary, every-day problems and mishaps, which are intensified by the added stress of Vladek's obsessions, foibles, and impositions. The contrast between the contemporary American setting and the Holocaust past is of course jarring, yet it is impossible to separate the two in any neat manner. The past not only interacts with, but erupts into, the present, and at times the present seems to be only a function of, or a diaphanous screen for, the past. This is obviously true for Vladek. But it is also true for his son, who becomes preoccupied with the story of his parents and with the need to come to terms with it in his life and to record and render it in his art.

Vladek does not want to remember. But at times his memories are compulsive and invade the present. One such memory is that of his dead child Richieu, Artie's older brother. Richieu was sent away from the family for safe-keeping, and, as an unintended result of this action, did not survive. Vladek feels guilt over the fate of his dead son, and Artie shares this guilt. This "guilt"—or rift in the existence—of the sur-

---

[23] In interviews, Spiegelman is himself suspicious of such a quasi-religious quest and its sociopolitical functions. Indeed, he is quite sensitive to the possible abuses of the Holocaust as a symbolic counter in a civic religion or a contemporary politics of identity. "In terms of the way the Holocaust has entered into Jewish American consciousness, there's something sad and dangerous in that, along with the existence of Israel as being important to American Jews, the Holocaust is one of their defining aspects, more so than Tisha B'av or Sukkot or something (I'm lucky I'm able to conjure up the right holiday names). It's like envisioning a future in which Christians walk around wearing crucifixes and Jews walk around wearing small gas chambers around their necks. It becomes this closed-off martyrology that doesn't necessarily open up into what it is to be a passive witness to ethnic cleansing." Jacobowitz, pp. 54–55.

vivor seems caused not by the mere fact that Vladek survived but by the abyssal contrast between his survival and the fact that a loved one, for no good reason, did not survive. Vladek's plight is especially pronounced when he calls Artie by the name of his dead brother, thus making his living son the host for a revenant. Book II is dedicated to Richieu as well as to Spiegelman's own child, Nadja, and Richieu's photograph is prominently displayed at the beginning of the book. (Two other "real" photographs are found in the books, one of Artie's mother with a child and, near the end of the second book, one of Vladek himself after his liberation from the camp. Vladek is still strikingly, indeed shockingly, handsome after his Holocaust experience, and he wears a dapper rendition of a camp outfit for his apparently exuberant display.)[24] Given the reader's knowledge of Richieu's fate and that of most of his family, the baby picture of a healthy, beautiful, somewhat blonde child is particularly disorienting and uncanny. It is a point of entry that functions as a stumbling block and a point of no return.

Much to his son's dismay, Vladek, in his flight from painful memory, has even destroyed Anja's notebooks. He has burned them because "these papers had too many memories" (M, p. 159). Vladek's burning of the traces of his first wife's past is both blatantly symbolic and overdetermined, as the reference to "too many memories" might be taken to imply. Vladek burns the books in order to forget the past and to obliterate (incinerate?) the memory of both Auschwitz and his wife. In this sense his assertion against Auschwitz (fighting fire with fire) is also a bizarrely inappropriate act of aggression against his wife. But his burning of the papers serves simultaneously to burn them into his being as emblems of an unworked-through relation to the past and to the dead wife, both of which will continue to possess him and help to undermine his second marriage (which he always compares unfavorably to the first). One might here suspect an unconscious desire to be punished in Vladek's ostensible attempt to get rid of the past in a manner that converts it not simply into a scar but into an open wound, hence assuring its painful, fatalistic return.

[24] Spiegelman notes: "It looks like he had a fine time having that portrait taken—he looks rather cheerful in an odd way. It's a troubling photo." He then goes on to make an intriguing comment on the role of the photograph in the text when he compares it to the tapes in the CD-ROM version: "His voice provides something in a way equivalent to that photograph. It's not filtered through his son; it's just there. Vladek was a good storyteller in his own right. The tapes have a strength for me." Jacobowitz, pp. 55–56.

Artie loses control when he learns of his father's act: "God damn you! You—you murderer! How the hell could you do such a thing!!" (M, p. 159). Artie apologizes for his outburst but still walks off muttering "murderer." This scene terminates *Maus* I without providing— or by insistently withholding—a resonant, conciliatory, or uplifting ending. Artie desperately wants memory to fill in the gaps and emptinesses of his life, but his hoped-for mnemonic redeemer fails to come. With uneven success and, more for his own sake than for his father's, he compels, even at times harasses, his father to remember. With his ever-present tape recorder, he can be as obnoxious to his father as his father is to him. And the judgments he passes on his father are typically harsher than those the old man is tempted to pass on his son.

Artie is prone to blame both his parents for his difficulties—difficulties that are, in part at least, those of the child of survivors.[25] At one point, however, the blame (or "guilt-trip") he lays on his mother is enormous. *Maus* contains a strange interlude, a comic within a comic. Vladek finds one of Artie's stories that "appeared in an obscure underground comic book" which Artie thought Vladek would never see (M, p. 99). Vladek is upset by it but says he understands and even tells Artie: "It's good you got it outside your system. But for me it brought in my mind so much memories of Anja" (M, p. 104). The comic, entitled "Prisoner on the Hell Planet: A Case History," includes the picture of Artie's mother with a child. Anja is in a bathing suit and somewhat overweight. One recalls that Vladek has admitted that she was not as attractive as the woman he left for her but that "if you talked a little to her, you started loving her more and more" (M, p. 18).

One assumes that the child in the photo is the young Artie, blessed yet also cursed by the presence of the lost mother. The "prisoner on the hell

[25] Spiegelman expresses his distance from children-of-survivor groups in a manner that indicates their limitations as well as some of their possibilities: "I was invited as a guest to one of these Second Generation groups to respond to some film by a child of survivors, so I did. Afterwards, a woman got up to make an announcement, saying that the Second Generation singles party was going to be held at Temple Emmanuel six weeks later. I realized, 'Wow, this is a problem,' because I couldn't imagine the kinds of pick-up lines that would be involved—something like, 'Which camps were your parents in?' I'm sure such groups are helpful to people and that I actually do have a lot in common with them, including my rather ironic distancing from the Holocaust. There's at least a certain type of commonality between children of survivors, but I'm really not interested in the blurring of uniqueness that's involved in finding commonality." Jacobowitz, p. 53. The obvious question is whether finding commonality has potentials not exhausted by the blurring of uniqueness.

planet" is clearly Artie, who appears in the series both as someone disturbed for good reason and also as a rather self-involved, self-pitying person, suggesting that the son of the survivor can also be a problem child. The first image after the photo is of Artie in a prisoner's outfit, recalling his stay in a mental hospital. He states: "In 1968, when I was 20, my mother killed herself. She left no note!" (M, p. 100). The unnecessary exclamation point almost makes this statement an accusatory plaint directed at the dead mother, whereby the son repeats the very act of aggression that he condemned his father for committing. The suicide takes place while Artie is away for the weekend with his girlfriend, and—in a strange displacement of so-called survivor guilt—he feels that relatives blame him for his mother's death. Artie is surprised when his father expects comfort from him rather than giving him support and comfort. He recalls the last time he saw his mother. She entered his room and asked: "'Artie . . . you . . . still . . . love . . . me . . . . don't you? . . .' I turned away, resentful of the way she tightened the umbilical cord . . ." As he, in his bed, turns away from her, he says: "'Sure ma!' . . . She walked out and closed the door!" The next images of Artie in the prison/asylum bear the words: "Well mom, if you're listening . . . Congratulations! . . . You've committed the perfect crime . . . You put me here . . . shorted all my circuits . . . cut my nerve endings . . . . and crossed my wires!. . . . You murdered me, Mommy, and you left me here to take the rap!!!" Fortunately, a fellow prisoner, assuming perhaps the reader's role, cries out: "Pipe down, Mac! Some of us are trying to sleep!" (M, p. 103) These words may be interpreted both as a critique of Artie's dubious desire to blame the (m)other (indeed the victim) and as an indication of one's own equally dubious desire to avoid all the issues he raises, including the valid ones.

What is particularly striking about "Prisoner on the Hell Planet," which is explicitly framed as juvenilia, is that the figures in it are human, yet they are ghoulish and rendered in a stark, if not brutal manner. They make less contact with humanity than the explicitly displaced figures of *Maus*.[26] And their role with respect to Vladek as well as Anja is not altogether filial or humane. Indeed they seem, even more than the other drawings in *Maus*, to be haunting, unworked-through traces of trauma or the outlines of still open wounds.

The figures in *Maus* are of course animals, and this gesture is the second source of profound shock in reading these books.[27] Bringing Auschwitz to the comics is one thing. Doing it through the medium of animal-figures is another. Moreover, the epigraphs to the two volumes provide strange and disconcerting introductions to these figures. The first volume carries as epigraph a quotation from Hitler: "The Jews are undoubtedly a race, but they are not human." The second volume has as epigraph a quotation from a "newspaper article, Pomerania, Germany, mid-30s." It reads: "Mickey Mouse is the most miserable ideal ever revealed . . . . Healthy emotions tell every independent young man and every honorable youth that the dirty and filth-covered vermin, the greatest bacteria carrier in the animal kingdom, cannot be the ideal type of animal . . . . Away with Jewish brutalization of the people! Away with Mickey Mouse! Wear the Swastika cross!" Clearly, Spiegelman is quoting these words ironically and shoving them back

[26] One might perhaps risk a cross-temporal and cross-cultural parallel and apply to these American images the words Spiegelman uses to describe his recent work, *The Wild Party:* "When I look back for a 1920s visual style with which to illustrate the book, it's actually a kind of Weimar Republic expressionism. On the other hand, the Weimar Republic also seems like exactly what I was describing: this desperate attempt to find a democratic, intellectually and psychically stimulating response to the horrors that foreshadow more to come. And that's part of what's wonderful about it." "In Pursuit of the Pleasure Principle: Art Spiegelman talks to Elena Lappin about comics and his nostalgia for the world before the genocide. 'I don't want to be the Elie Wiesel of the comic book'," *The Jewish Quarterly* 42 (1995), p. 10.

[27] Adam Gopnik overstates his case when he asserts: "It's extremely important to understand that *Maus* is in no way an animal fable or an allegory like Aesop or *Animal Farm*. The Jews are Jews who just happen to be depicted as mice, in a peculiar, idiosyncratic convention. There isn't any allegorical dimension in *Maus*, just a convention

down the speakers' throats. But irony in this case is equivocal and can easily misfire or be misread, especially in the light of the actual use of animal figures in the books. Still, if one were tempted to object that Spiegelman himself does in a sense figure Auschwitz (or Mauschwitz) as Mickey-Mouse land (although he intentionally did not draw the endearing, infantilized types of animals that appear in Disney cartoons), it would be equally important to note that his more challenging move is to bring Auschwitz to Mickey-Mouse land, that is, to bring the Holocaust past to the America that must have seemed to survivors like a Disneyworld in its distance from their experience.

Jews are represented as vermin: animals that seem to be a little too large for mice yet not quite the size of rats. Germans are cats: vicious, wild, malevolent cats that look more like werewolves than furry house pets. Poles are pigs. "Gypsies" are moths (Gypsy moths!). (While moths are mobile "pests" that are often exterminated, the "Gypsy" is stereotypically figured as a fortune teller, not directly as a member of a group oppressed and "exterminated" by the Nazis during the Shoah [M II, p. 133].) Americans are friendly if somewhat goofy dogs, and other nationalities are either predictable (the one Frenchman is a frog) or relatively nondescript (Swedes as reindeer of some sort). Artie's wife Françoise, who is French and converted to Judaism, is, after some deliberation (or self-reflexive banter) on Artie's part, represented in the same way as other Jews. While the depiction of certain nationalities seems rather obvious and may in its obviousness even function to hollow out and subvert stereotypes, the representation of Jews, Germans, and Poles presents serious problems.

The choice of animals of such a decidedly tendentious sort invites two criticisms. On the one hand, it is rather unfair to the (literal) animals to present them in the guise of human stereotypes. A pig, for example, is a PIG, with all the connotations of what it is to be a PIG, only from an anthropomorphic and invidious point of view. On the other hand, it is also dubious to represent entire peoples or nationalities in

---

of representation." Gopnik, p. 31. Yet how would the meaning of *Maus* have changed if Spiegelman had used the "peculiar, idiosyncratic convention" of representing Nazis as mice and Jews as pigs or vicious cats, or had he offered the cat image for Israelis? Gopnik raises a more disturbing issue when he writes: "It still must be said that the book succeeds so well in part because it evades the central *moral* issue of the Holocaust: How could people do such things to other people? The problem with the animal metaphor is not that it is demeaning to the mice, but that it lets the cats off too easily." Gopnik, p. 33.

terms of one-dimensional animal caricatures and "bestial" stereotypes.

Still, the animal representations are problematized in *Maus*; indeed,
they are problematized in ways that question ethnic and national identities. Mice sometimes have tails and at other times do not. There are,
moreover, "real" animals that contrast with the figurative ones. The ver-
min-like Jews are afraid of "real" rats in a bunker (M, p. 147). The Germans have vicious dogs. And Artie's analyst has a photo of a cat on his
desk. The animal metaphor is framed as a metaphor even if all its characteristics are not sufficiently controlled or justified by this explicit framing. There is, however, one instance in which there is a marked departure
from the animal figure, and instead a human child (whose head is hidden) is depicted. This occurs is in a forceful image of a German holding
the child by a leg and smashing it against a wall (M, p. 108). The next image ironically juxtaposes the silhouetted figures of the German standing
over the legs of the collapsed, upended child and Vladek (at this point
still ignorant of Richieu's fate) telling Artie how, on hearing of the incident, he thanked God his own children were safe in hiding.

Furthermore, nuances are introduced into the animal figures that
mitigate one's initial response to stereotyping. This is less true for Germans than for others. Germans tend to remain the categorical perpetrators, and the cats undergo little modulation either graphically or
conceptually. This undifferentiated representation of Germans is dubious. But the mice and the pigs are another story. The mice become
pathetic and moving figures, especially in certain scenes. Here Spiegelman may do much to reverse a negative stereotype and to transvalue
the image of the vermin. The most powerful images often involve
mice: the Germans beating Jews (M, p. 80); the puzzled Vladek and
Anja, wondering which way to go, as they stand at a crossroads resembling a swastika (M, p. 125); Jews burning in a pit at Auschwitz (M
II, p. 72); Vladek at Dachau during a typhus epidemic, walking on
dead bodies as he tries to get to the latrines (M II, p. 95); or Artie, himself at a drawing board atop a pile of dead bodies, as he awaits being
interviewed on TV about his first volume (M II, p. 41). I would make
special mention of one pathetic vaudeville scene involving Vladek's
formerly rich friend, Mandelbaum, in Auschwitz. Mandelbaum is reduced to a hopelessly clownish, Beckettian figure. His pants are too big
and he is forced to use one hand to hold them up. With the other hand
he holds a bowl, and under his arm is tucked a shoe that is too small

SO THE GERMANS SWINGED THEM BY THE LEGS AGAINST A WALL...

AND THEY NEVER ANYMORE SCREAMED.

for him. He states: "I hold onto my bowl and my shoe falls down. I pick up the shoe and my pants fall down. . . . But what can I do? I only have two hands!" (M II, p. 29).

ANJA AND I DIDN'T HAVE WHERE TO GO.

WE WALKED IN THE DIRECTION OF SOSNOWIEC – BUT *WHERE TO GO?!*

The depiction of people as animals at times has bitterly ironic sides. In one sequence Vladek compares the human body's response to being shot with that of a mad dog a neighbor of his once had. "The dog was rolling so, around and around, kicking, before he lay quiet. And now I thought, 'How amazing it is that a human being reacts the same like this neighbor's dog'" (M II, p. 82). Yet the accompanying drawing shows a dead mouse on the ground in a helpless position resembling that of the dog.

A striking departure from the use of animal figures is the role of animal masks. When figures wear explicit animal masks (for example, Artie, his TV interviewers, or his analyst), it remains unclear whether there are human faces beneath or whether there are masks all the way down. This *mise en abîme* or bottomless multiplication of the mask may be one of the most radical gestures in problematizing identity. In a more restricted sense, Jews wear pig masks when they pass for Poles. Artie wears a mouse mask for his TV interview, and his interviewers

also wear masks. One obvious reason for these masks is the artificiality of the interview, the factitious character of the interviewing process, and the falseness of the environment in which such activities take place, especially in contrast to the problems that obsess and plague Spiegelman. The scene begins with Artie at his drawing board atop a mound of dead bodies. In a cascade of facts and dates, he recounts the death of his father in August 1982; the birth of the baby (Nadja) he and his wife Françoise are expecting in May 1987; the gassing of over 100,000 Hungarian Jews in Auschwitz between May 16 and May 24, 1944; the publication of the first part of *Maus* in September 1986 after eight years of work; and his mother's suicide in May 1968. He adds: "Lately, I've been feeling depressed" (M II, p. 41). Then he is called to the TV interview. The first interviewer, wearing a pleasant dog (American) mask, asks him for the message of his book. The second, wearing a cat (German) mask, aggressively asserts that "many younger Germans have had it up to here with Holocaust stories" concerning things

that "happened before they were even born." The third, an Israeli in a mouse mask, asks how he would represent Israeli Jews, to which Spiegelman responds with an animal variant of the Sabra image: "I have no idea . . . porcupines?" Then a nondescript, cigar-smoking impresario offers him a deal for a *Maus* vest to start off a line of endorsed products. (M II, p. 42) At this point Spiegelman is reduced to a small, whimpering child and goes off to see his analyst who, like him, is wearing a mouse mask. (Does this imply that the analytic session is as artificial as the TV interview?) One of his more memorable statements to the analyst is emblematic of the role of the double bind in *Maus:* "Samuel Beckett once said: 'Every word is like an unnecessary stain on silence and nothingness.' " After a pause Artie adds the observation: "On the other hand, he *said* it" (M II, p. 45).This pause is marked by the only image in *Maus* not accompanied by words.

Aside from Artie's wife, the only French person in *Maus* is one of the prisoners in Dachau, where Vladek arrives after the forced march from Auschwitz near the end of the war. The frog feels the need to speak with another being, and English is the only language he and Vladek have in common. The Frenchman is not a Jew and so is able to receive packages from home, whose contents he shares with Vladek. After the war, Vladek exchanged letters with him, but these he "threw away together with Anja's notebooks."[28] He tells Artie: "All such things of the

---

[28] In the first volume of *Maus* (p. 159), Vladek says he burned Anja's papers. There is an apparent inconsistency when he refers in the second volume to throwing the notebooks away along with the letters from the Frenchman. This inconsistency may function to indicate the uncertainty of memory as well as to counteract the tendency to place too much weight on the burning of the papers. It may also be aleatory. One scene

war, I tried to put out of my mind once for all . . . until you rebuild me all this from your questions" (M II, p. 98).

Although there is little modulation in the representation of Germans, there is a complex rendering of the activities and policies of the Nazis with respect to Jews during the Holocaust. Here the education *Maus* provides is commendable even if it does not go into the treatment of other oppressed groups such as "Gypsies," homosexuals, or Jehovah's Witnesses. The reader of *Maus* will come to know much about Nazi practices of discrimination, ghettoization, incarceration, and extermination, particularly with respect to the Jews of Poland. Moreover, he or she will also become familiar with Jewish life in Poland, especially among the relatively well-to-do who were faced with a massive change in conditions of existence under the Nazis and their Polish sympathizers. Vladek's father-in-law is a very wealthy person with much influence, but all his wealth and influence do not save him or his wife from deportation and death.

Poland was the site of the death camps, and the killing fields of Poland have a prominent place in *Maus*. Indeed, the Poles (along with Jews) receive the closest and most sustained attention in *Maus*. Spiegelman's parents were from Poland, and the evocation of the Polish setting is careful and nuanced. Prevalent in Poland was a virulent anti-Semitism and at times a propensity to cooperate with, or at least support the policies of, the Nazis. Yet *Maus* (unlike Lanzmann's *Shoah*) acknowledges the existence of Poles who were willing to aid Jews even at great personal risk.[29]

Many pig-faces appear among the cruel kapos in the camps, and the Polish population, especially in the countryside, is often antagonistic to Jews. Before Vladek and Anja are captured, their Polish housekeeper states: "It's the Nazis stirring everybody up." Anja retorts: "When it

---

in which Spiegelman does explicitly raise questions about memory concerns the role of the orchestra at Auschwitz that played as inmates marched to work. Vladek does not remember it, while Artie points out that its existence is very well documented. Spiegelman actually departs from Vladek's memory in the interest of historical accuracy by picturing the orchestra in the corner of a panel (M II, p. 54).

[29] In an interview Spiegelman compares the Poles to contemporaries who are passive witnesses to horrible events about which they seem able to do little or nothing: "Well, maybe *Maus* will create more sympathy for non-Jewish Poles. We've all become that. Up until a few years ago, I was saying, we're all Jews, even Yasir Arafat, Elie Wiesel, whoever. But now, I'm beginning to think that many of us are Poles. The Poles were the victimized witnesses. They weren't the central dynamic. Some acted well, some acted badly." Jacobowitz, p. 55.

comes to Jews, the Poles don't need much stirring up." The house-keeper answers: "Mrs. Spiegelman - - how can you say such a thing. I think of you as part of my own family." To which Anja adds: "I'm sorry, Janina. I didn't mean you! I'm just worried!" (M, p. 37). Yet Anja could just as well have included the housekeeper in her generalization, for when she and Vladek in flight later come to her for help, Janina slams the door in their faces (M, p. 136). In Auschwitz, the vicious kapo who beats prisoners is a Polish peasant. Yet he befriends Vladek because he can teach him English, which he thinks will be useful if the Allies win the war. Anja has a comparable experience with a Polish woman kapo. After being liberated, Vladek has no desire to return to Poland. Anti-Semitism remains rife in postwar Poland, and Jews who return to their property are driven off or even killed. Friends tell Vladek: "Whatever you do, don't go back to Sosnowiec. The Poles are still killing Jews there" (M II, p. 131).

Before their capture, however, Vladek and Anja are helped and sheltered by various Poles: Vladek's father-in-law's former janitor, a peasant woman, and especially Mrs. Motonowa, who hides the couple in her apartment and must even conceal them from her husband during his rare visits, although she is well paid for her aid and does tell them to leave when she mistakenly fears a visit from the Gestapo. The lesson seems to be that Jews may be helped by Poles when the Poles are able to derive some profit from it, but they may also be turned out if there is perceived danger. Vladek and Anja are ultimately handed over to the Nazis by Poles who take their money and are supposed to smuggle them into Hungary—Poles who are themselves later sent to Auschwitz by the Nazis who no longer need them. Here Poles appear as victims who are nonetheless unwilling to forge solidarity with Jewish victims, whom they instead try to victimize in their own way. The most uncompromised Pole Vladek meets is a priest in Auschwitz, who is genuinely interested in his fate and to whom he later refers as a saint (M II, p. 28). Yet the primary form this interest takes is based on a belief in numerology, as the priest interprets various number combinations to assure Vladek that he will survive.

There are a few allusions to the dubious side of the Jewish councils. For example, Vladek, unlike a couple of his relatives, does not want to work for the *Gemeinde* because of what it was doing to Jews. When a Jewish leader announces that Jews must appear to register at a stadium, one of the people in the crowd says: "I'm not going. It's a Nazi trap. And our Jewish committee is helping those murderers" (M, p. 88). There are also appearances by Jewish policemen who do some of the dirty work of the oppressors. But one will not find much in *Maus* concerning the complexities of the issues surrounding the Jewish councils and the Jewish leadership, including the manner in which the Nazis themselves created double binds for their victims by actively and cynically trying to make accomplices of the Jews, placing members of the Jewish councils in impossible positions, and confronting them with no-win choices.

There are, I think, two questionable reasons and at least one good reason for the use of the animal metaphors and masks. Echoing certain of Spiegelman's comments, Miles Orvell writes:

> The rationale for the visual typology is at least twofold: first, as the epigraph to *Maus* (quoting Adolf Hitler) ironically suggests, the Nazi ideology itself was dehumanizing, one that turned its victims into less than human beings. "The Jews are undoubtedly a race, but they are not human." Second, in telling *Maus* from the Jews' perspective, Spiegelman is representing the world in the simplified but starkly authentic way the victims of the Nazis experienced it: the Jews were like mice to the terrifying cats of the Nazis; many of the Poles were, to the Jews, like pigs in their comfortable complacency. The world was a theater of stereotypes, of masklike signs of danger or indifference. (Orvell, pp. 119–21)[30]

The problem with Orvell's argument is that it goes beyond the critical framing of stereotypes and ideologies and threatens to take them up in the commentator's own voice. On the one hand, there is an appeal to "dehumanizing" Nazi ideology at however ironic a remove; on the other, there is an appeal to the "simplified but starkly authentic" representation of the putative experience of victims. One thus has an invocation of two drastically different subject-positions to arrive at both a complementarity of perspectives and a desired conclusion: Nazis dehumanized victims, and Jews experienced the world as would mice. Thus the use of animal masks or stereotypes

[30] Michael E. Staub's analysis is similar to Orvell's (see Staub, pp. 27–28). In reporting his exchange with a Polish curator who questioned the representation of Poles as pigs, Spiegelman states: "He said: 'Do you realize that it is a terrible thing to call a Pole a pig? It's worse than it even sounds in English. Do you realize that the Germans called us *schwein*?' So I said, 'Yeah, and the Germans called us vermin. These aren't my metaphors. These are Hitler's.'" Dreifus, p. 37.

is fully justified. One may object that Nazi ideology in figuring Jews as vermin represented them not simply as less than human but as radically other than human in a manner that turned them into scapegoats and perhaps paradoxically into sacrificial objects. Orvell offers no evidence that Jews experienced themselves as mice in relation to their persecutors, and it is significant that even in *Maus* no Jew states that he or she feels or felt like a mouse. By contrast, some Jews during the Holocaust did use the more sacrificial image of sheep-to-the-slaughter, whether to describe their plight or to urge action against it—Don't go like sheep to the slaughter!—and postwar commentators, such as Raul Hilberg, at times appealed to this image to characterize and criticize Jewish leadership, especially the Jewish councils. In any case, Orvell's argument may be taken to bring out the dubious nature of unmediated identifications, even with the subject-position or the perspective imputed to the victim. The dangers of his conclusion signal the need for the commentator to work out a different subject-position or set of subject-positions that does not simply coincide with one or more (actual or ascribed) participant-positions. Finally, Orvell's view relies on some of the most prejudicial anthropocentric assumptions. Some Poles behaved not like pigs but like human stereotypes of pigs. Here the crucial point may be that the very idea of "bestial" behavior is a human projection that conceals anxiety about the extremes to which specifically human viciousness may go. It is not animals who are bestial but human beings in certain situations. Animals may kill but they do not systematically torture, experience carnivalesque glee at the suffering of victims, seek "sublime" elation in violence, or scapegoat the weak. These are human "achievements."

Spiegelman elsewhere gives an obvious and defensible, if limited and still somewhat problematic, reason to justify the use of animal figures: their role as a distancing device that may paradoxically serve as the most direct mode of access to phenomena for those who have not in fact experienced them.

First of all, I've never been through anything like that—knock on whatever is around to knock on—and it would be a counterfeit to try to pretend that the drawings are representations of something that's actually happening. I don't know exactly what a German looked like who was in a specific small town doing a specific thing. My notions are born of a few scores of photographs and a couple of movies. I'm bound to do something inauthentic.

Also, I'm afraid that if I did it with people, it would be very corny. It would come out as some kind of odd plea for sympathy or "Remember the Six Million," and that wasn't my point exactly, either. To use these ciphers, the cats and mice, is actually a way to allow you past the cipher at the people who are experiencing it. So it's really a much more direct way of dealing with the material. (Groth, *The New Comics*, pp. 190–91)

Vladek is perhaps the central character in *Maus*. He has been through hell. Of his entire family, only a younger brother in Russia is, like him, a survivor of the Holocaust. Of the rest of the family, only photographs remain (M II, p. 116). Vladek is an especially difficult figure for both his son and the reader: he is a victim who must be respected, yet he is not likable. Indeed he is the epitome of the problematic survivor. Before the Holocaust, he had unattractive personality traits that persist, are intensified, and are added to as the result of his traumatic experiences. He is self-centered, obsessive, and intensely money-conscious. As a sheik-like young man whom friends compared to Rudolph Valentino, he drops a woman who is not wealthy for Anja, who comes from a very wealthy family. While he is courting Anja, he looks in her closet on the sly "to see what a housekeeper she was." He observes with pleasure: "Everything is neat and straight just the way I like it." Yet he finds pills and, with evident concern, makes notes in order to be able to check on them. "If she was sick, then what did I need it for" (M, p. 19).

In America the relatively well-off Vladek is a burden to everyone around him: his second wife, his son, his daughter-in-law. Françoise observes: "It's so claustrophobic being around Vladek. He straightens everything you touch—He's so anxious" (M II, p. 22). Vladek has the habits of a scavenger and saves every little scrap that he finds. (Artie repeats this gesture with respect to the residues and ruins of the past.) Mala, Vladek's second wife, leaves him only to return and feel trapped by him and his demands. He keeps strict control over her budget and does not give her money for personal items. Artie tells her: "He's always been—uh—pragmatic." Mala retorts: "Pragmatic? Cheap!! It causes him physical pain to part with even a nickel." She refuses to attribute Vladek's unattractive traits to his traumatic experiences. "All our friends went through the camps. Nobody is like him." Artie adds to her sentiments: "It's something that worries me about the book I'm doing about him . . . In some ways he's just like the racist caricature of the miserly old Jew." Mala rejoins: "Hah! You can say that again" (M, 131). Here Artie faces the disconcerting possibility that, at least in certain cases, the stereotype may seem to represent reality or, conversely, a person in "real life" may, performatively and perhaps unconsciously, take the stereotype as a scripted model for existence.

One of the most embarrassing incidents for Artie and Françoise comes just after Mala leaves Vladek and he is preoccupied with bringing partially used packages of her food, which he cannot eat, back to the supermarket in order to get reimbursed. Artie: "Sigh. I'd rather kill myself than live through all that. . . ." Françoise: "What? Returning groceries?" Artie: "No. Everything Vladek went through. It's a miracle he survived." Françoise: "Uh-huh. But in some ways he didn't survive." This exchange takes place while the couple is waiting in the car at the supermarket while Vladek manages to convince the store manager to give him six dollars worth of food for one dollar after explaining to him "my health, how Mala left me, and how it was in the camps" (M II, p. 90). In this scene the distance between victim and survivor is accentuated, for the experience and the belated effects of victimage may act as recurrent impediments to survival. Moreover, there is the intimation that the victim may manipulate his status to "con" others and gain dubious advantages for the self.

Returning home from the supermarket, Vladek reveals his intense prejudice against blacks. Françoise stops for a hitch-hiker, and Vladek exclaims: "A hitch-hiker? and—Oy—it's a colored guy, a Shvartser! Push quick on the gas" (M II, p. 98). Vladek continues to grumble in Polish about picking up the "Shvartser," and after the hitch-hiker leaves, he scolds Françoise and says he had to watch the man so that he would not steal groceries from the back seat. Françoise responds: "That's outrageous! How can you, of all people, be such a racist! You talk about blacks the way the Nazis talked about the Jews!" Vladek rejects the analogy: "Ach! I thought really you are more than this, Françoise. It's not even to compare the Shvartsers and the Jews" (M II, p. 99).

One of the unacknowledged ways in which Artie tends to identify with and relive the more problematic sides of his father is in his own relationship to his mother. Artie obviously has been sensitized to feminist issues and would not be as blatantly and crudely overbearing as Vladek. For example, Artie discusses problems with his wife with an openness and air of equality that one does not find in his father. But Artie's mother, Anja, tends by and large to be a significant absence or at best a marginalized presence in the book, and Vladek's destruction of her papers seems to have taken its toll on his son in ways that are not always conscious. There is a sense in which Artie seeks a memorial to the missing mother, a necessarily inadequate gift of mourning that tries to compensate both for her suffering in life and for her untimely, unjustified death. But Artie's attention tends to be focused on his father even when he is lamenting the loss of his mother. Anja seems to become a phantasmic archive that Artie hopes will provide him with a point of entry into the elusive, seemingly redemptive past that he tries to recapture. Indeed, at times she seems to *be* her lost papers, and when they are destroyed, she almost shares their fate. When her role becomes more pronounced than an absence or a cameo part, it serves questionable functions (as in the "Prisoner on the Hell Planet" sequence). What may threaten to occur here is that Artie may become an accomplice of his father in the sacrifice not only of the mother's memories but also of the memory and the role of the mother. There even seems to be a silent accord between father and son that forms a bond between them at the expense of the mother.

Mala, Artie's kindly and long-suffering stepmother (whose name seems suspiciously dissonant in its "evil" connotations), has never taken the mother's place. Nor is that place taken by Artie's wife. Françoise has more than a cameo role and often seems to be in accord with, or complementary to, Artie. For example, she shares his manifestly critical reactions to his father yet nonetheless tries to mitigate them. These reactions function to conceal the affinities between father and son both for Artie and for the reader, and Françoise's role here may prompt insight. But Françoise does not displace the mother, and her very Frenchness gives her a somewhat exotic position that helps to place her at a safe distance from any comparisons with the lost mother. She is also in the difficult position of a convert to Judaism, which is indicated by the uncertainty about whether to represent her as a mouse. The mother herself exists for Artie largely as an absence that makes itself felt. The father-son relation takes center stage, and the son is most often obsessed with the father's ghostly presence, which transmits a harrowing past that has not been laid to rest, as well as with his own effort to bear witness to that past-present while trying to prevent it from dominating his life.

One of the successes of *Maus* is in inducing the reader to accept, indeed empathize with, Vladek while nonetheless extensively displaying his off-putting features and limitations. One comes to respect the survivor without sacralizing him or enabling his trials to excuse everything about him. One also comes to understand better the relation between father and son and the difficulty the son has in not reliving and repeating the traits of the father. The one person who is mentioned in the story but of whom we have no concrete image is Artie's child, Nadja. Book II ends with the image of the tombstone of Vladek and Anja, yet the reader remembers that Nadja also exists and has not been discussed. How will she relate to her father and, through him, to the memory of her grandfather and everything he went through? Will the difficulties Artie has inherited from his father also be passed on to his child? These unsettling questions introduce another temporal layer into the story, for *Maus* is not simply about the past or the relation between the present and the past but also about the future, which is shaped by past and present in ways that are not altogether knowable or predictable. Nadja's absent presence reminds the reader that memory-work always bears on the present and future.

The larger ethicopolitical and aesthetic question is the effect of the interplay between image and word in the possible impact of *Maus* on collective memory, especially among the young who will be exposed to the Holocaust only through mediated or secondary memory and largely through the media of popular culture. Does the conjunction of image and word provide a more effective medium of transmission than the use of the word alone?[31]

---

[31] One might initially be tempted to compare *Maus* with two other works: Haim Bresheeth, Stuart Hood, and Litza Jansz, *Introducing the Holocaust* (New York: Totem Books, 1994); and Stewart Justman, *The Jewish Holocaust for Beginners* (New York: Writers and Readers Publishing Inc., 1995). But these works resemble one another more than they do *Maus* and may serve to highlight its achievement. They are relatively straightforward in their discursive representation of the Holocaust, at times editorialize, and do not attain either *Maus*'s complex interplay of word and image or its self-reflexive relation between past and present. Moreover, *The Jewish Holocaust for Beginners* does not employ cartoons but a combination of photographs and paintings by Rebecca Shope. In a statement worthy of parodic insertion in *Maus*, the back cover notes: "The paintings by Rebecca Shope are so intensely charged that they provide a perfect counterpoint to the text. And if you have any doubts, there are the photographs. . . ." *Introducing the Holocaust* combines cartoons, sketches, maps, graphs, and photographs, and it attempts in certain limited ways to emulate *Maus*. In appar-

On one level *Maus* employs what a film like *Shoah* eschews: graphic images of the process of discrimination, oppression, and "extermination." These images are displaced in that they operate through metaphor and allegory in a contemporary re-enactment of an Aesopian gesture. But they are nonetheless powerful and even disturbing enough to provide offset but somehow realistic representations that trigger the imagination and are required as springboard or counterpoint so that an even more displaced, indirect, and allusive method, such as Lanzmann's, may have an impact. *Maus* creates in the mind a set of little demons that disturb the tranquillity of one's "memory palace," that prevent it from becoming too "normal" or cozy and overly glazed with the products of silicone valley and their historiographical counterparts. Even if one is unable to be confident about its constructive potential in inhibiting the recurrence of the type of events it portrays, *Maus* is still commendable in its ability to disturb and place in radical question an unjustified and forgetful complacency.

One of the most challenging (and vexed) dimensions of *Maus* is its use of the carnivalesque as a modality of memory with respect to the Shoah. The primary form of the carnivalesque, both during and after the Shoah, has probably been so-called gallows humor: humor saturated with bitter, disruptive (not suspensive) irony and remote from any reconciling, harmonizing, or conciliatory role.[32] Humor of this sort is tensely caught up between melancholy and mourning and varies in the ways it negotiates their intricate relationship. The wake is an obvious case of the role of gallows humor in mourning itself, and it signals the problem of the more limited or less institutionalized functions of humor in mourning and, more generally, in the response to a devastating past that remains a force in a difficult present. The differences in the very tenor of laughter are themselves intimately related to the various possibilities in the interaction of melancholy and mourning (or acting-out and working-through more generally). They point to the more intricate variations and the continual interplay between remain-

---

ent seriousness, its back cover announces: "Just as Steven Spielberg's Oscar-winning film *Schindler's List* brought the horror of the camps once again to the world's attention, this important and powerful book provides a clear and forthright guide to the Holocaust for readers today. The book has been brilliantly illustrated by Litza Jansz, in the graphic tradition pioneered by Art Spiegelman in his highly evocative *Maus*."

[32] For an initial approach to this problem, see Terrence Des Pres, "Holocaust Laughter?" in *Writing and the Holocaust*, ed. Berel Lang (New York: Holmes & Meier, 1988), pp. 216–33.

ing captive to a past and trying to live in a present while creating openings to a more desirable future. Indeed the entire problem of the carnivalesque and humor is bound up with the uneven, often interrupted, and at times failed movement from victim to survivor and agent.

I have noted the limited role of gallows humor in *Maus*. It is virtually nonexistent in recalling Vladek's experiences during the Holocaust itself. One gets little sense of how it helped camp inmates or ghetto dwellers to try to cope with impossible situations, no doubt because it seems to have had little place in Vladek's life. Its role with respect to the aftermath of traumatic events is more in evidence but still very restricted.[33] With respect to mourning, even gallows humor must be combined with the serious work of memory in a context of grieving and sorrow that is both alleviated and intensified by irony, incongruity, and jokes. *Maus* is indeed a labor of mourning in this respect, for its carnivalesque dimensions are always embedded in, and at times overwhelmed by, the dire past with which it contends.

The most obvious carnivalesque side of *Maus* is its attempt to represent towering (or abyssal) events worthy of the most "elevated" tragedy in the "low" or popular genre of the comic book. Conversely, it "raises" the comic (or the comix) to the level of the "highest" and most "serious" art or thought. Here the activity of the son reenacts, respects, and tries critically to get beyond the repetitive impasses of the father. Vladek himself (as represented in *Maus*) seems utterly devoid of a sense of humor and has virtually no perspective on himself. Perspective is offered to the reader, however ambiguously, through certain of Artie's comments and reactions and, more significantly, through Spiegelman's mode of representation, most blatantly in the massive frame provided by the comic-book format and its Aesopian devices. Aside from this important structural feature, the most pronounced thematic mode of carnivalization in *Maus* is the frequent juxtaposition of scenes from the present and scenes from the past, which creates a double or multiple consciousness in the reader and generates both a jarringly ironic discrepancy and an uncanny sense of déjà vu that heighten one's awareness of the poignancy or impossibility of certain situations. To a significant extent, the present is always haunted by memories, revenants, or repressed aspects of the past, for example,

[33] It is, however, very pronounced in Spiegelman's paratextual comments, notably in his interviews.

in the manner in which Artie, for his father, is always wearing the phantom-like shroud of his dead brother, Richieu.

Probably the weakest but most blatant modes of the carnivalesque are in the present trials and tribulations of father and son where the humor, never devoid of disconcerting irony, is nonetheless close to the sitcom and embroiled in the more commonplace difficulties of the family romance. These dimensions of *Maus* are saved from triviality by their implication in a past that manages to color the present in a seemingly indelible way. Still, the gallows humor of *Maus* remains subdued and often sombre in its negotiation of the relation between past and present. One never has the boisterous, round-house humor found, for example, in Mel Brooks's *The Producers*, where the response to the past remains insistently secular, as in *Maus*, but the resources of gallows humor reach riotously insolent and ribald extremes. These extremes provoke both tears and belly laughs: they threaten to burst the bounds of decorum, perhaps upsetting those for whom the subject, in its seriousness or even quasi-religious significance, is simply beyond the pale of the grotesque and the Rabelaisian. (This discomfiture or even outrage is possible despite the fact that *The Producers* is quite careful in critically framing its more outrageous initiatives, for example, by staging an audience reaction to the Nazi-era musical comedy (the play within the play) that takes the form of stunned outrage. This initial reaction modulates into laughter only when the musical that is intended by "the producers" as a sure-fire failure becomes a success when it is perceived as hilarious parody and camp. It is nonetheless significant that *The Producers* never directly addresses the Holocaust but leaves it an implicit element of the Nazi regime.) In *Maus* the humor stays subdued and rarely does more than evoke an empathetic smile in the reader— a smile always constrained by graphic awareness of the forces agitating against it. But the notion of *the* reader is of course suspicious, and here it would indeed be useful to have actual empirical studies of the responses of different groups and individuals to *Maus*, including responses to its more carnivalesque dimensions. My own feeling is that *Maus*'s approach to the carnivalesque is quite restrained (to some extent in keeping with the interview material on which Spiegelman drew), but its range is great enough to raise the question of the limits and possibilities of the carnivalesque, as it relates to memory and mourning, in the aftermath of Auschwitz.

The most problematic aspect of *Maus* may not be the carnivalesque attempt to make Auschwitz a topic for the comics or even doing it through the medium of animal figures. In fact, the aesthetic, ethical, and even religious problems raised by this attempt, despite their importance, may readily serve as a screen to cover an even knottier problem which Spiegelman may share with Lanzmann. I am referring to the subject-position of the child of the survivor or, more generally, of the Jew of a later generation, especially someone tempted to convert the Holocaust into a founding trauma and thus a paradoxical, perhaps impossible source of meaning and identity.[34] Indeed this position can, whether justifiably or not, be taken up by those who become involved in problems of the Holocaust through inquiry, personal contact, and various modes of transference.

The question of how to negotiate the subject-position of one born later is both everywhere in *Maus* and nowhere confronted or thematized in an explicit and sustained manner. In this respect the critical self-reflexivity of *Maus* tends to be arrested at a certain point or to become indeterminate. This everywhere-and-nowhere status of the problem posed by the position of one born later attests to its difficulty and perhaps to the readiness with which it may itself be conjoined with some form of sacralization or desire to redeem the self.

Artie has an insistent and pervasive preoccupation with recording his father's story, which is dangerously close to becoming the master narrative of his own life. But he nowhere sits himself down and asks about his own motivations and reasons or directs at himself the dogged scrutiny to which he subjects his father. Indeed, in certain ways, he becomes a Jew or assumes a Jewish identity (even enacts a frustrated messianic desire for redemption through memory) through his concern with the Holocaust—a concern that nonetheless escapes sufficient critical examination. At best there is the hint that Nadja may come to give her father as "tough" a time as he gave Vladek, perhaps with greater hopes of working through a past whose phantoms and unresolved conflicts may readily be transmitted across generations to create intricate and often misunderstood problems in the descendents of those involved in unbearably traumatic events.

But it is important to remember that Spiegelman's intention was not to provide Artie with resources that would indeed have facilitated

---

[34] Lanzmann was a teenager during World War II and took part in Resistance activities. He was not himself deported or interned in a concentration camp. In relation to the Holocaust, his position is, in significant ways, analogous to one born later.

reader identification with him, and the limitations of Artie's self-critical insight may serve a distancing function. Spiegelman himself has in interviews addressed the issue of why he was preoccupied with the Holocaust and undertook *Maus*. He began with his desire to do something truly significant: "I wanted to deal with subject matter that could matter . . . I really wanted to start on something that would take a sustained effort, something that would take me further." But *Maus* was also motivated by Spiegelman's own need to offer something to his dead mother. Indeed, he mentions these two reasons in quick succession, as if they were associated. "Another cause is, when I was a kid I remember my mother wishing she could write about her experiences and not being able to. Not feeling able to. I remember vaguely her saying, '. . .and then someday maybe you'll write about this stuff.' And that was an impulse, an input. It was a concern that my mother had that my father doesn't have. He has no desire to bear witness" (Groth, *The New Comics*, p. 192). While the father seems to be the obsessive center of Artie's concern in *Maus* and the mother seems to be marginalized or even sacrificed to the relation between father and son, here for Spiegelman the very motivation of the text is the relation to the mother as well as the son's desire to be a good-enough secondary witness. Indeed there is an evident correlation between the writing that the mother was unable to do, which she passed on to the son as an unfulfilled intention, and the destroyed papers that haunt the son as indicative of a lost legacy and an obligation. The genesis of *Maus* and its particular significance might be situated between these two absent pieces of maternal writing that serve as a mournful appeal to the son—an appeal simultaneously from childhood and from beyond the grave.

Alain Finkielkraut has written of the imaginary Jew, the individual who has not been brought up as a practicing Jew but who vicariously assumes Jewishness in a tangled rapport with the traumatic events of the Shoah and its aftermath of suffering.[35] Recently, historians such as Charles Maier, Henry Rousso, and Peter Novick have criticized a putatively obsessive concern with the Holocaust and related events. Maier has referred to a neuropathic surfeit of memory, Rousso to a Vichy syndrome, and Novick to an identity-forming appropriation of the Holocaust on the part of American Jews that may at times serve du-

---

[35] *The Imaginary Jew,* trans. Kevin O'Neill and David Souchoff, intro. David Souchoff (1980; Lincoln: University of Nebraska Press, 1994).

bious functions.[36] These critiques run the risk of both pathologizing a necessary concern with memory and normalizing limit-events that must continue to raise questions for collective memory and identity. Still, what may be retained from their discussions is the importance of specifying the conception of memory one attempts to work out as well as the need to inquire, critically and self-critically, into one's own subject-position and the nature and functions of one's concern.

Maus (in conjunction with its paratexts) may be read in a manner that prompts one to recognize the significance of these issues and to confront the question of how they should be addressed. Indeed the very images in *Maus* may be seen not as imaginative representations of the unrepresentable but as condensed and at times disconcerting mnemonic devices that help to recall events one might prefer to forget, and the complex relations between image and word, father and son, mother and son, history and art serve as reminders of the difficulties and variable functions of memory-work that is addressed to extreme experience and limit-events. Nonfictional "art" may here have to engage the problem of memory-work in a manner that enables the recreation of possibilities for the imagination that otherwise threatens to be overwhelmed, put out of operation, or jolted into a manic state of free play in the face of certain "experiences" and events. In this respect, *Maus* may be argued to function in multiple ways as a complex work of memory and mourning on the margin between auto-ethnographic, historical reconstruction and art.

[36] Charles Maier, "A Surfeit of Memory? Reflections on History, Melancholy, and Denial," *History & Memory* 5 (1992), 136–51. Henry Rousso, *The Vichy Syndrome: History and Memory in France since 1944*, trans. Arthur Goldhammer (1987; Cambridge: Harvard University Press, 1991); Eric Conan and Henry Rousso, *Vichy, un passé qui ne passe pas* (Paris: Fayard, 1994). Peter Novick, "'Lessons,' 'Memory,' 'Uniqueness' and Other Absurdities of American Holocaust Discourse," lecture delivered at Cornell University, 4 October 1994. Novick is working on a book-length manuscript on the American Jewish reception and use of the Holocaust.

CHAPTER SIX

Conclusion: Psychoanalysis, Memory, and the Ethical Turn

This book has not provided a continuous narrative or a unified theory. It has attempted to approach a set of problems from a variety of related perspectives. Each chapter is an essay intended to be a dialogic intervention in an ongoing debate, and discussion is often shaped by particular, critical exchanges with other inquirers. The procedure is one of critique—often immanent critique—and self-criticism that strives for a reformulation of issues without pretending to put forth a free-standing argument or position that deceptively dispenses with its context of elaboration. Perhaps my most prominent incentive has been to articulate the relationship between history and psychoanalysis in a manner that does not eventuate in a dubious pathologization of historical processes or personalities but instead links historical inquiry to explicit ethical and ethicopolitical concerns bearing on the present and future. The particular problem of memory is set within this broader context. Moreover, a specific reading of an artifact, such as a film or novel, is itself an attempt to remember the artifact in a certain way, and it may fruitfully be informed by a selective, nonformulaic use of psychoanalysis that is oriented toward an exchange between past and present with implications for the future.

Perhaps the broadest question raised by the works I have discussed, especially insofar as they render extreme fact in inhospitable form or provide hybridized versions of documentaries in formats usually associated with fiction, is the complicated set of relations among traumatic event, memory, and imagination. Extremely traumatic series of events beggar the imagination, and such events often involve the literalization of metaphor as one's wildest dreams or most hellish night-mares seem to be realized or even exceeded by brute facts. Such facts go beyond the imagination's powers of representation. Indeed, when things of an unimaginable magnitude actually occur and phantasms seem to run rampant in "ordinary" reality, what is there for the imag-ination to do? Such events cannot be intensified through imaginative recreation or transfiguration. A major problem in working through them may well be that, in attempting to arrive at their empirical di-mensions and counteract the role of phantasms, one may nonetheless encounter events whose empirical reality itself went to phantasmic ex-tremes. To the limited extent it is possible, working through problems in this context may require the attempt to reinforce dimensions of the "self" that can somehow both come to terms with and counteract the force of the past, as it returns in the present, in order to further the shaping of a livable future.

During the occurrence of traumatic events, the imagination may at times provide momentary release or an avenue of escape, but after the event the imagination may be overwhelmed by hallucinations, flash-backs, and other traumatic residues that resist the potentially healing role of memory-work. For both survivors and those born later, the imagination may seem to be superfluous, exhausted, or out of place with respect to limit-events; even their allegorical treatment, transfor-mation, or reduction in scale poses difficult, perhaps intractable, prob-lems of tact and judgment. Notably for those born later, these events may, through a kind of posttraumatic effect, prompt a generalized hy-perbolic or exorbitant style that at times becomes indiscriminate and verges on a paradoxically bland sensationalism, which may under-mine critical judgment and obscure, or provide too one-sided a reso-lution of, the problem of the actual and desirable relations between excess and normative limits.

Adorno's famous and often misunderstood comment about the barbarity of writing poetry after Auschwitz is itself best seen not as a *Verbot* (prohibition) but as a statement concerning the difficulty of legitimate creation and renewal in a posttraumatic condition, and it is also better applied to the role of the imagination as well as its interac-tion with memory than to poetry in any generic or delimited sense. Similarly, my own theoretical reflections do not assert absolute limits, much less prohibitions or taboos, but at most indicate obstacles and challenges with which writers and artists have had to come to terms in supplementing documentary with more "artistic" approaches to the Shoah. These reflections also indicate the necessity of performing critical work on memory in the hope of renewing imaginative possibilities and reopening the question of the future—a necessity that brings art into a particularly close, provocative, and mutually questioning relation with history.

In this context critically tested memory may appear as the necessary starting point for all symbolic activity, even though it is continually threatened by lapses, holes, and distortions. In any event, the question of memory may come to the forefront of attention or even be exaggerated precisely because of the difficulty of remembering events that defy the imagination and are not fully encompassed by conventional methods of representation. This difficulty is exploited by those commentators, such as negationists, who have self-interested reasons for raising extreme doubts about memory, undermining the credibility of witnesses, and denying aspects of the past. Indeed, if memory threatens to become inaccessibile, subject to continual doubt, or constituted as an equivocal object of desire, the danger is that imagination—deprived of the sustenance and the safeguards that memory provides—will, if it does not atrophy, alternate between melancholic repetition and superficial manic agitation. Empathy itself, as an imaginative component not only of the historian's craft but of any responsive approach to the past or the other, raises knotty perplexities, for it is difficult to see how one may be empathetic without intrusively arrogating to oneself the victim's experience or undergoing (whether consciously or unconsciously) surrogate victimage. The notion of muted or secondary trauma that is allowed to register in one's approach is an admittedly inadequate attempt to address the problem of how to approach certain questions with empathy while not renouncing all critical, and possibly self-preservative, distance.

What Kant discussed as a conflict of the faculties may seem, with respect to limit-cases, to result in one "faculty," the imagination, at least provisionally leaving the field because there is no contest in which it may engage. Memory may even come to occupy the place of the imagination in posttraumatic contexts. What is required may be both to remember and to check memory with all the resources of critical inquiry in order to approach as closely as possible events that necessarily involve gaps, distortions, and limited evidence at least with respect to the experience of trauma itself. Here "recovered memory syndrome" is not a pathology that may serve to incriminate victims or invalidate psychoanalysis. It is rather a subcase or even a metonymic exemplar of a larger problem concerning the difficulties of memory with respect to traumatic events that are invested with devastating phantasms, generate anxiety-ridden uncertainties, create disorienting holes in experience, and can only be reconstructed and worked through after the fact. But the problematics of trauma should not lead one to mystify problems or to discount the work of both memory and reconstruction with respect to limit-events. There is much that can be reconstructed and remembered with respect to the Holocaust and other historical "catastrophes," and the challenge is not to dwell obsessively on trauma as an unclaimed experience that occasions the paradoxical witnessing of the breakdown of witnessing but rather to elaborate a mutually informative, critically questioning relation between memory and reconstruction that keeps one sensitive to the problematics of trauma.

Two crucial psychoanalytic concepts for any attempt to relate history and memory in the aftermath of traumatic limit-events are mourning and melancholia. In Freud's classic study, "Mourning and Melancholia," it would seem that melancholia is ambivalent: both a precondition to (or even necessary aspect of) mourning and that which can block processes of mourning insofar as it becomes excessive or functions as an object of fixation.[1] Melancholia is an isolating experience allowing for specular intersubjectivity that immures the self in its desperate isolation. In the best of cases, it may allow for insights that bear witness to crisis-ridden or even traumatic conditions and have broader critical potential. In Freud, it is a state in which one remains possessed by the phantasmically invested past and compulsively, narcissistically identified with a lost object of love.

Melancholia may be necessary to register loss, including its lasting wounds, and it may also be a prerequisite for, indeed a component of, mourning. In accord with so much of the Christian and Romantic traditions, one may even value the poetry of melancholy and the extraordinary demands imposed by a feeling of inconsolable loss or an

---

[1] In addition to Freud's essay, see Eric L. Santner, *Stranded Objects: Mourning, Memory, and Film in Postwar Germany* (Ithaca: Cornell University Press, 1990); Alexander and Margarete Mitscherlich, *The Inability to Mourn: Principles of Collective Behavior,* trans. Beverley R. Placzek (New York: Grove Press, 1975); and Peter Homans, *The Ability to Mourn: Disillusionment and the Social Origins of Psychoanalysis* (Chicago: University of Chicago Press, 1989).

imitatio of an idolized other.[2] Yet mourning, although continually threatened by melancholia, may counteract the melancholic-manic cycle, allow for the recognition of the other as other, and enable a dissolution or at least loosening of the narcissistic identification that is prominent in melancholy. In mourning one recognizes a loss as a loss yet in time is able to take (partial) leave of it, begin again, renew interest in life, and find relatively stabilized objects of interest, love, and commitment. Moreover, one remembers and honors the lost other but does not identify with the other in a specular relation that, however ecstatic or self-sacrificial, confuses the self with the other.

To be effective, mourning would seem to require a supportive or even solidaristic social context. One may question how effective a one-to-one clinical relation can be, not only for broader social and political problems, but also for durable and desirable transformations of the individual. Social processes of mourning losses and dead loved ones may be the only effective ways of partially overcoming melancholia and depression or at least of preventing them from becoming all-consuming and incapacitating. Support groups could facilitate memory-

---

[2] The Romantic may at times harbor within him- or herself a displaced Christian seeking redemption through a secular absolute (such as love, art, or totalizing political revolution) and turning (or simply being) melancholic in the face of its loss or unavailability. Or, as T. E. Hulme put it, Romanticism is "spilt religion." It should, however, be noted that Romanticism was an internally complex and divided movement that included self-critical elements that were not stereotypically romantic. (The work of Paul de Man and his students is especially alert to these elements.) Moreover, the entire notion of secularization as involving displacement of religious elements does not undercut the significance of the constitutional principle of separation between church and state, which functions on a different level of conceptualization and practice. Indeed one's defense of such a principle may be reinforced insofar as one is sensitive to the less obvious but at times potentially dangerous ways in which secular life may embody displaced religious quests for salvation or extremely negative reactions to groups perceived as posing threats to purity or integrity. With respect to psychoanalysis, it should be further observed that the notion of secularization does not imply, as Freud at times seemed to believe, that psychoanalysis could serve as a secular master discourse that provided the key to demystifying and decoding religion. Rather the relation between psychoanalysis and religion(s) should be seen in terms of the possibilities and limits of mutual translatability, and psychoanalysis itself might be argued to involve more or less disguised and encrypted displacements of religion (as Freud also at times recognized). Translatability would be understood as a real problem, including the possibility that certain religious practices or discourses might be richer than existing forms of psychoanalysis in the manner in which they address certain problems, including those formulated in psychoanalytic terms as acting-out and working-through. In any case, the notion of secularization should not be taken to justify a reductive and uncritical use of psychoanalysis in attempting to understand or account for religious phenomena.

work and mourning; the question is how they might relate to broader social and political processes of transformation. There are no easy answers, but psychoanalysis may offer a slim basis for posing questions.

The correlation of certain of Freud's concepts may be explicated by presenting melancholia as a form of acting out and memory as a modality or component of working through problems. Memory in this sense may become a manner of recalling misguided ventures and critically taking leave of less desirable aspects of the past as well as of attempting to honor other aspects or make them the bases of constructive action in the present and future. The historical study of the limit-event may itself help to generate a readiness to feel anxiety in nonparanoid doses that may put one in a better position to think the possibility of the unthinkable and to counter conditions that foster the occurence of traumatizing events; such study may thus provide a new twist to the saying that to be forewarned is to be forearmed. Here I would underscore the point that I have avoided notions—especially seemingly neutral or medicalized technical notions—of normality and pathology in favor of explicitly normative valorizations and modes of ethicopolitical criticism. In this sense working-through has been valorized in my account, but acting-out has not simply been devalorized or summarily dismissed. And the relation between acting-out and working-through has not been seen in terms of an optimistic scenario or uplifting narrative in which one may ultimately heal all wounds, achieve full ego-identity, transcend the past, and live happily and fully in the present. Rather, I have noted that, particularly in cases of trauma, the past and its phantasmic modifications undeniably have possessive force, and acting-out may be not only necessary but perhaps never fully overcome. Indeed, it may be intimately bound up with working through problems. But it should not be isolated, theoretically fixated upon, or one-sidedly valorized as the horizon of thought or life. Moreover, working through the past is itself in good part an ethical process, and it may be most effective when it is situated in social and political contexts.

In their useful and important book, J. Laplanche and J.-B. Pontalis address directly the problems of acting-out and working-through.[3] They define acting-out "according to Freud" as "action in which the subject, in the grip of his unconscious wishes and phantasies, relives

---

[3] See *The Language of Psycho-Analysis* (1967; New York: W. W. Norton & Co., 1973).

these in the present with a sensation of immediacy which is heightened by his refusal to recognize their source and their repetitive character" (p. 4). They also observe that Freud most often referred to repetition in the transference as acting-out and that acting-out betokened the return of the repressed (pp. 4–5). Of working-through they write:

> Process by means of which analysis implants an interpretation and overcomes the resistances to which it has given rise. Working-through is taken to be a sort of psychical work which allows the subject to accept certain repressed elements and to free himself from the grip of mechanisms of repetition. It is a constant factor in treatment, but it operates more especially during certain phases where progress seems to have come to a halt and where a resistance persists despite its having been interpreted.
>
> From the technical point of view, by the same token, working-through is expedited by interpretations from the analyst which consist chiefly in showing how the meanings in question may be recognised in different contexts. (p. 488)

Working-through thus counters compulsive acting-out, but it does not provide full enlightenment or definitive liberation from the constraints of the past. Indeed it is best seen as a necessarily recurrent process that responds to recurrent modes of self-deception and ideological implication. Moreover, it should be noted that Laplanche and Pontalis mitigate the opposition between acting-out and working-through by noting that "working-through is undoubtedly a repetition, albeit one modified by interpretation and—for this reason—liable to facilitate the subject's freeing himself from repetition mechanisms" (pp. 488–89). Working-through would thus seem to involve a modified mode of repetition offering a measure of critical purchase on problems and responsible control in action that would permit desirable change. It is thus intimately bound up with the possibility of ethically responsible action and critical judgment on the part of someone who strives for the position of an agent and may thereby counteract his or her own experience of victimhood and the incapacitating effects of trauma. Indeed, a crucial question is how one may further the difficult process of moving from victimhood to survival, witnessing, and agency. A related problem is how to recognize one's own transferential implication in events one has not lived through without projectively assuming the role of victim or survivor. Laplanche and Pontalis also indicate that working-through is not a purely intellectual process but requires a form of work involving not only affect but the entire personality. For them "working-through might be defined as that process which is liable to halt the repetitive insistence characteristic of unconscious formations by bringing these into relation with the subject's personality as a whole." Unfortunately, they provide little insight into the possibility of more broadly social or even political modes of interaction and activity that might engage processes of working-through.

Laplanche and Pontalis intimate that working through problems in any comprehensive sense requires the active recognition that there always remains in thought and in social life a "stain," impurity, or residue of the past that cannot be entirely eliminated or made good. The unassimilable remainder may change over time and undergo transvaluation or recycling with changes in normative orders. But one of the lessons of both deconstruction and psychoanalysis (especially in its Lacanian form) is that it is dubiously utopian and possibly destructive to believe one can simply get rid of this residue of the past. And aspects of one's response to it may well be uncontrolled and unconscious, involving acting-out and the compulsive return of the repressed. Particularly when one avoids recognizing the sources of anxiety in oneself (including elusive sources that are not purely empirical or historical in nature), one may be prone to project all anxiety-producing forces onto a discrete other who becomes a scapegoat or even an object of quasi-sacrificial behavior in specific historical circumstances. Jews were taken to be an impurity, "stain," or phantasmic source of anxiety-producing contamination in the *Volksgemeinschaft* (community of the people), and the "final solution" was in one sense motivated by a desire to be *Judenfrei*, entirely and definitively free or purified of the polluting other. Even the ambivalence of one's response to the other (involving fascination and attraction, including erotic attraction) tended to be resolved in an overwhelmingly negative, hostile, and abusive direction.

The very fact that German culture owed so much to the Jews and that one could even speak of a putative German-Jewish symbiosis made the relation between Germans and Jews similar to that between enemy brothers, but the enmity came predominantly from the German side of the relationship. Jews were divided (at times internally divided) between the extremes of assimilation and Zionism, but even Zionists might recognize the value of German culture and attempt to make their own best employment of it. Indeed Jews' shock and disbelief over what was happening in Nazi Germany were bound up with the feeling of many Jews that they were an integral part of German culture, that German *Bildung* was their *Bildung*.[4] Here the case of Victor Klemperer is particularly striking, for his diaries reveal him as a Jew who, under difficult and tenuous living conditions during the Nazi regime, retained an identity as a German and even a German patriot; indeed, he saw the Germans as a "chosen people" and the Nazis as un-German.[5]

Klemperer and others more or less like him were not entirely deluded, for before the Nazi ascendancy there were many positive initiatives and outstretched hands from the German side that counteracted anti-Semitism. For example, Progressives and Social Democrats developed principled, political opposition to prejudice. Marx showed signs of so-called Jewish self-hatred, but Ferdinand Lassalle not only achieved a powerful leadership position in the labor movement but was loved and respected by many non-Jewish workers. One may also recall that Karl Jaspers did not follow the route taken by Martin Heidegger. During the Nazi regime, Jaspers remained devoted and loyal to his Jewish wife and, throughout his life, retained the Enlightenment ideal of a German-Jewish symbiosis. His perspective may in certain respects have been naively utopian or even self-deluded, but it is memorable nonetheless. Moreover, his 1946 *Die Schuldfrage* [*The Question of German Guilt*] was one of the earliest attempts to come to terms with the German past in the wake of Auschwitz. To be sure, this study may be subject to criticism, especially with the benefit of hindsight, but it at least attempted to grapple with problems that others are still trying to obfuscate or avoid—as the views of certain contributors to the *Historkerstreit* alone would demonstrate.[6]

[4] On this issue, see John V. H. Dippel, *Bound upon a Wheel of Fire: Why So Many German Jews Made the Tragic Decision to Remain in Nazi Germany* (New York: Basic Books, 1996).

[5] Victor Klemperer, *Ich will Zeugnis ablegen bis zum letzten: Tagebücher 1933–1941* and *1942–1945*, ed. Walter Nowojski and Hadwig Klemperer (Berlin: Aufbau-Verlag, 1995).

[6] For the problem of stereotyping in general and for German-Jewish relations in particular, see the important work of Sander L. Gilman, especially *Difference and Pathology: Stereotypes of Sexuality, Race, and Madness* (Ithaca: Cornell University Press, 1985) and *Jews in Today's German Culture* (Bloomington: Indiana University Press, 1995). See also Anson Rabinbach and Jack Zipes's excellent collection, *Germans and Jews since the Holocaust* (New York: Holmes & Meier, 1986). For the relationship between Hannah

The image of a polluting or contaminating other is a phantasmic, phobic projection related to one's own anxieties, but those who harbor it may be quite "normal" and socially adaptive, even celebrated, insofar as prejudice is legitimated in society and reinforced by institutions. One's critique of this image must in this sense be ethical and political and eschew a narrowly psychological conception of psychoanalysis itself. And one's very psychoanalytic understanding of it may be related to the view that such an image involves a displaced ritual and sacrificial dimension that can be counteracted only if it is recognized as in some sense involving a returning repressed. But its role in society is of course overdetermined and is not explainable by any one set of forces or factors.

In his book, *Hitler's Willing Executioners: Ordinary Germans and the Holocaust*, Daniel Jonah Goldhagen is obsessed by a question to which he returns time and time again: How could the Nazis (or more simply, for Goldhagen, the Germans) possibly have done what they did to the Jews: not only tried to kill every man, woman, and child but often behaved with gratuitous cruelty, humiliating and degrading gestures, brutality, and even carnivalesque glee?[7] Even if one objected strongly to Goldhagen's rashly generalizing ascription of the "mind-set" that induced this behavior to virtually all Germans at the time and acknowledged that similar behavior and outlooks were prevalent in other groups in areas such as Austria, Latvia, Lithuania, Poland, Romania, and Russia, one may recognize his question as a pointed and important one. Goldhagen's own answer is not up to the question he raises, for he sees such behavior as explained by long-standing "eliminationist antisemitism" which is itself not further explained and comes close to an uncritical, stereotypical conception of German national character. But one may nonetheless insist on the importance—even the ineluctably haunting quality—of the question Goldhagen raises. Many

---

Arendt and Karl Jaspers, as well as other issues touched on here, see Steven E. Aschheim, *Culture and Catastrophe: German and Jewish Confrontations with National Socialism and Other Crises* (New York: New York University Press, 1996), chap. 6. The groundbreaking work of George Mosse is also relevant; see, for example, Mosse's *Germans and Jews : The Right, the Left, and the Search for a "Third Force" in Pre-Nazi Germany* (New York: Howard Fertig, 1970) and *Toward the Final Solution: A History of European Racism* (New York: Howard Fertig, 1980).

7 New York: Alfred A. Knopf, 1996. Without attempting to thematize and interpret them, Goldhagen reports many carnivalesque and celebratory gestures that are mixed with Nazi torture and degradation, for example, on pp. 220, 236, 245–48, 256–57, 259, 286–87, 291, 294, 299, 306, 308–10, 320, 387, 400, 440–41, 452–53, 548 n32, and 577n35.

reviews of his book do not include such an insistence. For example, in the generally cogent, judiciously critical, and well informed analysis of Omer Bartov, a basic counterargument concerns the uniqueness of the Holocaust: "What was—and remains—unprecedented about the Holocaust is a wholly different matter, which Goldhagen avoids treating: the industrial killing of millions of human beings in factories of death, ordered by a modern state, organized by a conscientious bureaucracy, and supported by a law-abiding , patriotic, 'civilized' society."[8] One may agree with Bartov that bureaucratically organized, industrialized mass killing is indeed an important component of the Shoah, which has been placed in sustained relief in the work of Raul Hilberg, Zygmunt Bauman, Tzvetan Todorov, and Bartov himself among many others. And one must continually insist that the Shoah was indeed an overdetermined series of events for which there is no single explanatory key. But there is also a sense in which the brutality, cruelty, and elation involved in acts of perpetrators are not entirely explained by the bureaucratic or technological imperative. The bureaucrat's relation to a cold and vicious "superego" involving literal or figurative distance from the dehumanized, debased other may well be one component in a larger, tangled constellation of forces. And bureaucracy itself may involve more or less hollow but still compulsive ritualistic elements and pockets of behavior that do not conform to the Weberian ideal type or formally rational model of bureaucracy. Nor does this ideal type fully explain the less antiseptic, more direct, face-to-face viciousness involving beatings, torture, and degrading acts such as beard-burning, strip-searching, beating with rods or whips, forcing to eat or drink excrement, and so forth. It also fails to address the more elated and carnivalesque forms of torment in which certain Nazis delighted. Moreover, these forms do at times appear through the words of Hitler or even Himmler.[9] And they are equivocally amalga-

[8] "Ordinary Monsters," review of *Hitler's Willing Executioners: Ordinary Germans and the Holocaust, The New Republic*, 29 April 1996, p. 38.
[9] The following statement from *Mein Kampf* mingles (pseudo-)scientific, political, ritual, and erotic anxieties: "With satanic joy in his face, the black-haired Jewish youth lurks in wait for the unsuspecting girl whom he defiles with his blood, thus stealing her from her people. With every means he tries to destroy the racial foundations of the people he has set out to subjugate. Just as he himself systematically ruins women and girls, he does not shrink back from pulling down the blood barriers of others, even on a large scale. It was and it is Jews who bring the Negroes into the Rhineland, always with the same secret thought and clear aim of ruining the hated white race by the necessarily resulting bastardization, throwing it down from its cultural and political

mated with bureaucratization and a (pseudo-) scientific discourse concerning hygiene and medicalization in which the active agents are such entities as germs and blood. (Indeed notions such as "germ" and "blood" themselves functioned in different registers, including the phantasmic, ritualistic, and magical.) I think certain aspects of Nazi behavior and motivation can only be understood, however partially and with no pretense to full explanation of the Shoah, by seeing them in terms of anxieties about ritual contamination and the desire to seek purification through a displaced, disoriented mode of sacrificialism and victimization, involving at times a redemptive quest, a negative sublime, and carnivalesque elements.[10] These factors were in no sense unique to the Holocaust or to Germans, but they are nonetheless important, and they acquire distinctive characteristics precisely as a returning repressed that is divorced from any official religion, encrypted in a secular, neopagan ideology, and inserted within a modern, industrialized, bureaucratized context where they seem utterly uncanny and out of place.

In contrast to the resolution of ambivalence in a negative direction or its conflation with self-serving modes of equivocation, one may argue that certain ambivalences should be maintained and played or worked out in nondestructive, mutually challenging, even life-enhancing ways. Here the active affirmation of the complex value of certain modes of difference and even of anxiety-inducing otherness—including disconcerting difference and otherness within the self—is crucial. But the basic ethicopolitical question is how to distinguish between modes of difference that deserve affirmation and those that

---

height, and himself rising to be its master." *Mein Kampf*, trans. Ralph Manheim (1925; Boston: Houghton, Mifflin Company, 1971), p. 325.

[10] Here, whatever its limitations, the work of Mary Douglas, notably *Purity and Danger: An Analysis of the Concepts of Purity and Taboo* (1966; London: Routledge, 1984), as well as that of other anthropologists investigating related problems, may be relevant to the study of the Shoah. And Julia Kristeva's *Powers of Horror: An Essay on Abjection* (1980; New York: Columbia University Press, 1982), despite its turn to an aestheticizing interpretation of, and even apology for, Céline, remains valuable for its insight into ritual anxiety about contamination and the quasi-sacrificial, extreme, manically elated, scatological responses it may evoke. An interest in such problems would have added a valuable dimension to the important book of Michael Burleigh and Wolfgang Wippermann, *The Nazi Racial State: Germany 1933–1945* (New York: Cambridge University Press, 1991). See also Jacques Derrida's important *Gift of Death* (1992; Chicago: University of Chicago Press, 1995; trans. David Wells). Derrida stresses the excess or "sublime" transcendence of ethics in sacrifice and discusses the role of the sacrificial gift without thematizing the problem of victimization.

should be criticized and overcome in defense of better kinds of ambivalent interaction, hybridization, or (in the psychoanalytic sense) compromise formations that resist reduction to pure binary opposites or to the decisive victory of one purified entity or group over another through Social-Darwinian survival of the fittest. Certainly, the vital role played in German and, more generally, Western culture by Jews and other groups oppressed by the Nazis may be argued to be intertwined with the kinds of social and cultural difference any viable society must not only learn to live with or tolerate but actively support as possibly creative and challenging constituents of a complex world. But a group like the Nazis, dedicated to the conquest of power, militaristic expansion, and the elimination or enslavement of other groups deemed inferior, "evil," or radically unassimilable, represents a kind of difference that is not worthy of affirmation. How to criticize and struggle against such a group without adopting tactics comparable to its own poses a continuing problem for democratic politics, which was not adequately solved in Weimar Germany. One goal of careful inquiry and critique is to find ways of averting violence or at least limiting its use to a dire last resort in opposing a greater violence.

How to respond to various kinds of difference is a question that has recently been on many intellectual and political agendas, and the familiar "mantra" of race, class, and gender should not lead one to think that the problems signaled by these terms are themselves hackneyed or unworthy of sustained attention. Among these problems is how to distinguish among kinds of difference rather than to engage in an indiscriminate celebration of difference *per se*. Class relations present certain differences one would want to overcome insofar as they are illegitimate and create vastly unequal chances in life. In class formations, differences of wealth and income are often exploitative or unjust and bound up with hierarchies of status and power. Race, which may function to obscure without resolving class antagonisms, also presents differences that should be overcome insofar as they are prejudicial, and the very concept of race is dubious in light of its history and pseudo-scientific pretensions. But certain cultural differences related to "race," such as African American music or Native American ecological practices, may be worth remembering and developing, although not in ways that reinforce stereotypes or discrimination. It is less clear whether one would want to retain aspects of the gendering of social relations. At the very least one might want to argue for the distinction between gender and sex and for the end of patterning gendered relations on sexual difference. Instead, one might defend the unhitching of gendered assumptions from certain activities, such as occupations, as well as for the dismantling of the massive polar opposition between the private and public spheres, with the former generally coded as feminine and the latter as masculine. (Such a dismantling would not imply the rejection of all forms of privacy.) One might also defend different modes of sexuality that are neither gendered nor embedded in a normative hierarchy that privileges heterosexual relations.

A more general approach to defensible differences may be formulated in terms of cultural multiplicity based on social justice. Such differences would of course include collective or shared memories of past experiences that are specific to groups and help define their cultural heritages. Justifiable multiplicity would be predicated on economic and social conditions recognized by interested parties as just preconditions for the expression and elaboration of cultural differences, and those differences would not reinforce inequalities but at least enable their contestation. Economic and social rights, including equality of opportunity and the satisfaction of basic needs, are among such preconditions. This perspective does not imply total relativism. Rather, it entails a distinction between two understandings of incommensurability. The first postulates incomparability and a total, nonnegotiable lack of communication between culture-specific groups. Jean-François Lyotard has formulated this notion of incommensurability in terms of a differend, a radical difference that cannot be adjudicated through common norms or legal procedures.[11] This condition should, I think, be seen as a possible limit-case rather than as a general postulate concerning group relations, and it is questionable even as a limit-case when the differend is asserted by an intolerant dominant group rather than by an oppressed or marginalized one (for example, by the Nazis with respect to Jews). When an oppressed group is in a position to affirm a differend, its meaning may vary from an extreme measure prefacing revolt or revolution to a demand that is not nonnegotiable but sets very high initial conditions for negotiations.

The second sense of incommensurability is rather different. It implies that there is no metalanguage or higher-order normative struc-

[11] See *The Differend: Phrases in Dispute*, trans. George Van Den Abbeele (1983; Minneapolis: University of Minnesota Press, 1988).

ture into which differences may be translated or in terms of which they may be resolved. But it does not eliminate the possibility of mutual translatability or normative argument and adjudication, with the risks of both understanding and misunderstanding such an exchange engenders. An analogy here would be the relation between two "natural" languages (such as English and French) which may indeed be translated into one another in an economy of losses and gains although there is no "original" or superior language to serve as a court of appeal. It is this second sense of incommensurability that is required by a critique of essentialism or foundationalism, and the first sense might be seen as its extreme limit. The problem would then be how to "negotiate" issues in the face of incommensurable differences, some of which might be taken as valid (for example, differences among groups involving differentially valorized yet equally valid and mutually respected activities, such as dance, theoretical reflection, music, and narrative). Moreover, this view of incommensurability does not eliminate the possibility that groups might share important features of life on other levels (notably the normative, legal, and constitutional) and that through interaction (not imposition or identification with the aggressor) the different might become the shared. Any complex, diversified (perhaps even any conceivable) political entity would manifest a dynamic combination of the incommensurable and the shared that would vary over time.

Furthermore, while it is very important to recognize and even affirm certain irreducible residues and nontranscendable differences, it is also important not to become fixated on them in an abstract, decontextualized fashion that induces a discursive repetition compulsion whereby every analysis loops back to them or their analogues and aporias. In other words, all thought should not be a matter of endlessly returning to irreducible alterity, unsublatable negativity, or (as noted earlier) trauma whereby processes of working-through are stymied and specific cases become mere illustrations of an encounter with the uncanny other, the real, the undecidable, and so forth. The tendency to become captivated by a discursive repetition-compulsion, through which one acts out a real or phantasmic absence or felt loss, remains important in recent critical theory, and it attests to the difficulty and complexity of certain problems. This tendency may at times be found in certain forms of deconstruction and psychoanalytically oriented criticism (for example, the recent work of Shoshana Felman) as well as in some critics of deconstruction (for example, Slavoj Žižek, in whom the appeal to unsublatable negativity or the traumatizing Lacanian real seems to occur with the terrifying regularity of a recurrent nightmare). One desideratum here is to relate necessary and significant theoretical reflection to a sustained engagement with specific problems that are not addressed through relatively set theoretical moves or patterned practices.

At points in this book, I have suggested a linkage in recent work of acting-out not only with possession by the repressed past, repetition-compulsions, and unworked-through transference but also with inconsolable melancholy and the generalization of trauma or its transformation into the sublime. Such a linkage may undermine desirable transformative social and political thinking or make it seem largely gratuitous and arbitrary. Working-through would require a careful, discriminating, nondismissive critique of this linkage, which would nonetheless account for its insistence and limited value. In this respect, it is indeed important to distinguish between structural trauma, or the condition of possibility that generates a potential for trauma, and empirical forms of historical trauma. As noted in Chapter 2, everyone is subject to structural trauma, which has been figured in a multiplicity of ways (from the *felix culpa* of original sin as a consequence of the fall to the rupture of primary narcissism, the entry into the symbolic, and the encounter with the Lacanian real). Trauma in this sense cannot be "cured" or overcome and can only be lived with in various ways. One may argue that historical trauma (like structural trauma) should not be pathologized and may be confronted in various ways, but (unlike structural trauma) it may conceivably be averted or prevented. However, historical events of the seismic nature and magnitude of the Holocaust may, in transgressing a theoretical limit, pose a challenge to this distinction: the structural (or the existential-transcendental) seems to crash down into the empirical. Thus one has the tendency to figure these events as utterly unique and sacralized or demonic, as an index of God's intervention in history or, on the contrary, of his death and the upsurge of diabolically radical evil. But this tendency should be resisted, and the problematic but crucial role of certain distinctions should be affirmed and explored in the face of extreme threats to them.

I have also stressed the importance of taking the concept of working-through out of a narrowly therapeutic framework and relating it to ethical and political considerations. This move does not imply a moralization of all thought, a simple dichotomy between good and bad objects, or the construction of certain actions of distraught people as purely voluntaristic and unqualifiedly blameworthy. But it does require the notion that working-through is a desirable process, that ethical considerations are always relevant but may be difficult—perhaps at times impossible—to apply in complex cases (for example, those of certain inmates in concentration or death camps), and that a goal of thought and action is to make them applicable, for example, by furthering processes whereby both objective conditions and the degree of responsible control in behavior make ethical considerations applicable. It also requires a concern for the conditions and exercise of critical judgment, since working-through implies the possibility of judgment that is not abstractly posited, apodictic, or *ad hominem* but informed, argumentative, self-questioning, and related in mediated ways to action. In this sense it is bound up with the role of distinctions (including the very distinction between acting-out and working-through) that are not pure binary oppositions but marked by varying and contestable degrees of strength or weakness. Working-through thus becomes a regulative ideal whose actual role in history is a matter of inquiry and argument and whose desirability is affirmed but acknowledged as problematic.

Freud related working-through to the process whereby the past is recalled in memory rather than compulsively repeated or acted out, and there are of course a variety of possibilities between the two that deserve extensive investigation and subtle formulation. These intermediary possibilities include more or less pronounced forms of arrested or partial mourning, which is never free of the traumatic residues of the past. Indeed, someone may see a recurrent nightmare as a memorial to dead friends and thus be ambivalent about trying to overcome it because its significance goes well beyond acting out a merely disturbing residue of the past. Moreover, memory itself is bound up with ethical questions of vengeance, justice, and forgiveness. One would like to separate vengeance from the other two demands and sentiments. But it is unclear how vengeance—or the mitigation, sublimation, and transformation of the desire for it—relates to the movement from acting-out to working-through and whether a desire for vengeance always marks or motivates the demand for justice, notably on the part of victims or their intimates. For example, the desire for at least symbolic and belated vengeance, as well as a demand for justice, agitates Daniel Jonah Goldhagen's argument in *Hitler's Willing Execu-tioners,* and very active in his words and emotional reactions is his transferential relation to his father: a survivor, (like him) a Harvard professor, and (he tells us) the one person who is closest to his own in-terpretation of the Holocaust.[12]

Justice may not satisfy the desire for vengeance, especially when jus-tice is constrained to undergo the delays, deferrals, formal detours, and technicalities of a legal system. Yet vengeance may be sublimated into a demand for justice or counteracted if not overcome by the vic-tim's gift of forgiveness—a gift most deserved when perpetrators or those closest to them eschew evasion, denial, and self-exculpating apologetics, engage in acts of memory bound up with attempts to grieve or mourn for victims, and genuinely try to make up for past wrongs. One might also maintain that the demand for, and viable re-alization of, justice and the ability to extend the gift of forgiveness are components of working through problems, notably for victims of trau-ma and, in different ways, for those who respond empathetically to them. Recognition of this demand and genuine attempts to implement it, as well as the ability to acknowledge the injustice of one's acts and to accept forgiveness, would be required of perpetrators. Here the maxim is not "forgive and forget" but rather: remember in a certain way so that forgiveness becomes possible and letting-bygones-be-bygones constitutes a hope for the future.[13]

Descendants of perpetrators may—perhaps should—undertake the work of memory and mourning not because they are guilty for the

---

[12] See *Hitler's Willing Executioners,* pp. 479–80 and 604.

[13] Particularly with respect to the suffering attendant on trauma, justice in any strict sense is impossible because there is no common measure between what was done to victims and any conceivable compensation for it. But here too the dual meaning of commensurability comes into play, and commensurability in the second sense of nec-essarily imperfect translation is a better guide than notions of equality between offense and compensation in terms of a common measure or universal equivalent. Thus cer-tain acts, including reparations and the public acknowledgment of injustice on the part of perpetrators or those taking up their dire legacy, may be acknowledged by vic-tims as acceptable even if never fully satisfactory or adequate. Here the temptation is great to conflate a transhistorical absolute with historical possibility and to insist that no regime or form of justice could ever be adequate or even acceptable with respect to the traumatic suffering of victims. But this form of absolutism would be dogmatically theory-driven; it would also dictate a monological response to victims and amalga-mate all initiatives on the part of perpetrators from extreme obduracy and denial to good-faith efforts to make up in whatever degree possible for past wrongs. These his-torical differences do not make all the difference, but they make some valid difference nonetheless.

deeds of their ancestors but because they have a limited liability for the consequences of these deeds (for example, the fact that one may be living in a house expropriated from a Jew), may work through (more or less unjustified) feelings of guilt or vague disorientation, and strive for critical distance (or basic evaluative and emotional difference) with respect to the ideology and motivation that led to the acts of perpetrators. It is perhaps in light of these considerations that one should understand Habermas's statement in the Historians' Debate:

> There is first of all the obligation that we in Germany have—even if no one else any longer assumes it—to keep alive the memory of the suffering of those murdered by German hands, and to keep it alive quite openly and not just in our own minds. These dead justifiably have a claim on a weak anamnestic power of solidarity, which those born later can only practice in the medium of memory which is constantly renewed, often desperate, but at any rate alive and circulating. If we brush aside this Benjaminian legacy, our Jewish fellow citizens, the sons, the daughters, the grandchildren of the murdered victims, would no longer be able to breathe in our country. That also has political implications.[14]

One should add to Habermas's statement the proviso that other peoples have memory-work to do with respect not only to the Shoah but to other traumatic events that mar national histories or international relations and create faulted traditions whose memory is necessarily ruined or riven. Moreover, Habermas himself would no doubt agree that the role of survivor and witness, which may be more than enough for victims, is not sufficient for those fortunate enough to be born later. Those born later should neither appropriate (or belatedly act out) the experience of victims nor restrict their activities to the necessary role of secondary witness and guardian of memory. Any politics limited to witnessing, memory, mourning dead victims, and honoring survivorship would constitute an excessively limited horizon of action, however desirable and necessary these activities may be.

---

[14] "On the Public Use of History," in *Forever in the Shadow of Hitler?*, trans. James Knowlton and Truett Cates (Atlantic Highlands, N.J.: Humanities Press, 1993), p. 165; translation modified. Suggestive for understanding the intergenerational transmission of family secrets and often ill-defined feelings of guilt are the concepts of the "phantom" and encrypting developed in Nicolas Abraham and Maria Torok, *The Shell and the Kernel*, vol. 1, ed. and trans. Nicholas T. Rand (Chicago: University of Chicago Press, 1994).

My comments imply that there is a need in critical theory for an explicitly ethical turn in the attempt to argue for certain judgments and lend credibility to related analyses, even if their cogency or applicability cannot be proved conclusively and is always subject to qualification in the face of complexity. It is also important to recognize the force of tendencies that resist or impede such an ethical turn. I would mention at least four assumptions or ideological convictions that block such a turn and that remain active in critical thought and practice, notably in the academy.

First, there is the separation of spheres of thought and action in modern society, including the disjunction of the ethical, the cognitive, and the aesthetic. This separation may be questioned not in the interest of a totalizing whole or a fully harmonious reconciliation of seeming opposites but in defense of a conception of tensely complex relations that should be empirically investigated and at times transformed or rearticulated in the direction of more desirable and challenging tensions.

The separation of the ethical and the cognitive was and is a premise of positivistic science. The disjunction of the ethical and the aesthetic was enshrined in art for art's sake, and it became conventionalized and professionalized in formalist criticism. Still, in art for art's sake, for example in Baudelaire, there was a covert ethical imperative in the very demand for a sharp distinction or even opposition between ethics and art. Indeed, *l'art pour l'art* was in important ways a protest against a society in which narrowly productive and utilitarian values tended to predominate with the result that art in general, and poetry in particular, were marginalized insofar as they could not be commodified. In at least certain variants of formalism, this ethical or ethicopolitical dimension may be muted or virtually nonexistent, as the notions of the autonomy of art and of its appreciation or criticism become the bases for standard operating procedures of artists and critics.

Here is an example of critical commentary in which the autonomy of the aesthetic is simply assumed without any felt need for argument. It comes from Louis Menand's review of Anthony Julius's book, *T. S. Eliot, Anti-Semitism, and Literary Form*:

> The argument of *T. S. Eliot, Anti-Semitism and Literary Form* is easily summarized: T. S. Eliot was an anti-Semite; his anti-Semitism is integral to his poetry, and there is nothing in the nature of poetry that renders the anti-Semitism less anti-Semitic for being expressed in the

form of poetry or that renders the poetry less poetical for including anti-Semitic expression. The final point is the critical one for Julius, and it is what distinguishes him from every other writer who has treated the subject of Eliot and the Jews. For Julius deplores, bitterly, the anti-Semitism, but he refuses to regard it as a blemish on the poems. "Anti-Semitism," he says, "did not disfigure Eliot's work, it animated it. It was, on occasion, both his refuge and his inspiration, and his exploitation of its literary potential was virtuose." There is, to put it another way, no artistic difference between Bleistein and the hyacinth girl. The one is as poetically realized as the other. Exposure to anti-Semitism is simply part of the experience of reading Eliot. When we bracket the prejudice, we miss the experience.[15]

The plangent complacency of this paragraph, as well as the polite *frisson* it produces, conceals its contestable assumptions. One may agree with Menand that anti-Semitism is integral to at least some of Eliot's poetry and that it is commendable on Julius's part not to try to explain Eliot's anti-Semitism away or to purify the poetry of it, for example, by mistakenly seeing the poetry as making use of anti-Semitism only as an objectified, carefully framed theme. One may also agree that "nothing in the nature of the poetry renders the anti-Semitism less anti-Semitic for being expressed in the form of poetry." But one may stop short at the next assertion that "there is nothing in the nature of the poetry . . . that renders the poetry less poetical for including anti-Semitic expressions." This assertion is dubious, not because one would want to negate it by asserting that poetry is less poetical when it is anti-Semitic, but because Menand's assertion assumes that there is such a thing as the nature of poetry and that one may isolate the poetical from other features of language and practice. In other words, Menand treats the poetical as an ingredient that one may separate out, by some linguistic analogue of chemical processing, from other ingredients, such as ethics or politics, and thus isolate its nature and effects. This decisively analytic, thoroughly conventionalizing view disavows the role of responses that relate the poetic to other aspects of language and practice and that see it as ineluctably interacting with the ethical and the political. Moreover, it obviates even raising the question of whether Eliot's poems as well as the "experience" of reading them would have

[15] "Eliot and the Jews," *New York Review of Books* 43 (6 June 1996), p. 34.

been better had they been animated not by anti-Semitism but by a morally superior outlook.[16] At the very least Menand's approach ignores the confusion in judgment one experiences when one confronts the issue of how to evaluate poetry in which anti-Semitism is an important motivation or inspiration—confusion stemming from the problematic interaction of the poetic, the ethical, and the political.

A second prevalent way of excluding the pertinence of the ethical is through the notion of authenticity as an ontological or, at times, subjective category. Authenticity is a matter of being true to the self and not being self-deceived (or, for Sartre, in bad faith). As such it is not an ethical or moral virtue but a transcendence of ethics. In Heidegger *Eigentlichkeit* is not a function of subjectivity, as authenticity tends to be in the early Sartre, but it is explicitly opposed to moral values, which are denigrated as subjective projections and contrasted with the ontological. Authenticity for Heidegger is a matter of being true to the call of Being, whatever that may be. Authenticity is, moreover, often allied with sublime and heroic values that are beyond ethical evaluation: in *Being and Time,* with being-towards-death and choosing one's hero. These aspects of *Being and Time* help, I think, to explain its openness to the use Heidegger made of it in 1933–34 to justify his commitment to the Nazis and their attempt to overcome the mediocrity of modern Western civilization.

I also think there is something of the appeal to the authentic and the sublime in Derrida's apology for the fact that Heidegger after the war remained silent about Auschwitz: "Perhaps Heidegger thought: I can only voice a condemnation of National Socialism if it is possible for me to do so in a language not only at the peak of what I have already said, but also at the peak of what has happened here. He was incapable of doing this. And perhaps his silence is an honest form of admitting he was incapable of it."[17] In these disconcerting reflections, the assumption seems to be that a judgment must be "on the level" of one's most elevated and exacting philosophical work as well as of the phenomenon in question (Auschwitz?), although the approximation of the two might give one pause. The result is the invocation of inappropriate

16 Similar questions may be posed to Julia Kristeva's analysis of Céline in *Powers of Horror,* which Menand's analysis in certain ways resembles.

17 "Heidegger's Silence," in *Martin Heidegger and National Socialism,* ed. Günther Neske and Emil Kettering, intro. Karsten Harries, trans. Lisa Harries (1988; New York: Paragon House, 1990), p. 148.

heroic or sublime aesthetico-philosophical criteria, or at least the implication that the only authentic response is one that competes with sublimity, in a case where the most relevant concerns are ordinary ethical and political ones, such as acknowledging one's past and one's present response to it.

The third basis for de-emphasizing ethics is the conflation of morality with moralizing in a pejorative, self-justifying, and high-handed sense. This very restricted conception of morality is, I think, prevalent at least in certain critical reactions, and often allied with an emphasis on an aesthetics of the sublime.

The fourth tendency does not exclude ethics but finds beauty or even sublimity in radical transgression and the flouting of ethics. The most cogent variant of this outlook objects to normalized or conventionalized ethics and employs transgression as shock therapy. But the plea for radical transgression may itself be autonomized and all norms may be indiscriminately dismissed as objectionably normalizing. As Tzvetan Todorov has observed in *Facing the Extreme: Moral Life in the Concentration Camps*[18]: "Such notions as the 'beauty' of crime, murder as art, the dandy who wants his life to be governed by aesthetic rather than ethical rules have been solidly ensconced in Europe since the nineteenth century" (p. 101). Here one may also quote Max Weber's famous lines in "Science as a Vocation," which formulate a position that Todorov would like to challenge in his attempt to rehabilitate ethics in the form of ordinary virtues and to give it a central place in critical discourse:

> Since Nietzsche, we realize that something can be beautiful, not only in spite of the aspect in which it is not good, but rather in that very aspect. You will find this expressed earlier in the *Fleurs du mal*, as Baudelaire named his volume of poems. It is commonplace to observe that something may be true although it is not beautiful and not holy and not good. Indeed it may be true in precisely those aspects. But all these are only the most elementary cases of the struggle that the gods of the various orders and values are engaged in. I do not know how one might wish to decide "scientifically" the value of French and German culture; for here, too, different gods struggle with one another, now and for all times to come.[19]

[18] New York: Henry Holt, 1996.
[19] *From Max Weber: Essays in Sociology,* trans. and ed. H. H. Gerth and C. Wright Mills (New York: Oxford University Press, 1958), p. 148.

Weber expresses in more pathos-laden (and unguardedly national-istic) terms the assumptions implicit in the notion of the differentiation of spheres or orders in modern society, and his words indicate the dif-ficulty in formulating cogently and defending a different perspective on problems in which the ethical would be neither dissociated from other modes of thought and judgment nor harmoniously reconciled with them in some Platonic heaven or stereotypically Hegelian higher synthesis. In any case, to the extent that the four assumptions or con-victions I have mentioned are indeed prevalent, there is a great deal to unlearn and to rethink in order for ethics and the ethicopolitical to take a prominent place in critical discourse.

One of the more problematic and speculative dimensions of my own analysis in this book has been the notion of secularization as a process of displacement involving at times a return of the repressed. Much work has been done on nationalism as a civil religion that took on many of the trappings of religion and inspired a comparable commit-ment that at times overrode considerations of class, gender, and race. Even more work may be necessary to do justice to the various roles of nationalism in modern life. A particulary virulent and intolerant na-tionalism was certainly a pronounced aspect of Nazi ideology, and its Social-Darwinian drive and its desire for purity in the *Volksgemein-schaft* were not totally different or isolated from developments in oth-er countries or regions of the world. My own focus in this book has been on less obvious and perhaps more avoided dimensions of secu-larization. Most noticeably, I have presented a displaced sacrificialism as a crucial instance of the returning repressed that is acted out, often blindly. I have also related this sacrificialism to a secular sacred or neg-ative sublime that I have suggested was active in the motivation of at least certain Nazi perpetrators. It involved a horror at contamination or defilement by an impure other and an anxiety-ridden impulse to get rid of the putative source of contamination. My view here is itself not only analytic but also ethical in import, for it implies the importance of recognizing and recalling such a sacrificialism in order to resist or attempt to undo its recurrence. As I noted earlier, I do not think that a secularized or encrypted ritual or disorienting sacrificial reaction was the sole cause, the most important cause, or even the unique element in the Shoah. But I do think it is important for trying to understand cer-tain aspects of perpetrator motivation and action.

I would also like to specify that my suspicion and critique are di-rected toward that aspect of sacrifice which involves victimization, scapegoating, and regeneration if not redemption through violence. This dimension has been very important historically in influential modes of both thought and practice. Indeed one difficult question is whether there can (at least within a tradition in which certain Christian presuppositions have been so forceful) be sacred and ecstatic experience without victimization, including surrogate victimization or shattering immolation of the self. A related question is whether such experience, if it is possible, can be conjoined with viable forms of social and political practice and not be all-consuming or obsessive. These quesions have not received sufficient attention even by important figures who have touched upon them (such as Georges Bataille, René Girard, or Julia Kristeva).

One point worth making here is that the sacred and sacrifice are not exhausted by victimization, scapegoating, and the motif of regeneration through violence. Sacrifice itself also includes the role of oblation or gift-giving. While the gift is frequently the sacrificial victim and is offered to the god or god-like figure, it is possible to distinguish the gift from the victim, validate only the gift-giving, and even argue that gift-giving is a mode of possibly ecstatic (or "sublime") performativity that may counteract or displace victimization and in relation to which victimization may be seen as a degraded form. This argument is at least plausible when the agonistic side of gift-giving is restricted to relative equals or peers and the relation to those in a position of weakness or vulnerability is one of generosity and kindness. This economy of the gift was recognized by thinkers as different as Nietzsche and Marcel Mauss, and it provides at least one basis for rethinking the role of the sacred and its possible displacements or analogues in secular society.

I have argued that mourning involves memory-work in the attempt to convert haunting presences into honored dead who can be laid to rest but not simply forgotten or dismissed. I also have intimated that mourning itself should be recognized as a gift of which not everyone is deserving. The problem is that there may be dead who cannot be laid to rest, either because their loss is irremediable and inconsolable, or because they do not deserve to be honored, or both. With respect to inconsolable loss or the insistent recurrence of traumatic residues, one can only recognize the partial value of attempts to valorize these experiences, for example, in the poetry of melancholy and the agony of the passion play, and insist that one be attentive as well to the efforts of victims to rebuild a life and to make use of counterforces that enable them to be other than victims, that is, to survive and to engage in social and political practices related to the renewal of interest in life (for example, having children). One may even contend that, in the face of severe trauma, a requirement of working-through may be the active recognition that not everything can be worked through (at least in the sense of overcome). With respect to the dead who may not deserve mourning and a proper burial, one might contend that there are other forms of working-through, such as critique involving normative issues and the elaboration of nonfetishistic narratives—narratives that do not deny the trauma that called them into existence. These forms would be directed at the disengagement of people from unjustified emotional and narcissistic investments (or "cathexes") and nostalgic longings for putative lost glories (such as those of Hitler and his regime). Here one task of future thought would be the exploration of the possibilities and limits of the concept of working-through, notably including its relation to critique, narrative, and normativity.

One may also point out that an ethical or normative turn is itself necessary but not sufficient in an attempt to work through problems, particularly if it is construed in terms of individual self-understanding and behavior. To have a social role, it must be articulated with political concerns. Addressing such concerns requires a combination of the roles or subject-positions of scholar and critical intellectual, a combination that does not dispense with rigorous scholarship or conflate critical reflection with partisan propaganda but does render allowable or even desirable modes of thought that often are discouraged in the academy.

One aspect of intellectual activity with a clear bearing on political issues is the role of critical theory in a field or discipline and its relation to cross-disciplinary problems that are not confined to any one constituted discipline but may receive different inflections in various disciplines. Theory, in the sense I am employing the word, involves the sustained attempt to pose critical questions to research in terms that address its basic assumptions and presuppositions as well as the uses to which it has been and may plausibly be put. It should not be conflated with the formulation of decontextualized "laws" and strategies of interpretation, explanation, and reading or with methodology that provides rules or stipulates procedures that are effective in obtaining delimited, clear-cut results. Rather, theory should have a dialogic and critical relation to research by raising provocative questions about its procedures and being itself open to reformulation on the basis of what is disclosed by research into specific social, historical, and cultural problems. Among such questions are the possibilities and limits of modes of objectification that are often taken to be synonymous with research. An intimately related question is that of the subject-position(s) and voice(s) of the researcher and the manner in which they may be critically transformed in the research process.

Subject-position is a crucial notion that, despite its jargonistic sound, conjoins social and psychoanalytic concerns and critically mediates between an essentializing idea of identity and an ill-defined, ideologically individualistic, and often aestheticized notion of subjectivity. A crucial issue is how any researcher in the humanities and social sciences is implicated in a transferential relation in which one is both situated in a contemporary existential context and tends to repeat, at least discursively, the processes that one studies—a relation that is negotiated in ways that may variably reinforce or place in question one's existing subject-positions. Here one may propose a revised notion of objectivity not in terms of a perspectiveless view from a transcendental position of absolute mastery but in terms of the attempt to counteract inevitable (and at times thought-provoking or heuristically valuable) processes of projection and to work viably through one's implication in the problems one investigates. One may also suggest the need to examine carefully the actual and desirable relations between performative and constative dimensions of research (or related activities) in different fields or disciplines.

What I have termed one's transferential relation to the object of research is particularly intense with respect to extremely traumatic series of events, and one may, in some combination, deny, act out, and attempt to work through the attendant problems. (The transferential problem revealed itself as particularly intense in the case of Goldhagen's *Hitler's Willing Executioners* and the laudatory or critical reactions to it.) I have already indicated that my own conviction is that, in cases of extreme trauma, one may never entirely overcome acting out problems, even in a repetitively compulsive manner. But one may attempt to check acting-out through the role of memory and critical perspective, which are constituents of working through problems. Still, difficulties arise in the very terminology one uses, for no names are innocent or politically neutral. It makes a difference whether one calls events the Holocaust (capital "H"), the Nazi holocaust (lower-case "h"), Judeocide, the Shoah, the Nazi genocide, *le pire*, and so forth. And naming as well as elaborating one's conception of problems is highly charged politically. Not every topic or area of research may be such an obvious minefield, but any topic or area raises pointed questions for the researcher insofar as it is not completely and deceptively treated in a totally objectified manner and subjected to narrowly empirical and analytic techniques of representation. Indeed, insofar as one relies exclusively on such techniques, which within limits are necessary for valid historical reconstruction, one may well indulge in dubious interpretations or renderings which are not checked and to some extent controlled by explicit critical and self-critical theoretical questioning.[20]

History is a field that is particularly resistant to theory in this sense, while literary criticism at times has been given to theorizing as a self-propelled, unqualifiedly performative movement of thought that lacks specificity and generates its own internal aporias and resistances. Here one may juxtapose quotations from a leading historian and a foremost theorist.

John Pocock has made very important contributions to historical research and even taken an interest in certain forms of speech-act theory to inform his investigations. But one of his writings is rather curious. In it, Pocock relies on an invidious distinction between the working historian and the reflective intellectual, as if the two roles were inherently incompatible. And his words imply a sharp divide between research and an exchange with the past that bears on contemporary ethicopolitical concerns without necessarily being projectively "presentist." Indeed, his argument seems to eventuate in an anti-intellectual intellectual history that adamantly denies or represses the manner in which the very self-constitution of the field of intellectual history is intimately bound up both with theoretical problems and with a dialogic relation to the past having implications for the present and future.

> It is possible to define "intellectual history" as the pursuit by the "intellectual" of an attitude towards "history," and to write it as a series

---

[20] On these issues, see my *Representing the Holocaust: History, Theory, Trauma* (Ithaca: Cornell University Press, 1994), and "History, Language, and Reading: Waiting for Crillon," *American Historical Review* 100 (1995), 799–828.

of dialogues between the historian himself, as intellectual, and his probably French or German predecessors, in the attempt to arrive at a "philosophy of history" or something to take the place of one. Such "intellectual history" will be meta-history, meaning that it will be reflection about "history" itself. But it is also possible to imagine a "working historian" who desires to be a historian but not (in this sense) an intellectual, who desires to practise the writing of history but not to arrive at an attitude towards it, and who does not look beyond the construction of those narrative histories of various kinds of intellectual activity which she or he knows how to write. . . . It is such a working historian of this kind whom I have presupposed in this article.[21]

In stark contrast, Paul de Man writes:[22]

Literary theory can be said to come into being when the approach to literary texts is no longer based on non-linguistic, that is to say historical and aesthetic, considerations or, to put it somewhat less crudely, when the object of discussion is no longer the meaning or the value but the modalities of production and of reception of meaning and of value prior to their establishment—the implication being that this establishment is problematic enough to require an autonomous discipline of critical investigation to consider its possibility and its status. . . . (p. 7)

If these difficulties are indeed an integral part of the problem then they will have to be, to some extent, a-historical in the temporal sense of the term. The way in which they are encountered on the present local literary scene as a resistance to the introduction of linguistic terminology in aesthetic and historical discourse about literature is only one particular version of a question that cannot be reduced to a specific historical situation and called modern, post-modern, post-classical or romantic. . . . Such difficulties can be read in the text of literary theory of all times, at whatever historical moment one wishes to select. . . . (p. 12)

[21] "A New Bark Up an Old Tree," *Intellectual History Newsletter* (1986), p. 8.
[22] *The Resistance to Theory*, foreword by Wlad Godzich (Minneapolis: University of Minnesota Press, 1986). For a somewhat different reading of de Man on theory and reference, as well as for the analysis of trauma, see Cathy Caruth, *Unclaimed Experience: Trauma, Narrative, and History* (Baltimore: Johns Hopkins University Press, 1996). One may question the extent to which Caruth's version of trauma theory, as an ambitious rewriting of de Manian deconstruction, is able to get beyond the repetition compulsion other than through allegories of excess, incomprehensibility, and empty utopian hope.

De Man continues:

> Technically correct rhetorical readings may be boring, monotonous, predictable and unpleasant, but they are irrefutable. They are also totalizing (and potentially totalitarian) for since the structures and functions they expose do not lead to the knowledge of an entity (such as language) but are an unreliable process of knowledge production that prevents all entities, including linguistic entities, from coming into discourse as such, they are indeed universals, consistently defective models of language's impossibility to be a model language. . . .
>
> Nothing can overcome the resistance to theory since theory is itself this resistance. (p. 19)

There is much in these comments that is worth taking seriously and commenting on extensively. Especially significant is de Man's attempt to demystify the sublime by relating it to mechanical tendencies and deflating its relation to elation or exhilaration. For the present purpose, I would simply note that de Man seems to construe literary theory as an autonomous, self-referential inquiry into pure conditions of possibility and their attendant resistances and aporias. This construction is bound up with a near fixation on structural trauma. De Man also appears to rely on an abstract, objectivist notion of linguistics and to undercut, if not render superfluous, investigation into the actual and desirable uses of language or, more generally, of signifying practices in history. Conditions of possibility tend to be autonomized and thereby detached from sustained critical inquiry into the presuppositions and assumptions of actual historical procedures and activities involving social agents, including uses of language that have practical implications. Moreover, the opposition between linguistic universalism (however defective) and reductive historical particularity functions to exclude an understanding of historicity in terms de Man himself at times broaches: historicity as displacement or repetition with (at times traumatic) change, a process whereby problems recur with significant variations that must be addressed in their specificity. The result of de Man's view may well be the identification of history with arbitrariness or aberration and the incapacity or reduced ability to address in nonreductive but informed fashion the very ways in which the establishment of meaning in various historical and cultural contexts is indeed problematic. One thereby threatens to define oneself into an agonized position of political and social irrelevance.

What tends to drop into the large crack separating Pocock's and de Man's formulations is the interaction among research, theory, and ethicopolitical concern in the critical attempt to come to terms with specific problems. What is at issue here is not a middle way or a *juste milieu* but the need to work out a different way, at the very least a different articulation of discourse with possible relations to practice. Discourse in this sense would involve the mutually provocative interaction between theoretical questioning and research that has an empirical and historical dimension. The ethical impetus behind this approach might also force a reconsideration of the very meaning of ethics and its relation to politics: ethics open to the crucial interaction between work and play (or the serious and the carnivalesque), and politics understood not simply as power but in terms of normatively guided life in common. Indeed, seen in an ethicopolitical sense, concern with transference in research need not induce a show-and-tell session or even a movement toward autobiography, particularly when that movement is strained, trivializing, or self-indulgent in view of the object of inquiry. Of course those with direct experience of traumatic events may bring that experience to bear in what they write, and often such writing or discourse is itself crucial in the attempt to come to terms with the past.But it is also the case that one's implication in a set of problems can exist and be explored by virtue of the fact that one is indissociably a scholar, an ethical agent, and a citizen or political being.

INDEX